3rd Edition
Revised
1978

HERBS
AND THE FRAGRANT
GARDEN

For Use and Delight

A salad fit for a king
I sing;
With chives and marjoram, lemon thyme—
A crime
To leave out parsley and sprigs of mint—
A hint
Of sage and bay will crown the head
(in soup or stew)
Of the newly-wed!
For few
Can resist the charm
Of a sprig of balm
Or the hope of becoming a paragon
By the tactful use of tarragon!

HERBS
AND THE FRAGRANT
GARDEN

MARGARET BROWNLOW
B.SC.(HORT.),N.D.H.

With colour illustrations and poems by the author

DARTON, LONGMAN AND TODD
LONDON

Darton, Longman and Todd Ltd
89 Lillie Road, London SW6 1UD

This revised edition © 1978 Darton, Longman and Todd Ltd

First edition 1957
Second edition (revised and enlarged) 1963
Third edition (further revised) 1978

ISBN 0 232 51396 1

Printed in Great Britain by
Fletcher & Son Ltd, Norwich (text) and
Lowe & Brydone (Printers) Ltd, Thetford (colour plates)

TO MY MOTHER

CONTENTS

	Page
LIST OF ILLUSTRATIONS	9
FOREWORD BY SIR EDWARD J. SALISBURY	13
INTRODUCTION TO THE SECOND EDITION	15

Chapter		
I	THE QUEST OF HERBS	17
II	THE HISTORY OF HERBS	27
III	THE HERB GARDEN	43
IV	CULTIVATION, HARVESTING AND DRYING, AND NOTES ON HERBS IN OTHER CLIMATES	59
V	THE USES OF HERBS	75

REFERENCE SECTION

TABLE OF FLOWERING TIMES	89
CLASSIFIED LISTS OF AROMATIC SHRUBS, SCENTED SHRUBS, AND NORTH AMERICAN HERBS	93
ALPHABETICAL LIST OF HERBS, AND AROMATIC AND SCENTED SHRUBS	95
BIBLIOGRAPHY	207
INDEX	209

ILLUSTRATIONS

Line drawings

    Plan of herb garden 1   *page* 45
    Plan of herb garden 2   46
    Plan of herb garden 3   46
    Plan of herb garden 4   47
    Plan of herb garden 5   48

Colour Plates

Plate	Subject	Location
Plate 1	Lavenders	*between pages* 48 and 49
Plate 2	Culinary Herbs	
Plate 3	Culinary Herbs	
Plate 4	Culinary Herbs	
Plate 5	Culinary and Aromatic Plants	,, ,, 80 and 81
Plate 6	Culinary, Medicinal and Aromatic Herbs	
Plate 7	Medicinal Herbs	
Plate 8	Medicinal Herbs	
Plate 9	Medicinal Herbs	,, ,, 96 and 97
Plate 10	Medicinal Herbs	
Plate 11	Poisonous Drug Herbs	
Plate 12	Poisonous Drug Herbs	
Plate 13	American Herbs	,, ,, 112 and 113
Plate 14	American Herbs	
Plate 15	Aromatic Shrubs	
Plate 16	Scented and Aromatic Shrubs	
Plate 17	Scented Shrubs	,, ,, 144 and 145
Plate 18	Scented Shrubs	
Plate 19	Aromatic Herbs	
Plate 20	Aromatic Herbs	
Plate 21	Aromatic Herbs	,, ,, 160 and 161
Plate 22	Aromatic and Medicinal Plants	
Plate 23	Aromatic and other Plants	
Plate 24	Salvias	
Plate 25	Sages and Decorative Salvias	,, ,, 176 and 177
Plate 26	Mints	
Plate 27	Thymes	
Plate 28	Pelargoniums (scented Geraniums)	
Plate 29	Various Plants	,, ,, 192 and 193
Plate 30	Various Plants	
Plate 31	Various Plants	
Plate 32	Various Plants	

My Herb Garden

My garden will have tranquil Lavender.
Blue-mauve and pink and musical with bees
To edge my paths. And here bright fragrant Thymes
Perfume the air when trodden; near to these
The gentle Chamomile with apple scent
And pungent Pennyroyal like water-mint,
With lilac sprays delicate against the stone . . .
Curry and Santolina blossoms glint
Like pure-wrought gold against their silver tresses.
My garden will have jewelled Bergamot—
Warm crimson, royal purple and the flush
Of rose; and when the summer sun is hot
Rich aromatic airs will fill my garden
Of Sage, sweet Thyme and Marjoram for the pot
(Lovely their leaves outlined with winter frost
Or morning dew). Then Rosemary shall stand
About the house, mist-blue with April blossom.
Southernwood and spiced Geraniums close at hand
Filling the mind with distant memories,
Mysterious and varied shall be there,
With hints of that first garden far in time,
When the Creator, walking round could share
His pleasures with the gardener; and a glimpse
Of the last river garden, pure and fair,
When foliage of the Tree of Life shall be
Valued to heal the nations' enmity—
Eternal garden of tranquillity.

Foreword
By SIR EDWARD J. SALISBURY, C.B.E., D.SC., L.D., F.R.S., F.L.S., V.M.H.L.
Director of Kew Gardens from 1943 to 1956

The Herb lore of the past has always had a fascination for many who are unattracted by the more austere pleasures of the flower collector and botanist. It is to these that Miss Brownlow's book will especially appeal and I am constrained to comply with her request that I should furnish a foreword by our common appreciation of non-botanical charms. For the purposes of this book the author deems a plant to be a herb when it is either useful for its culinary value, for its aromatic qualities or for its real or supposed medicinal virtues. Miss Brownlow is clearly appreciative of the subtle differences in flavour and scent provided by the herb garden and it is well that appreciation of these qualities should be encouraged in an age that is all too prone to stultify its palate with cocktails before a meal and will accept an apple, or a rose, for its colour alone regardless of its lack of flavour, or of scent. Here in these pages we can read of Alecost and Allspice, Basil and Betony, Bistort and Borage, Chamomile and Clary through all the musical alphabet of their popular designations, till we come to Lovage, Rampion and Rue, Vervain and Yarrow. The reader can be initiated into the recondite distinctions in flavour of the diverse Mints, the variety of Sages or the scents of the several Thymes. A herb garden can in fact provide its owner with joys that appeal to all the senses and these pages will help to enhance its pleasures and provide guidance for the enrichment of its contents.

The lore of herbs has its roots in the prehistoric past and as an oral tradition may well go back to the time when Stone Age Man was the subject of experimentation, both culinary and medicinal, by Stone Age Woman. How little do we pause to think upon what a long tally of human suffering, of trial and error, must rest the accumulated knowledge of the poisonous, the merely unwholesome, the innocuous and the nutritious that we possess today. How exhaustive has been this survey through the ages, imposed in part by curiosity but more often by sheer necessity, is impressed upon us by the few herbs that modern research has revealed to us as possessing pronounced qualities that had not already been recognized as potent by primitive peoples. The contribution of modern times has been rather the isolation and identification of active principles and the elucidation of their real, as distinct from their supposed physiological effects. But to all who are interested in plants even the myths, as well as the knowledge, of our forefathers often sheds light on the dark places in the pattern of the past.

E. J. SALISBURY

Introduction
to the Second Edition

During the five years since this book was first privately published I have met or have had letters from many who have appreciated it and found it helpful. I am grateful to all these friends of *Herbs and the Fragrant Garden* who have made themselves known. I also have a sense of gratitude to those who have helped with kindly criticism.

In this second edition there are two additional plates of scented shrubs, with notes about them, and two plates of American herbs, with comments on their uses and location. The unconventional style of plate has been replaced by lithographic illustrations. This method involves an entirely different technique in drawing, and allows the inclusion of greater detail, more subtlety in colour and a different arrangement of the plants on the plates. Therefore the plants have in many cases been re-illustrated for their new medium, and this has involved collecting fresh material, in addition to two hundred kinds grown here.

This late season has produced some quirks amongst vegetation. There were still flowers on *Lonicera fragrantissima* and *Corylopsis spicata* in May, while *Elsholtzia stauntonii* emerged unhurriedly in October, and *Crocus sativus* strolled into bud in November. The illustrator has many other problems to face, not the least that in hot weather buds can open, bloom and drop at a handcanter, in a matter of an hour or two when one's back is turned as a large herb-viewing party arrives almost simultaneously with a thunderstorm.

These illustrations have been done to pass on some of the pleasure obtained from the herbs, and to enable them to be identified from one another, and to become familiar friends.

I am indebted to Mr John Sambrook, who has always been encouraging, and who reviewed the first edition understandingly over the radio. I have paid visits to the Royal Horticultural Society's gardens at Wisley and the Chelsea Physic Garden with the interest of the plant-hunter, and value the help received. F. P. Knight, Esq., V.M.H., the Director of Wisley, and the Librarian of the Lindley Library have given helpful assistance. Amongst others whose provision of specimens has been invaluable are Mr T. Hilling, Mr and Mrs John Sich, Mr G. W. Robinson of the Oxford Botanic Gardens, and Mr P. F. Yeo of the Cambridge Botanic Gardens.

I have paid valuable visits to Kew, and Mr R. D. Meikle has given much useful help, particularly on the subject of synonyms. For information on herbs in other parts of the world, I am grateful to Mrs H. W. Neil of Littleton, Colorado, Mrs Lester Rowntree of California, Mrs P. Faggetter of Mitcham, Victoria; the Curator of the Botanic Gardens at Stellenbosch, the Government Botanist at Brisbane, and Mr J. P. Salinger, Horticultural Advisory Officer at Wellington.

I am indebted to the New York State Museum and Science Service, Albany 1, New York, for permission to redraw the plants in Plate 13 and three in Plate 14 from *Wild Flowers of New York*, Memoir 15. The Smithsonian Institute also kindly allowed me to make drawings of three herbs on Plate 14 taken from Mrs Walcott's Wild Flower plates; in both cases the geographical information given was useful.

I am indebted to the following for permission to make use of copyright material: to Messrs Jonathan Cape Ltd. for information from Mrs M. Grieve's *A Modern Herbal;* to Mr Gerald Howe for material from *Leaves from Gerard's Herbal*, by Marcus Woodward; to Messrs Longmans Green & Co. Ltd. for material from *The Old English Herbals* by Eleanour Sinclair Rohde, and to the Medici Society regarding the same author's *Herbs and Herb Gardening*, all mentioned in the Bibliography.

Mrs Dennis and her helpers here have kept work running smoothly during my withdrawal into studio conditions; and when I emerged, Mrs Dennis has always been ready with help in proof-reading and with practical ideas.

Mr T. Michael Longman's individual interest in the book has made a pleasure of the business link between author and publisher.

M.E.B.

The Herb Farm,
Seal,
Sevenoaks.
December 1962.

CHAPTER ONE

The Quest of Herbs

I have in my mind the unknown lady (or gentleman) who writes (or approaches) saying, 'I have a plant in my garden with a strong scent. Is it a herb? What can I use it for?'

Life is too short for the full drama. The correspondent is asked to send me a sprig, and at length some morsel of vegetation appears. If we are fortunate, it bears the post-pressed remnants of flowers and a haunting vestige of aroma, so that a successful post-mortem may be conducted.

But the personal questioner demands more. One asks with, we hope, quiet patience, 'Yes, of course. What is the plant like?' 'Well, it has—er—green leaves and the flowers are not very big.' This does at least rule out elecampane and bergamot; we have progressed.

'Can you tell me what the leaves are like—long or round, heart-shaped or feathery?' 'Not very long, you know, and roundish; perhaps a bit feathery at the edges, too, and they're green.' This is not altogether illuminating, and patience with a few worn threads asks hopefully 'What are the flowers like? Are they perhaps two-lipped, or like a daisy, and what colour?' 'I don't think I've noticed the flowers much, they're not very showy, you know.'

In a final desperate fling we probe as to the aroma. 'Could you, please, tell me something about the scent? Is it like lemons or caraway, floor polish, leather suitcases, new-mown hay or coconuts?' 'I'm sorry, I can't quite tell you.' Then, after deep thought, 'But it's a very nice smell.'

I hope that in future it will sometimes be restful to say 'Would you care to look through the plates and find the nearest to your herb?'

The British public are considered inarticulate and are just exactly so when asked to describe a plant. A reticence creeps in that would be a credit to the Silent Service, and any familiarity with botanic terms such as umbels, racemes, cordate leaves or whorls seems, somehow, not the thing.

I have every sympathy with such people for it is entirely advisable to make sure of the name and uses of a herb before feeding it open-handedly to the family. It is for this reason that one plate not only shows the decorative value of the drug herbs but is also a warning that it is inadvisable to mistake hemlock for—say—chervil.

Life also is short for detailed correspondence giving advice on The Compleat

Herb Garden by return of post. There are now occasions when it may be possible to replace the 'Dear Madam (or Sir)', It is interesting to hear about your proposed herb garden. On your heavy soil it is helpful to work in some compost and a dressing of lime . . . for your sunny paved terrace *Thymus serpyllum* 'Coccineus major' and *Artemisia lanata pedemontana* would be delightful . . . for the shady border *Hypericum patulum henryi* . . . for grey foliage *Perovskia atriplicifolia* and *Helichrysum angustifolium* are excellent' . . .—with a more laconic style, perhaps in moments of stress reduced to 'Dr. Madam, Thanks for yrs. of 28th inst. . . . Please refer Hbs. & the Fragrant Gdn. pages 2 and 3 for ans. to Qu. A; and Glossary P. – for Qu. B; Illust. Plate – Rampion for Qu. C.,' . . . Or not, as the case may be.

Uplifted from these lower reasons for writing this book, there was during the First World War a strong trend of interest in herbs. During the 1939–45 war British-grown medicinal herbs were in great demand, and in the forefront of many country people's minds.

Culinary herbs, too, attained prominence to flavour variants of Woolton Pie and other patriotic delicacies. When foreign spices and condiments were in short supply sage, for instance, kept the traditional flavouring flag flying in sausages, strangely companioned by odd and cosmopolitan meats till pork returned to keep correct company once again.

Since the war, with the great increase from all walks of life of travel abroad, the secrets of continental cookery are explored and many would like to add that *je ne sais quoi*, having identified it, to their ordinary dishes.

Again, a clamour of continental cooks arises, and will not be stilled until the apathetic house doyen can produce cerfeuil, estragon and oregano. Threats of resignation and imminent departure if these necessities are not procured may well account for many a hasty visit to herb farm or garden. Such excursions will almost certainly have been preceded by nose-dives into the appropriate dictionary, found upholding the aspidistra (or, in modern vein, the saintpaulia).

One of the most frequent remarks in conversation is 'Herbs seem very interesting, but we know so little about them, and would like to know more.'

Indeed, for five hundred people who know the names tarragon, marjoram, caraway and angelica one would probably only find one who knows what the living plant looks like, and who could describe it.

Again, there is great confusion and mis-naming over the identity of many herbs. Lemon thyme, lemon balm and lemon verbena are most frequently confused; and good gardeners who would scorn to mix up lupins and delphiniums will confuse borage with alkanet, anchusa, comfrey and even lungwort. This is understandable, since illustrations of these herbs do not, for instance, abound on coloured seed-packets, to which best-selling line we owe a considerable amount of unconscious horticultural education. With herbs, in order to get the appropriate flavouring it is, obviously, vital to know the proper plant.

Beyond these considerations, there are horticultural fashions as there are in 'A lines' and 'New Looks', and chamomile and thyme lawns and knot gardens are in the forefront, written about and mentioned over the air. Again, with the second Elizabethan era, many people's minds went back to the first period, when the herb garden was the garden proper. In this way, interest was revived, with a nostalgic longing for what is imagined as the tranquil order and slow rhythm of life in those days.

Herbs, again, have power not only to give us a sense of proportion as we look back in time, and perhaps therefore some historic sense of security, but they have tremendous power to evoke memories, more often perhaps pleasant, poignant or restful than bitter.

This is one reason for the renewed interest in breeding and growing well-scented roses, sweet peas, carnations and other favourites. Aromatic plants, with a more subtle appeal, are popular for the same reason.

It is increasingly realized that aromatic plants can give particular pleasure to the blind, deprived of the deep joy we have of thrilling to the vibrant scarlet of oriental poppies, or the translucence of guelder-rose berries. The blue of delphinium spires, azure flames against a dark hedge, or the sunset-toned, incurving folds of a gold-hearted Talisman rose are our privilege.

Those without sight have a heightened sensitivity to the world of fragrance and scented public gardens with plant names labelled in braille are a feature in an increasing number of towns, among them Hove, St. Leonards, Chorley, Isleworth, Edmonton, Bath, Sevenoaks, Southport, and many others.

There are many personal instances of this aspect of the value of herbs. I recall a tea-party of blind children, when they were given sprigs of scented plants to enjoy and hold, and of the tightly-clutched, bruised sprigs that were considered treasures. Again, a lady having undergone an operation to improve her sight was not allowed to use her eyes for a period, and an understanding friend, knowing her pleasure in gardens, and the recuperative power this can have, took a bunch of labelled sprigs. He wrote later to say that she had had a diverting time with the herbs, teasing her nurses over not knowing the names, while she herself was preserving the sprigs to take home and strike, where possible, as cuttings for her pleasure in her own garden.

Again, the educational value of herbs is increasingly recognized in colleges and schools. Herbs are rooted deep in history, and the Bible pages hold many names that are household words to us. The bitterness of wormwood and gall, the cleansing hyssop, the wicked flourishing like a green bay tree are proverbial. It is more complimentary to refer to a friend as a palm or fir tree, as the righteous appear to thrive like these. It is therefore of great value to have a mental picture of the plant to match a knowledge of the phrase.

Again, Shakespeare and other poets have numerous references to the uses of plants. Pharmaceutical chemistry (in the elementary distilling of essential oils), domestic science (in the drying and uses of culinary herbs and those for scenting linen) and the winter preservation of plants, as well as the direct botanical aspects of herbs, are all relevant. For instance, it adds point to the classification of plants in families when it is realized that a certain range of essential oils is present in the *Umbelliferae*, and that these have economic and personal value and interest. Again, it introduces an element of widespread value to know that the *Solanaceae* contain not only plants well known as vegetables, the potato and tomato, but those in which poisonous alkaloids predominate, such as *Datura* and *Hyoscyamus* the henbane, which, rightly used, have great healing efficacy.

Nature study has more practical point if it can be shown that even ordinary daisies are used (as I know by practical experience during the war) to make a tincture for relieving asthma; or that eyebright with its cheerful yellow 'eye' in the flower, is used nowadays in the eye-lotions, while the wild clary, one of the sages, also means 'clear eye', and seeds can help to remove grit or dust from the eye.

The country-lover, out for a picnic on the Downs, having absentmindedly forgotten the sliced cucumber, and finding that the cool scent arising from under the picnic-rug is not mere wishful thinking, can pick leaves of the salad burnet to add to the sandwiches and provide the missing flavour. It is, of course, better to grow the garden kind, as it is more lush and prolific in growth, and of a more tender texture; but the wild form is not to be despised in emergencies.

When visiting ancient buildings, castles, abbeys and churches where there have been gardens for many centuries, it is interesting to see which herbs appear to be naturalized on the crumbling walls or in the vicinity. Pellitory-of-the-wall, greater celandine, periwinkles and deadly nightshade (the latter growing abundantly in Knole Park, near Knole House) may often be found.

The names of herbs hold fascination in themselves, and we have met those who would like to plant a herb garden because of the intriguing qualities of pellitory-of-the-wall, pennyroyal, costmary, elecampane and lovage. The names in themselves have a poetic flow, and even when the appearance of the plant does not live up to the quality of its name as with pellitory-of-the-wall (which merely encrusts itself with masses of minute green flowers), it adds depth to one's comprehension to know what the plant was used for.

Around Knole House and in many other places is found pellitory-of-the-wall, perching in crannies where wind-blown dust must be the chief source of soil-particles for its life. We can imagine bygone generations using a decoction for according to Gerard it 'Helpeth such as are troubled with an old cough.' The stem of the greater celandine, which exudes an orange juice, would be broken and squeezed on a wart that was detracting from a local beauty. Those who had frequently dined only too well would sooner or later have recourse to deadly nightshade as a liniment or plaster against gout. This plant, often called belladonna, is also naturalized in Knole Park and forms large clumps which look handsome, with their fine leaves and shining black berries, amongst the bracken or in the quarries. During the war we collected considerable quantities to meet the pressing need, as the drug has many beneficial uses in circulatory troubles, asthma and other disorders.

The pleasing mauve wheels of periwinkles radiate from wayside banks and copses near old shrubberies, and we can picture these plants being cultivated as a protection against 'wykked spirytis'. Pleasantly, it was called 'ye Juy of Gro wnde', or joy-of-the-ground, and used both as a remedy for cramp and as a conserve, against nightmares; also against 'envy and terrors and that thou mightest have grace'.

The ivy-leafed toadflax (*Linaria cymbalaria*) festoons the churchyard walls of St. Nicholas, Sevenoaks, and is found in many similar places. The small lilac 'snap-dragon' flowers and slightly succulent leaves make out an unusual plant which was formerly used in salads. At Beaulieu Abbey hyssop and savory are naturalized on the old walls.

I have covered a wide area in search of herbs and aromatic plants, and have lighted on some with the thrilled wonder of the far adventurer. The Botanic Gardens at Oxford yielded special delight, for the Labiates are warmly represented, and in September *Salvia involuerata bethellii* glowed in effulgent magenta, daring all who do not like that colour not to be impressed, even if not attracted. I liked it, and a whole group of others, introduced by the infinitely wide knowledge and appreciation of them shown by the Curator.

It was a misty September morning; I was shocked with pleasure at the impact of the crimson-smouldering virginian creeper, with Magdalen Tower in the background. I knelt there, sketching or making notes from early-breakfast onwards, in the silver mist.

A little later, I was told of an exciting rarity—a blue-flowered mandrake—in a certain garden. All night long the recesses of dreams were invaded with images of this gem. There it shone, the blue flowers luminous in the light of imagination.

Wakened not, as usual, by dawn but moonlight, I rose (for once at 3.30 a.m.) and as soon as possible was away on the mist-wreathed road. 'Pilgrim', the utility, was scudding along a high ridge of the North Downs when dawn, frequently overrated, flared up in a heart-warming coral and apricot.

I enjoy that alluring free cameo of the nautical life, capturing by its propinquity to great liners a modern savour of the magic and mystery of the east, of spices and Samarkand—the Woolwich Ferry. Sadly, I accepted that it was still closed owing to fog. The primeval roar of the white-tiled Blackwall Tunnel had to be safely negotiated instead. Then, as Chaucer would say, we 'priked' through the fog-veils for very many weary miles.

The sun had dispelled the fog-fantasy when I neared my destination. This pilgrimage had to be consummated alone. I was filled with the spell of mystery, the whisper of legend and romance echoing through the long centuries. Reverently, I entered the garden and located the site, guided to the right bed by—frankly—the characteristic, faintly decayed aroma of certain *Solanaceae*. I stilled my footsteps and gazed around.

Here was my herbal shrine. Yes; here stood a fine plant, thornapple leafed, with blue trumpets—pleasing scene of loveliness—beginning to open in the welcoming caress of the sun. Respectfully I stood before it; and with an odd blend of deference and doubt, began to draw and to colour the lovely flowing lines of leaf and flower. The questioning began at the calyx, cunningly inflated, which bore the oddest resemblance to *Nicandra physaloides*, encountered before in Oxford. But here was the label, only it was discreetly facing the plant—as a friend said afterwards, as though to ask the plant if it were really so.

My graphic efforts completed, I went in search of Authority, to have a definite ruling over the differences, obviously subtle, but well suited to the admirably-learned body responsible, between my lodestar, the reputed blue mandrake, and *Nicandra*.

In the meantime, Delegated Authority had gone out in person to the beds. Locating the personality, I approached, and with some diffidence put my question. I received the infinitely sad reply: 'The plant IS *Nicandra physaloides*, and I have this minute removed the label.'

The final delicate touch lay in finding the shoo plant . . . as a substitute for the alluring mandrake.

. . . .

There is an increasing number of people living in flats in towns who have just a paved yard or balcony, or even a window-ledge in which to exercise their gardening instincts. In such limited circumstances, where there is no real scope for vegetables or fruit (apart from mustard and cress on flannel or strawberry plants in a barrel), herbs provide the satisfaction of something home-grown.

As additions to the salad or the basis of an unusual savoury, or the foundation of a plate of herb biscuits, they make a talking-point. Above all, they give a hint of that special creative pleasure that is liable to be submerged in these synthetic, tabloid days.

I am always filled with respectful admiration when I travel through our suburbs and crowded areas by train or bus. I specify these two methods of transport because the true gardener, once distracted from the hazards of the road, is in danger of overshooting a policeman on point duty at the sight of a really beguiling window-box, or having as a Famous Last Word 'Look at that shrub on the roundabout—I think it's a *Philadelphus microphyllus*.'

Freed from these overruling cares of the road, I watch to see the gardener's instinct emerge. Here it may be a geranium or two on a window-ledge, with sooty leaves and lanky growth with lack of sun, but keeping their scarlet standard flying. On the other hand, there may be the triumph of a well-filled window-box, gay and challenging, with the royal glow of petunias, blue lobelias and poised fuchsias; or the fanfare of daffodils in the spring.

I think as I see these brave efforts that a few pots of herbs or a window-box outside the kitchen window, in addition to the cheerful show, would give pleasure and value of a different quality to the town-dwellers. Again, those with utility minds, who might scoff at the time and expense of flowers, would find fresh interest in growing and finding ways to use their herbs.

Others with an unstilled longing for the country and a real garden would find themselves able to have symbols, at any rate, at hand in the sight and scent of lemon thyme and marjoram, chives and rosemary.

For this reason I am devoting a section to window-box and general town gardening which will I hope be of detailed practical help.

For these reasons and others we find that at shows and exhibitions people who attend are always attracted by the herb stand. I have shown at Chelsea for eight years, with the primary object of providing an educational and decorative exhibit. At all times when the shows are well attended we are crowded with people wishing to make a closer acquaintance with the various herbs.

Many say that the quiet greys and greens, the soft purples and gold of the herb foliage provides a restful contrast to the glorious colours of most of the exhibits.

Again, the quality of fragrance and aroma, pungent, sweet or intriguing, makes a pleasing change in using another sense than that of sight.

Again, many have said that an exhibit in which each kind of plant has separate significance holds the attention longer than a stand of, perhaps, tulips or gladioli. One worships the blaze of glory from afar, then enjoys the contrast of the individual interest of the herbs.

It is because I have so often been in this unique position of learning personal reactions to herbs from a complete cross-section of real gardeners that I have written this book with many contacts in mind, and the questions commonly asked.

On seeing the exhibit, comments are many and varied, from 'cute' and intriguing to the superior amusement of those who entertain themselves asking us if we have brought up cow parsley and nettles. It is a little deflating to them to find that the 'cow parsley' is caraway with its white umbels of flowers, and the nettles are *Nepeta cataria*, while 'docks' resolve themselves into bistort or, more usually, broad-leaf sorrel.

Much surprise is always shown in finding that angelica and caraway can indeed be grown outside in this country, and the products used for cakes, while 'curry plant' and 'camphor plant' and wintergreen arouse interest because the scents are so well known in another connection, in the kitchen or medicine chest.

The wide range of mints always provokes comment, for so many say that they only thought there was one flavour of mint, and the rich variety provided by eau de cologne mint, apple mint, pineapple mint and the others, is appreciated and we are always then asked how they can be used. Quite frequently there is the comment 'I did not know there was a peppermint mint', a slightly illogical remark till one realizes that most people have never connected peppermint with mint plants, only with flavours.

The practical definition of a herb in our use of the word is not that of the botanist, for their meaning of the word is a non-woody plant. Since lavender, sage, rosemary and bay trees, for instance, are decidedly woody shrubs or trees, the botanists' meaning of the word is entirely different from that of this book.

For our purpose, a herb is any plant used for its flavouring qualities (the culinary and salad herbs); for its healing value (the medicinal herbs); or for its aromatic or scented properties.

The introduction, then, is a two-fold one. 'Sir, the anonymous herbage in your garden is lemon balm, marjoram and rue.' 'Yes, madam, here are your household names, angelica, caraway, horehound and tarragon in real life for you to meet.'

PASSOVER HERBS

On Dandelions quiet war is waged
(Those gold-crowned florets gaily whorled)
One moon-lit night this herb engaged
The central drama of the world.

Celestial blue the Chicory wheels
Speak of high Summer's picnic peace;
One hour it left the Hand that heals
For traitor's shame that shall not cease.

Horseradish, too, our homely herb,
Was blended in the Sop with these,
Given by compassionate Hand to curb
The jealous follower's deep disease.

Then came dark agony; then a light
More glorious than the flower's rich gold;
Heaven opened to us far more bright
Than Chicory's luminous flowers unfold.

CHAPTER TWO

The History of Herbs

The story of herbs is as old as history. In the early pages of Genesis we read 'Even as the green herb have I given you all things', a statement once again placed early in civilization by the discoveries of ancient writing at Ur of the Chaldees. In the Psalms, considerably later, there is the pleasant comment 'God who maketh the grass to grow upon the mountains, and herb for the use of man'.

These quotations imply that in earlier times all green plants were considered herbs, and it is as the practical use declines that the number of plants regarded as herbs is reduced also.

We have noted how wormwood and gall (from the opium poppy), hyssop and bay are mentioned in scripture. One of the earliest recorded is the mandrake, *Atropa mandragora*, prized for the scent of its fruits and for its romantic medicinal uses. It features in the story of Rachel, Leah and Reuben, and again in Canticles.

In the earliest days of history, in the Sudan, not later than 3000 B.C., incense was the most prized substance for trade after gold.

Perfumes were highly valued in the significant worship of the Tabernacle. An oil of holy ointment and a perfume were to be used, the former on the altar and the ark, also for the priests; the perfume, containing 'sweet spices, stacte, and onycha, and galbanum; . . . with pure frankincense' was to be placed beside the Testimony where God met his servant and friend, the High Priest. The perfume and oil were to be unique, and judgment lay on any who dared to make the same blends for their own pleasure. These compositions were to be holy—set apart. Frankincense was especially the symbol of prayer rising up to God.

These perfumes and spices are of eastern origin, unable to be cultivated outside in this country. Frankincense (known as *Boswellia thurifera*) is a forest tree with pinnate leaves and spikes of pink flowers, and its gum gives fine incense. Aloes (*Aloe vera*) have foliage rather similar to the low, palm-like *Agaves* cultivated ornamentally over here. They have reddish or golden flowers and are natives of Africa and elsewhere. Myrrh is a resin from various species of plants, one of which appears to be *Commiphora myrrha*, a spiny bush found by the Red Sea, in an almost impossibly barren and hot area, amongst other situations. Stacte is a liquid form of myrrh, according to some authorities, and is obtained from storax (*Styrax officinalis*), which has snowdrop-like flowers.

The shittah tree, yielding the aromatic wood, has yellow flowers and acacia-like foliage.

The balm of Gilead or balsam of Gilead comes from the *Commiphora opobalsamum*, yielding resinous juice. This is a small tree with trifoliate leaves and small reddish flowers, and was cultivated on the Mount of Gilead, but found wild in countries both sides of the Red Sea. Another plant, a Labiate, *Cedronella triphylla*, with a citron-like scent, is sometimes called balm of Gilead.

Cinnamon is obtained from an aromatic tree, *Canella alba*, and the bark yields the well-known and characteristic flavour. Calamus, the sweet rush, has foliage with cinnamon-like scent. Myrrh, cinnamon, cassia and calamus were ingredients of the holy oil of anointing.

The instructions for the equipping of the Tabernacle were full of meaning, and it is interesting to think round them. Why was the pomegranate chosen to be embroidered on the High Priest's robe? Because the flowers, of glorious crimson and orange-flame, were a reminder that all the gaiety and splendour of life, its vitality and beauty, were focussed in this highest service? And because the pomegranate, beyond the loveliness of its flowers, is valuable in every part? Almost in paradox, the fruit-juice is refreshing, and has refrigerant qualities in fevers, while the rind and leaves and the bark, are astringent and purgative. The flowers give a red dye, and the seeds are used in syrups and conserves. There is, too, great beauty in the subtle shading of the fruit.

By a strange coincidence, as I write this, a dwarf pomegranate, a friend's gift, is beginning to flower for me in the greenhouse. It is *Punica granatum nanum*, and at 3 inches high has three intensely bright flower-buds, which must represent considerable effort. It gives me a sense of the inspiration behind the specifications and of our unity with those seemingly far-off days, by the continuity of created beauty and significance.

Of other herbs with an early mention there is the description of manna from heaven as resembling coriander seed, small, round, white and pleasant to eat. Amongst other civilized delights for which the children of Israel languished when they complained bitterly in the wilderness was garlic.

The gourd shredded into the pot by the sons of the prophets was most probably the bitter colocynth, and in this way its valuable though unpalatable medicinal properties may have been discerned.

The acanthus, used by the Corinthians in sculpture on their pillars, is in the book of Job translated 'nettles'. The exquisite azure-blue, gold-centred water-lily, called *Nymphaea coerulea*, was used by the Jews for the design for the lily work carved on the chappiters of the Temple. It was also the sacred flower of Ancient

Egypt, symbolizing the spiritual life arising in perfection above the murk and mire.

One of the loveliest pictures of all time is the one in the Canticles or Song of Solomon likening the one loved to a perfumed garden, 'a garden enclosed'. Grown for their joy are 'an orchard of pomegranates, cypress, with spikenard and saffron, calamus and cinnamon, with all trees of frankincense, myrrh and also with all the chief spices, a fountain of gardens, a well of living waters, and streams from Lebanon. Awake, O North Wind, and come, thou South, blow upon my garden, that the spices may flow out. Let my beloved come into his garden, and eat his pleasant fruits . . . until the day break and the shadows flee away, I will get me to the mountain of myrrh and the hill of frankincense.' 'The vines with the tender grapes give a good smell.'

This poetry brings the wise king close to us in sensitivity and appreciation, for it is an experience now to go into a vinery in flower, when the first trusses of grapes are forming, for the unique and exquisite fragrance.

Ahab, that hard and ruthless king, had a single-minded wish to own Naboth's vineyard, to turn it into a herb garden, and the resulting conflict of interests led first to cynical crime and then to tragedy foretold to Ahab, ironically, in his projected place of peace, the herb garden, where the prophet found him.

In Isaiah's day the women wore, attached by chains, sweet balls which probably resembled the Elizabethan pomanders. The craftsmanship of a picture shimmering with reality and feeling comes to us also in the same book. 'The Lord said "I will take my rest, and I will consider in my dwelling-place like a clear heat upon herbs, and like a cloud of dew in the heat of harvest."' And in the same book we have a practical illustration of the ancient virtues of plants, when Hezekiah was healed of a serious boil by Isaiah's recommendation of a plaster of figs.

Hippocrates, whose name is immortalized in the doctors' Hippocratic oath, is said to have been born in Cos, an island off Asia Minor, but was of Greek origin. He pursued his researches, living around 460 B.C., and wrote medical studies. He is once mentioned by Aristotle and often quoted for his opinions on the virtues of plants.

Over three hundred years before Christ, the Greek philosopher Aristotle, who was the son of a doctor, lived and wrote. His successor was Theophrastus of Athens, who wrote a treatise *On the causes of Plants*, which has been considered the most important contribution to botanical science in antiquity and, some authorities even add, up to the Middle Ages.

Jesus was anointed with the costly, fragrant ointment of spikenard, which may have been the nard of spike lavender, or the product of a plant allied to the valerian, both of which yielded scented ingredients. Earlier on, at his birth, the symbolic gifts of the Wise Men had been gold, and frankincense and myrrh. When he outspokenly condemned the Pharisees for their wrong sense of proportion, he mentioned the herbs they were careful to tithe—mint and rue (used as a fumigant), anise (or dill) and cumin; but, tragically, they omitted judgment and the love of God, the great essentials for keeping the Commandments.

In Roman days, the second wife of Caesar Augustus lived at the Villa Livia, named after herself. Here, for her pleasure, she had a garden-room decorated all round with an exquisite fresco of a scented garden, with orange trees, oleanders, roses, carnations and many other flowers.

Pliny the Elder (c. A.D. 23–79) was a Roman, a man of tremendously wide learning and interests, who was a contemporary of Jesus and who wrote a Natural History in thirty-two books, of which the twentieth to twenty-seventh volumes were on medical botany. They showed the range of his enquiring mind, but revealed him as being credulous on many points. In his day mandrake and belladonna roots were sometimes humanely given to patients to chew as anaesthetics before an operation.

Dioscorides was a Greek medical man who served in Nero's army, and collected and collated much information on materia medica, which was popular in the Middle Ages. He described some 600 medicinal plants.

Galen, another familiar name whose opinions on medicinal plants are quoted, lived around A.D. 130–200. He was a Greek physician, born in Pergamos in Asia Minor, and had a considerable knowledge of Greek philosophy. He travelled widely, visiting the Alexandrian medical school. This school was famous for a long period, from around 306 B.C. until A.D. 642. Galen eventually settled in Rome. After Hippocrates, he is considered the most distinguished physician of antiquity.

As well as their uses for culinary purposes and for healing, and the delight and stimulation of their perfume, herbs played important parts in the old pagan rites, and were valued, in many cases, to ward off evil powers.

The wild *Verbena officinalis* or vervain (found wild on English chalk downs) with small mauve flowers, was considered to have numerous powers and virtues, being one of the Roman altar-plants, used symbolically by ambassadors in making pacts, worn against snakebites, and as a poultice against headaches, which latter use is still considered of value.

The *Leech Book* of Bald, in Anglo-Saxon, of A.D. 900, can (according to a medical authority) be regarded as the embryo of modern English medicine. It is written in the vernacular, by one Bald who may have been a friend of King Alfred, to whom prescriptions were sent by the Patriarch of Jerusalem, and to which Bald had access. This book is probably a third edition, comprising a blend of the ancient Britons' herb lore with that of Eastern origin. It has been estimated that the Anglo-Saxons had names for, and used, five hundred plants, while on the Continent only some three hundred and eighty are mentioned in a German herbal printed in 1485.

The well-known suffix 'wort' means herb, and their gardens were 'wyrtzerds' or 'herbyards'. For pleasure and use marigolds, sunflowers, and violets were grown, among many plants and flowers we know.

There are Saxon translations of a Latin manuscript dating very likely from the fifth century, *Herbarium Apuleii Platonici*, with illustrations which probably derived much from the herb drawings of ancient students described by Pliny. 'They drew the likenesses of herbs and wrote under them their effects.'

In Anglo-Saxon days, herb lore was blended with myth and superstition; Christian rites entangled with those of earlier, pagan periods. In the *Leech Book* of Bald, illness and disease were linked with malicious elves, and apart from human ailments, cattle could be 'elf-shot'. This is of interest, laid for comparison alongside some of the New Testament hints that illness and disease lie in the power of the forces of evil.

Amongst many other plants, mandrake and periwinkle were said to have great power against demoniacal possession. The nine sacred herbs, cited in a heathen lay of great antiquity, as having power against venoms included chervil, fennel, 'wergulu' the nettle, crabapple, mugwort, watercress, 'waybroad' the plantain and 'maythen' the chamomile.

Thus, herbs were valued for their directly curative properties; for their protective effects against antagonistic forces; and, too, for their effects on men's minds. Borage was said to be good against 'melancholie; it maketh one merrie'. Later on, in Gerard's *Herbal*, he quotes the old couplet

> I Borage
> Bring always Courage

which, remembering the cucumber scent of borage, reminds us of the present-day saying, 'cool as a cucumber'. Other herbs associated with power over the moods were the old Scottish saying 'Gather sweetbriar in June, for it promoteth cheerfulness', and 'To comfort the braine smel to camomill'.

These sayings were written down in the sixteenth century but were presumably oral traditions many centuries before. They raise interesting speculations, in the light of the modern rise of psychosomatic medicine, stressing the connection between unhealthy or depressed states of mind and body.

You will have had the experience of instinctively taking deep breaths when you have passed a cistus bush, giving off a warm, incense fragrance, or a sweetbriar on a sunny day after rain. With the deep breathing and the contact with reality outside yourself will come a relaxing of tension and feeling of well-being. Recently, I found that I had the same experience with the impact of surprised pleasure at the season's first sight of the cool, celestial blue of *Plumbago capensis*. It comes, again, on entering a greenhouse, aromatic with pelargoniums, giving forth a blend of citron, pines, rose, peppermint and balsamic incense on a February day, holding all the promise of spring. Again one breathes deeply and restfully, and well-being is renewed.

Again, borage has cooling physical properties, and if the 'melancholie' were due in part to the overheating oppressiveness of an August day, relief and lightness would come as a result of the drink or the dose.

Meadowsweet, water-mint and vervain, amongst others, were strewn on floors and these especially were said to bring contentment and happiness. Just as peppermints make one inhale deeply and so begin to bring release from cramping indigestion, water-mint might well have the same effect when bruising brought out its strong scent. Meadowsweet, apart from the quietly anaesthetizing effect of the cumerin in its flowers, always has a delightful power of suggestion, bringing to mind tranquil, cool water-meadows on drowsing summer days. Vervain was symbolically endowed with many powers, although it has no aroma to recommend it.

In the thirteenth century Bartholomaeus Anglicus, an Englishman, became a famous professor of theology in Paris and wrote *De Proprietatibus Rerum*, nineteen volumes on Natural History. The seventeenth deals with herbs and their uses, including references to the writers of antiquity who discoursed on herbs, such as Dioscorides. This book is the only original work on herbs written by an Englishman in the Middle Ages. It was written in Latin but translated into English and first printed by Caxton's apprentice, Wynken de Worde, in 1493.

There are some delightful quotations from this book in Eleanour Sinclair Rohde's *The Old English Herbals*, and we can sense the real love of roses, lilies, apples and many other plants possessed by this great simple and clear-minded man. He describes the taste of some apples as 'mery'; and of the lily says 'though the levys of the floure be white yet wythen shyneth the lyknesse of golde'.

During the Middle Ages the monastery gardens must have furnished most of the herbs used both in their own infirmariums and to cure ill people in the towns. Herbs, too, were grown in the gardens belonging to houses of any importance, and ladies and their maids tended and collected the herbs, making them into ointments, unguents and many healing preparations. Later on, the stillroom was a vital place in the country house, for, in addition to the directly medicinal uses of herbs, elaborate toilet waters, cosmetic preparations, sweet bags, flower syrups and many other preparations were made. It is remarkable to consider the time that must have been spent on all these creations. Flowers were candied, perfumed candles made, anti-moth powders blended, and most housewives prided themselves on the individuality of their recipes, often handed down as treasured secrets.

At the same time, a range of culinary herbs was grown, before the spices from the East lost their costliness and became readily available. Mint seems to have been grown in this country since very early times; it is mentioned, with fennel, by Chaucer. Savory, borage, lemon balm, purslane, hyssop and costmary, the latter mentioned by Spenser, were all appreciated. Lovage, with a strong celery scent and taste, was valued and, remarkably enough, used for scenting baths. Mint and other herbs were used for this purpose.

Following the printing of Bartholomaeus Anglicus's work on herbs in 1495, another book, Banckes's *Herbal* which appears to be an anonymous anthology of herbal lore, came out in 1525. In this Herbal the pleasant name Alleluia is given to wood sorrel (or wodsour). It is also, maybe, cheering to know that if we put dry roses to the nose they 'do coforte the braine and the harte and quencheth sprite'.

This was closely followed by the *Grete Herbal*, printed in 1526 by Peter Treveris, in Southwark. This appears to be a compilation and has a complicated history, being a translation from the French *Le Grant Herbier* itself a version of a Latin manuscript of 1458. There are rather pleasing injunctions on bugloss, which, if eaten, 'confermeth and conserueth the mind'; while powdered betony with wine was recommended taken 'at the tyme that the fere cometh'.

In medieval and later days, innumerable herbal wines, beers and versions of mead were made and relished. The famous Chartreuse of the monks was flavoured with a considerable range of herbs. Homely brews such as elderberry wine, elder flowers used to give ordinary wines a muscadine bouquet, cowslip wine drunk as a sedative, alecost (or costmary) was used to give a spicy flavour to ale.

It is interesting to trace the inclusion of various herbs in literature. A representative bouquet of herbs and flowers can be gathered from the pages of Shakespeare. The best-known reference perhaps concerns a certain bank 'where the wild thyme blows'; and 'rue, sour herb of grace', as well as 'There's rosemary and rue'; but mint, savory and marjoram, with 'hot lavender' were all mentioned by Perdita in *The Winter's Tale*, hyssop by Iago, and fennel by Falstaff.

There is the contrast between good and evil men in *Romeo and Juliet*—the apothecary, betraying his high calling, willing to barter lives for money, and Friar

Laurence, also skilled in the value of herbs, and with spiritual clarity of mind and insight on their right use.

I have always enjoyed Milton's *L'Allegro*, with its reference to 'The sweetbriar and the vine and the twisted eglantine', even though it appears that he was confused between woodbine the twining honeysuckle and eglantine, usually a synonym of sweetbriar. In the same open-air poem, speaking of rural delights, he mentions 'Herbs and other country messes which the neat-handed Phyllis dresses'.

Bacon's classic essay *Of Gardens* captures a leisured appreciation that is in contrast with our streamlined days. Perhaps it was partly that like some genius of the lamp he had only to command, and his cool alleyways and trimmed hedges would be planted and tended for him. One likes to feel akin to him when he suggests the planting of water-mint, thyme and burnet in paths.

In Elizabethan and Stuart days, knot-gardens, laid out with a clipped pattern, were favourite garden features. Savory, santolina, lavender and marjoram were amongst the plants used; and living sundials were also fashionable during the period.

During the mid-sixteenth century came a landmark in the literary world, for Turner, known as the father of English botany, wrote his herbal. It is pleasant to learn that at Cambridge he was a friend as well as pupil of Ridley, the famous martyred Bishop of London. Turner was at one time Dean of Wells, but on the accession of Mary he had to take refuge on the Continent, and from Cologne published the second part of his *Herbal*, having written the first part in England. He seems to have been equally famous for his tremendous contribution to the study of plants and their uses, and, at the time, for his Protestant views and somewhat unorthodox behaviour.

Turner's descriptions of plants are careful and detailed. I like the one about Cornflowers. '. . . Blewbottel groweth in ye corne, it hath a stalke full of corners, a narrow and long leefe. In the top of the stalke is a knoppy head whereupon growe bleweflowers about midsummer.' Reinstated later at Wells, Turner eventually retired and had a physic-garden in London.

Gerard, a contemporary of Turner's, had a wonderful garden in Fetter Lane, in the City, a nostalgic fact that makes one yearn for a back-glimpse of those days. A passionate urge comes over me to see London as it was when Gerard gathered mallow, shepherd's purse, woodruff, bugle and clary in and around Gray's Inn Lane. And I long for the privilege of searching for the pimpinell rose (or burnet rose) 'in a pasture as you goe from a village hard by London called Knights brige unto Fulham, a Village thereby', or finding 'Osmund the Water-Man', a Hampstead pond fern.

It appears that Gerard's endearing *Herbal*, published in 1597, owes much, unacknowledged, to an English translation of Doedens' *Pemptades*. Gerard's *Herbal* has, however, a delightful stamp about it, and it was popular because of its refreshingly gifted evocation of herbs and flowers. There they are, lovingly observed and described; dew-fresh and of interest to us because Gerard himself cared so much for them. His writing bridges the centuries for us.

I like his deprecating description of the admittedly sombre flowers of deadly nightshade, which he calls 'sleepy nightshade', a more tactful euphemism—'small hollow floures bel-fashion, of an overworn purple colour'; followed by 'berries green at first, but when they be ripe, of the colour of black jet or burnished horne, soft, and full of purple juice; among which juice lie the seeds . . .'

It is suggested that since Shakespeare lived for a time close by, he was almost certain, being a famous literary man, to have seen and enjoyed Gerard's garden.

During Elizabethan and Stuart days, gallant adventurers sailed to the New World, and sent back specimens and seeds of exciting botanical finds that they made. The introduction of tobacco and the potato are classic stories; it seems, too, that the American sassafras was introduced for its medicinal value, being used in Seville against the pestilence.

Parkinson is generally considered to be the last of the great writers of herbals. His great book *Paradisi in Sole* reveals a riot of captivating names, of enchanted blossoms, striped, enamelled, jewel-like in their profusion of beauty, infectious in the enthusiasm one catches even from quotations of his pages.

It appears that clove gillyflowers are carnations (spelt with gay abandon, also, gillow flower, gilliflower, or gillofloures, in collaboration with Gerard); yellow stock-gillofloures are wallflowers; and stocke gillo-floures are, just stocks. It is not perhaps surprising that the heady comradeship of such exquisite scents, spicy, provocative and alluring, should have linked our garden friends into a fraternity of gillyflowers.

If Gerard kindles my imagination of London as it was, Parkinson stirs into a kaleidoscopic whirl of canterbury bells and sweet williams, of paeonies, sea-holly and gentians; of special tulips, from Candie and Armenia, and others named Fool's Coat and Cloth of Silver; of rosemary, too, and lavender, tarragon, liquorice, patience, angelica and many other herbs. The list is humbling in its prodigality and in the mental delineation he can achieve of the treasures he grows in Long Acre.

Parkinson's great herbal, *Theatrum Botanicum*, was completed in 1640, when he was 73. It did not appear to have the same drawing-power as Gerard's *Herbal*, although it was the author's great life-work. Still, in his time, much folk-lore was included with serious remarks on the medicinal values of herbs.

Culpeper's name is well known in connection with his *Herbal*, dated in 1652. Culpeper stressed his belief in the astrological significance of herbs, which seems curious to us. He was apprenticed at first to an apothecary, then decided to practise on his own, in Spitalfields, in the dual role of herbalist and astrologer, drawing on himself the wrath of the College of Physicians by issuing his *Physical Directory*, a translation of the *London Dispensatory*.

The value of medicinal herbs was based to a considerable extent on the Doctrine of Signatures, which taught that plants carried on them evidence of the healing use of the plant or signs of the ailment for which it was a cure. William Coles, a contemporary of Culpeper, wrote *Adam in Eden*, and *The Art of Simpling*. He believed in the Doctrine of Signatures and says "Though Sin and Sathan have plunged mankinds into an Ocean of Infirmities Yet the mercy of God which is over all his Workes Maketh Grasse to grow upon the Mountaines and Herbs for the use of Men and hath given them particular signatures whereby a Man may read even in legible characters the Use of them.' 'Walnuts bear the whole Signature of the Head, the outwardmost green barke answerable to the thick skin whereunto the head is covered, and a salt made of it is singularly good for wounds in that part, as the Kernell is good for the braines which it resembles.'

Similarly, the pale patches on the leaves of lungwort (*Pulmonaria officinalis*) were considered to look like unhealthy lungs; and the plant, actually, is good for chest complaints. The yellow juice of *Chelidonium majus* suggested jaundice; and the plant has been used in infusion against this trying complaint; and, a lady in North Somerset has told me that she has used it to cure the 'yellows', a canine ailment.

There appear, however, to have been many instances when the fanciful application of this doctrine related to plants having little or no curative value at all; and perhaps in these cases the power of suggestion was the healing factor.

It is of course of interest to ruminate on the way man first learnt of the healing qualities of different plants. One can assume that in primitive times watching the animals browse on certain plants when they were below par would suggest to man the wisdom of taking the same things. There must have been considerable 'trial and error' and experiment when there was a low standard of the value of human life. And, as we have seen, a remarkable blend of real factual knowledge was combined with superstition and useless methods until the times of Coles or later. Much information was handed down as oral tradition before it was embodied in the numerous herbals described.

The Still-Room Books were a link between herbals and cookery books, for they contained a practical blend of recipes for medicinal, cosmetic and culinary purposes. Once again, one striking feature is the time that must have been taken up in the loving preparation of the various concoctions made; and the serious attention paid to all the details. I am always stabbed by the contrast which assails my imagination. Pictures of the lovely things that came out of the Elizabethan and kindred eras—poetry, drama, the light and colour of pageantry, the love of gardens and plants, the affectionate care bestowed on delicate recipes such as 'molds for apricock Plumbs', or 'to preserve double blew violetts for Salletts', or a 'Conserve of Red Roses'. And set against it, within a mile or two of the charming people engaging on these delicious and civilized delights, the horrors of the Tower or of Smithfield. I find the moral dualism (not out of place to be mentioned in a book that deals with the arts of healing mind, body and spirit) grim and suggestive.

But to resume—amongst famous compilers of Still-Room Books, Sir Kenelm Digby, that remarkably versatile man in an age of wide interests—he was a man of adventure, of scientific investigation, a medical man and herbalist—collected recipes as some might gather autographs, and immortalized his friends. In *The Old English Herbals* we read of some of them—'The Queen's Barley Cream'; Sir Paul Neal's way of making Cider', 'Meathe from the Muscovian Ambassador's Steward' (evidently an international diplomatic triumph, leading, one wonders, to an entente cordiale?).

Others were 'White Metheglin of My Lady Hungerford's which is exceedingly praised', and 'My Lord of Denbigh's Almond March-Bane'. There they are, mead, metheglin and marzipan, using herbs and honey, almonds or fruit flavourings.

During the eighteenth and nineteenth centuries other herbals were compiled, and they became more in the nature of botanical treatises though at the same time retaining herbal features. For instance, in 1710 William Salmon published the *English Herbal or History of Plants*, with details such as we should find in a modern flora; also their preparations, 'Galenick and Chymick'; a section on garden flowers, with notes on commercial horticulture, described as 'where you have their culture, choice, increase, and way of management, as well for profit as for delectation.' And the illustrations in such books began to be both accurate and lovely.

Gerard's *Herbal* had been illustrated with woodcuts; and some earlier illustrations had traditional derivations not from the plants in real life but from old manuscripts; for instance, possibly from a sixth-century manuscript of Dioscorides.

At the same time, the exquisite technique of the Dutch masters in their flower-compositions brought out the natural, if stylized glories of blossoms and foliage.

In 1737, Elizabeth Blackwell produced her lovely hand-coloured engravings combining the best qualities of both schools of illustration. Her husband Alexander wrote the text for the work they published, *A Curious Herbal, containing five hundred of the most useful plants which are now used in the practice of Physic*. In this book, which was widely praised, the plants were grouped according to their medicinal value. The book was still primarily a herbal, rather than a botanical work. The flower-studies, taken from life, show a profound love of detail, not in the arrogance of fantasy but the humility of recording and emphasizing the created loveliness.

In 1838 the *Flora Medica*, a botanical account of the more important plants used in medicine, in different parts of the world, was written by John Lindley, Ph.D., professor of Botany in University College, London, and Vice-Secretary of the Horticultural Society. His name is enshrined for us in the Society's Lindley Library.

During the last centuries, therefore, the interest in curative herbs was upheld, though it had become more of a special science. In the garden, the cultivation of vegetables introduced from abroad, the spread of landscape gardening, and of fascinating plant discoveries from abroad, combined to take the main attention from the herb border. Many old favourites were grown, however, rosemary, lavender and southernwood having a lasting appeal; and the scented pelargoniums were popular in Victorian times.

The great compilation of this century has been Mrs Grieve's *A Modern Herbal* in two volumes, edited by Mrs Leyel, and published in 1931.

During the First World War the importance of herbs was made prominent by the wish to reduce imports and the great need of curative drugs. Drying sheds were set up in many places, and wild drugs such as foxgloves, *colchicum* and belladonna were collected and dried, for pharmaceutical use. At this time Mrs. Grieve wrote many detailed monographs on the uses of the various plants, and on food from the hedgerows—tea and coffee substitutes to help in the acute days of rationing, and nuts and fruit of nutritive value.

The Herb Farm at Seal was founded in 1926 by the late Miss D. G. Hewer, who had a science degree. She began with an acre and took in more land in due course, growing lavender, peppermint, rosemary, and culinary herbs such as sage, mints, marjoram, angelica, lemon balm and thyme.

She was in a true sense a courageous pioneer. There were those with country traditions, whose forebears had talked of many herbs and used them, who wished to grow their own flavours, but did not know of any source of supply for herb plants and seeds, very slenderly stocked by ordinary nurserymen, and the Herb Farm offered an intriguing list.

There were those who enjoyed the fashion of using special cosmetics and soaps, perfumes and preparations such as elder and honey tablets, soothing ointment prepared from alecost, and other out-of-the-way blends. A shop in the West End by the nineteen-thirties independent of the Herb Farm, and subsequently under the aegis of a large combine, sold these preparations with éclat and introduced a blend of country freshness and fashionable sophistication.

Pot-pourris have always had a following, for the evocative pleasure of the fragrances, reminiscent of 'old times', of some home remembered in childhood, of old country houses, or, again, capturing the summer loveliness to hold during the bleak winter days. To those abroad, it brings the essence of the English summer countryside.

Pomanders in Elizabethan days and kindred eras were of various kinds. They were, in simpler form, oranges stuck with cloves and dried, and gave out a warmly aromatic scent. More elaborately, they were chased and perforated metal containers filled with a blend of spicy and perfumed ingredients according to the owner's fancy. They were carried about to impart a 'bouquet' to the air in unpromising surroundings and, it was hoped, to ward off pestilence, in the same way as the judge's bunch of rue carried to the assizes.

The making of pomanders became briefly a Kentish industry around here before the last war, and dried clove-filled oranges were made and sent to town by the hundred, to be finally embellished with cord or ribbon, and in some cases specially scented, to be hung in the home for pleasure and as a traditional link.

Apart from places like the Herb Farm, which preserved the intimate and personal atmosphere of traditional herb associations, there have been and are large-scale farms either combining with market-garden crops or specializing in the growing of lavender, sage, mint, parsley, and some medicinal drug crops such as peppermint, chamomile, henbane, belladonna and thornapple for appropriate purposes. The lavender would be destined for distilling, the culinary herbs occasionally for the fresh market, more often for drying and final preparation; the medicinal crops for oil extraction or drying.

The homoeopathic chemists have also required a considerable variety of fresh medicinal herbs. During the war we had a detailed schedule from an impeccable West End firm requesting in the main from one to five pounds of a great number or herbs, wild or cultivated. For instance, it involved sorting out and collecting the bulbous, creeping and meadow buttercups and supplying the whole fresh plant separately. The deadly nightshade with root; calendula the marigold, for a soothing ointment, aconite the monkshood and many others were required. As we surveyed the list, however, we blenched a little. Soberly, with full use of Latin names, we were asked for (so to speak, late and pickled in alcohol), ladybirds, woodlice, jellyfish and *Arania diadema*, the papal cross spider.

A managerial meeting was held on the subject. These were crucial days; any request for supplies must be seriously considered. Ladybirds were ruled out as being in the nature of Beneficial Beasts to Agriculture. Jellyfish . . . it meant hazarding the incredulity of a military post a few miles away; should we not have been hailed either as singularly inept spies or as not wholly balanced if we had asked quietly to be allowed to drive to Herne Bay or Hythe for jellyfish? Then, the mines? And just how are jellyfish landed, anaesthetized and committed to alcohol? We abandoned this enterprise also. Woodlice? We were, it seems tyros in the Culture of the Common Pill, Slater or Woodlouse. Count them your enemies, and they thrive; cultivate them, and they fade away.

The spider—the fellow who spins an elegant web, dew-bespangled, which comes in conflict with your face across the garden path on a September morning. We collected him (and her), to the tune of an ounce or two and I repaired to the fashionable precincts in London.

I glided to the counter with my offering, asked the elderly retainer if I could speak to the managing director, and was told: 'Madam, the Director is upstairs, expressing mistletoe berries!'

The centuries roll away; we have links with the Druids, with Bald and his Anglo-Saxon friends, a detached though gloomy interest in the witches' brew in Macbeth. We could find comradeship with the apothecaries, would have loved to go plant-hunting with Gerard, or evoked delight with Parkinson.

And during a war sickening with sulphurous missiles, once again the herbs bridged the centuries, needed, as in the first world war, to give flavour to the food, from a chives pot on a window-ledge to thousands of sages for a farmer to grow and dry for the butchers.

During the years since the war, imports of culinary herbs from France, Italy, Yugoslavia, North America and elsewhere have made it uneconomic in many cases to grow culinary herbs unless on an extremely large scale in this country, where labour has become so much more expensive, while that abroad, combined with the wild state of many herbs and the warm drying weather, makes conditions much more reasonable.

But the interest in herb gardens has become, as already mentioned, considerable; and fresh herbs are sent up to town to decorate a banquet; herbs are carried and scattered solemnly in procession for the Lord Mayor of London, the City Solicitor and other dignitaries on a ceremonial occasion. Not so long ago the Henry VIII Chapel in Westminster Abbey was decorated with rosemary, curry plant and lavender; with fennel, pineapple mint, and santolina and all manner of aromatic plants to mark a great occasion, when Her Majesty Queen Elizabeth II came to institute two new Knights to the Grand Order of the Bath, spanning the years with the humane and ancient order of Chivalry.

CHELSEA, 1955

She swept into the Show with her regal grace,
Past the high-banked azaleas, a fanfare of hope,
And light-winged, garnet brooms, to the strange calm place
Where sparkling streams cascade, fine-spun down the slope
Over chiselled waterfalls, into the tarns, flower-pearled.
She paused to enter into the alpine meads,
Primula, gentian-gemmed; then past unfurled
Heraldic splendours of spring, where the perfume leads
To the scented plants, still silver, translucent green,
Set off by the soft pink parterre; and here the Queen
Mother said quietly, 'Lovely herbs.' The sun
Dappled the leaves with dancing light and the day
Glittered with glory within as she passed on her way,
Royal bestower of courage for tasks begun.

CHAPTER THREE

The Herb Garden

THE SCENT OF PLANTS

It is entirely appropriate that the scented plants and the herb garden should be considered together. Some plants, for instance lavender, have aromatic leaves and scented flowers. It is, however, more usual to find the two qualities separate—cistus and southernwood have strongly aromatic leaves, but the flowers are not endowed with fragrance.

Generally speaking, the aromatic qualities are more subtle than those of fragrance. In some plants the air around is impregnated with the aroma, as with sweetbriars and pine trees; but usually this quality is not brought out particularly strongly apart from handling except after rain, which would bruise the scent-glands in the foliage; or under a warm sun or a hot day, which helps to volatilize the essential oil content and bring it out on the air. Then rosemary, santolina and lemon verbena, marjoram and pelargonium are noticed.

The fragrance of flowers varies, too; and obviously, one plant will not have the widely-permeating influence of a large bed. Amongst those whose fragrance seems to float widely are the musk hybrid roses, honeysuckle, making a whole lane exquisite in season; lime trees, having the advantage of height and quantity of flowers; and privet, exhaling its odd aroma—a little irreverently, like the emanation from a milk-chocolate-biscuit factory, but possessing for me the pleasing associations of summer holiday lanes and gardens by the sea.

Then there is philadelphus, the mock-orange, overpowering to some, but rather lovely in the garden; and the wistfulness of meadowsweet. The dianthus Rainbow Loveliness has as heart-breaking a scent as any—it stabs and heals at the same time.

For me, wallflowers have a wonderfully friendly and homely scent; and stocks also, perhaps with an unconscious domestic hint of cloves and so of apple pies and their associations.

Violets and primroses have an intimacy of clean goodness; while lilac and lily-of-the-valley have an elusive perfection, the seductive trail of the unattainable till we reach eternity.

The traditional spiciness of clove gilliflowers or carnations accords well with the herb garden; and the old-fashioned sweet peas, purple-violet and crimson, have the finest perfume. If one collects seed of the waved kinds and sows it, then collects again another year, some variants of the old-fashioned type usually occur.

There are now charming dwarf single sweet peas growing some 12 inches high.

Some are most drawn by the mystery of white jasmine; others by nicotiana (now produced in colours and with flowers that stay open during the day) or night-scented stock. The widely exhaled fragrance of lilies has a spiritual quality, charged with meaning that is repeated in the varied depths or purity of the flower.

There is all the renewed hope of spring in the first bunch-flowered narcissus bought at Christmas, holding a promise we can trust; and in the sweetness of hyacinths grown indoors to cheer the late winter days.

Have you thought of the contribution made by trees and hedges? Pines give out a healing type of scent, perhaps specially valuable as it suggests, with the tang of bracken, the freedom of heather-covered hills. Amongst firs, the *Pseudotsuga douglasi*, the Douglas fir, has a scent redolent of pineapples. Cypress and particularly thuja hedges impart a fruity tang to the air; and there is the indefinable freshness of box hedges. The far-flung fragrance of apple-blossom is delectable.

Whatever the design of the herb garden, these shrubs and plants can be brought into the scheme. Honeysuckle, wistaria, with a musky aroma, *Clematis montana* with starry flowers and a vanilla scent, white jasmine and climbing roses can be trained on the house, the shed or unsightly building, made to ramble over a pergola or arbour, or trailed on a trellis of suitable design. Sheltering hedges could include some of the aromatic subjects, such as thuja. For dwarf hedges, lavender and those others mentioned later can be employed.

The aromatic scented shrubs may also in some cases be trained on walls or fences; or grown as specimens. They can be particularly useful to provide shelter from prevailing winds, or to fill borders on the fringe of the scheme, interplanted with suitable perennial or annual herbs or scented plants—lungwort, hellebores, *Anchusa sempervirens*, for interest, or annuals such as night-scented stock. Some low aromatic shrubs also provide ground-cover, such as wintergreen and *Sarcococca humilis*, with scented flowers in spring.

Carnations, pinks, and viola (with a subtle, friendly scent all their own), are suitable for filling-in the groundwork of knot-gardens, and for clumps at the front of the border. During the summer, large groups of the various scented pelargoniums, pineapple sage and heliotrope can be planted-out, remembering that the average height will be 2 feet or so. *Humea elegans* is delightful, too.

TYPES OF GARDEN

The herb garden can be anything from a yard-square patch near the kitchen door to a formal and decorative garden 200 feet square. One great aspect that needs to

THE HERB GARDEN

Diagram of a circular herb garden plan:

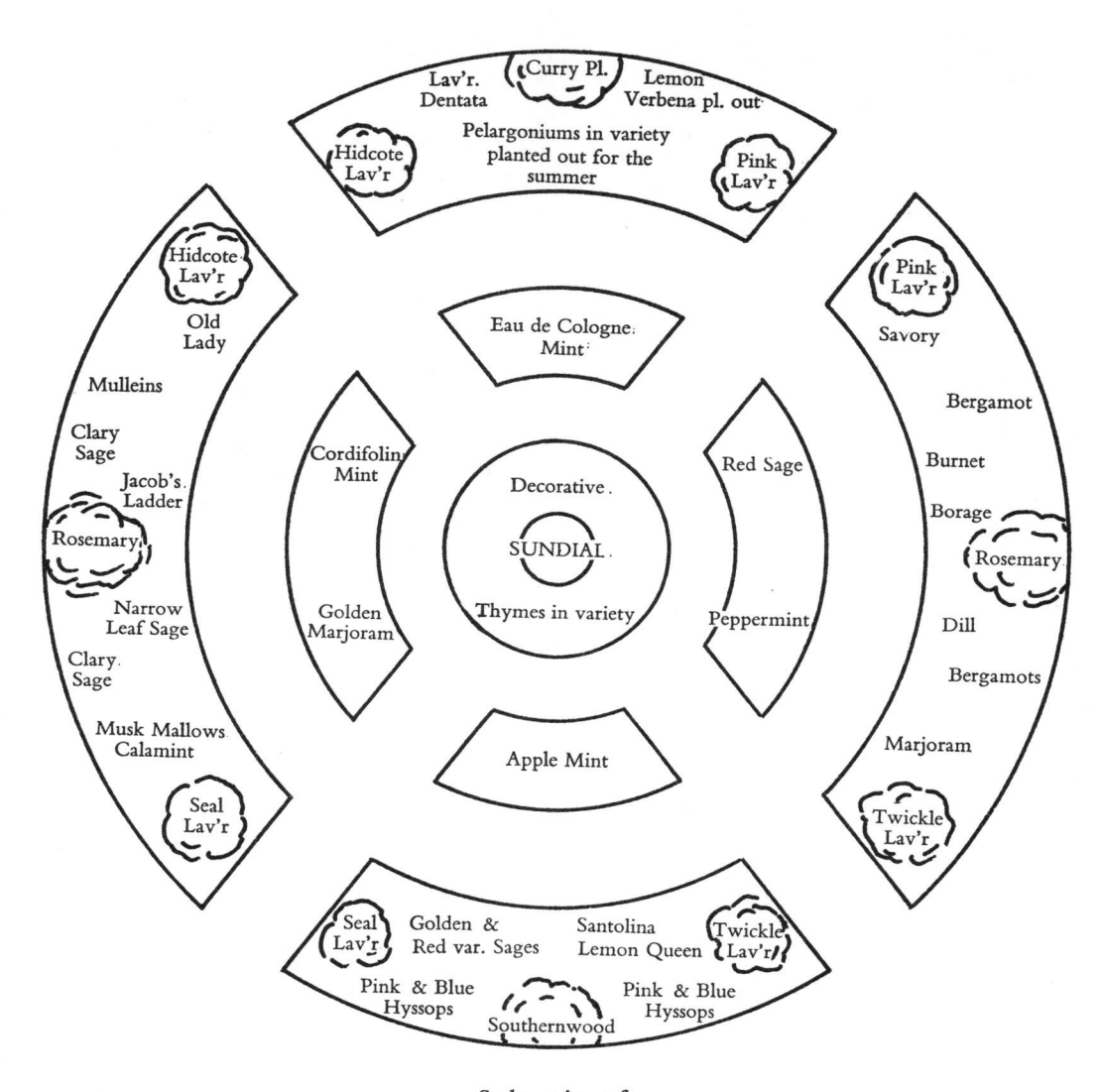

Top bed (outer arc):
- Lav'r. Dentata
- Curry Pl.
- Lemon Verbena pl. out
- Hidcote Lav'r
- Pelargoniums in variety planted out for the summer
- Pink Lav'r

Left outer arc:
- Hidcote Lav'r
- Old Lady
- Mulleins
- Clary Sage
- Jacob's Ladder
- Rosemary
- Narrow Leaf Sage
- Clary Sage
- Musk Mallows
- Calamint
- Seal Lav'r

Right outer arc:
- Pink Lav'r
- Savory
- Bergamot
- Burnet
- Borage
- Rosemary
- Dill
- Bergamots
- Marjoram
- Twickle Lav'r

Bottom bed (outer arc):
- Seal Lav'r
- Golden & Red var. Sages
- Santolina Lemon Queen
- Twickle Lav'r
- Pink & Blue Hyssops
- Southernwood
- Pink & Blue Hyssops

Inner beds:
- Eau de Cologne Mint (top)
- Cordifolin Mint (left upper)
- Golden Marjoram (left lower)
- Red Sage (right upper)
- Peppermint (right lower)
- Apple Mint (bottom)

Centre:
- Decorative SUNDIAL
- Thymes in variety

Scale—1 in.–4 ft.

I. This design would be given added interest if the paths were made of Chamomile (outer circle), Creeping Thymes (inner circle) and Pennyroyal (cross-paths). The top bed has half-hardy subjects planted out from the end of May till late September.

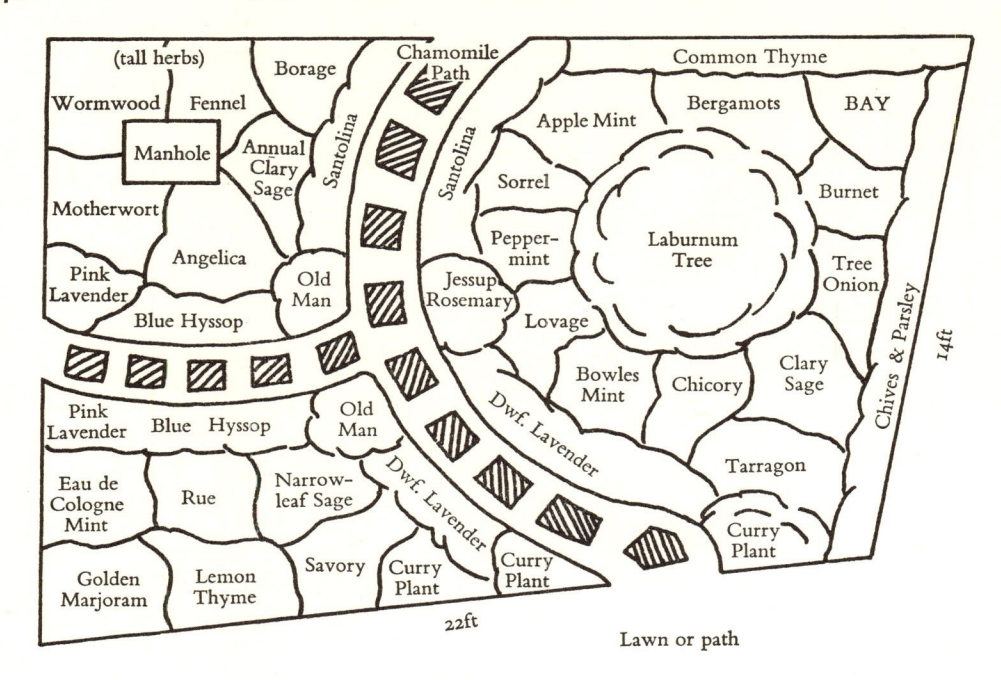

II. The path, in which "Noelite" or similar paving stones are used, embedded in Chamomile, follows the curving outline of the Laburnum tree. Interest and utility are blended.

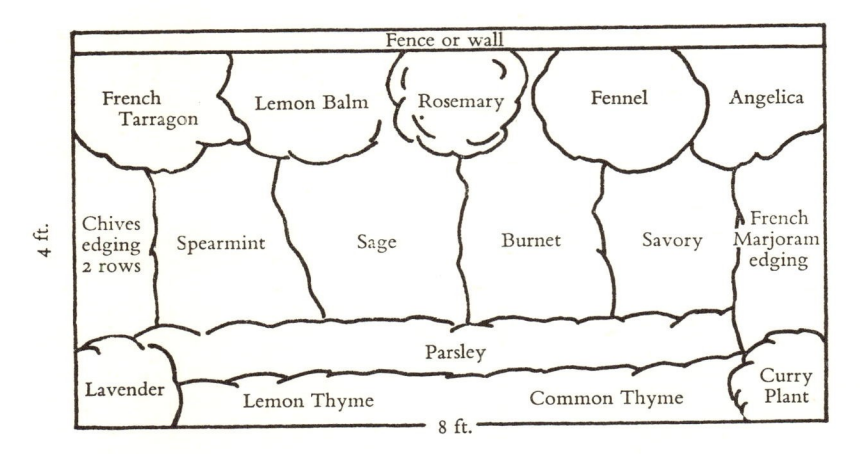

III. This small herb bed, located if possible near the house, is useful; the Mint is included where other space is not available but could be replaced.

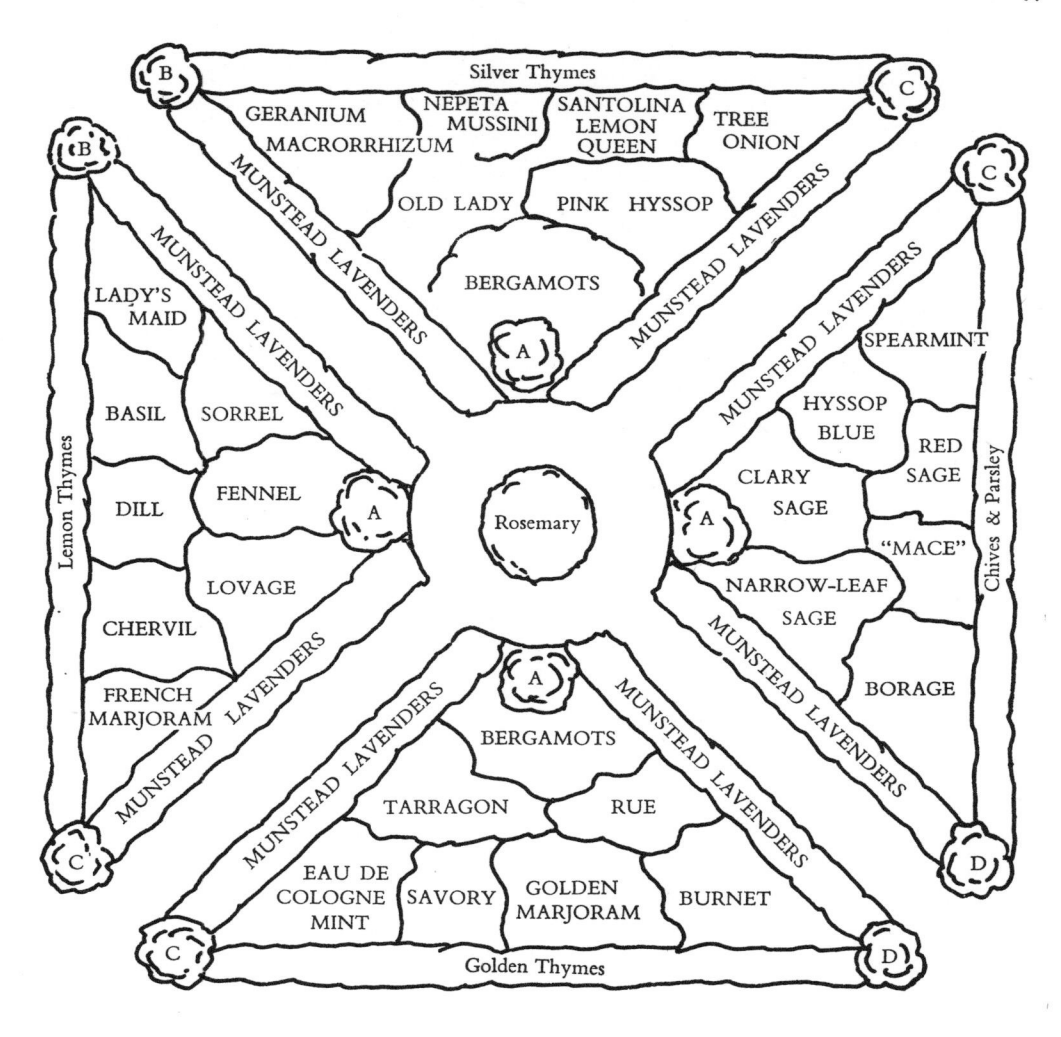

THE HERB GARDEN

(Diagram of a square herb garden, centred on Rosemary, divided by diagonal paths of Munstead Lavenders into four triangular beds. Labels around the diagram:)

- Silver Thymes (top edge)
- Golden Thymes (bottom edge)
- Lemon Thymes (left edge)
- Chives & Parsley (right edge)

Top triangle: GERANIUM MACRORRHIZUM, NEPETA MUSSINI, SANTOLINA LEMON QUEEN, TREE ONION, OLD LADY, PINK HYSSOP, BERGAMOTS

Left triangle: LADY'S MAID, BASIL, SORREL, DILL, FENNEL, LOVAGE, CHERVIL, FRENCH MARJORAM

Right triangle: SPEARMINT, HYSSOP BLUE, RED SAGE, CLARY SAGE, "MACE", NARROW-LEAF SAGE, BORAGE

Bottom triangle: BERGAMOTS, TARRAGON, RUE, EAU DE COLOGNE MINT, SAVORY, GOLDEN MARJORAM, BURNET

Centre: Rosemary

Corner markers: A. Seal Lavenders B. Curry Plants C. Southernwoods D. *Santolina* (Cotton Lavenders)

Scale—1 in.–4 ft.

IV. This delightful 20 ft. square herb garden is centred on a Rosemary bush. Cross-paths are edged with dwarf Lavenders, and outside edges to beds look neat planted with Thymes, and Chives with Parsley. Paved or grass paths may be interplanted with Chamomile, Creeping Thymes and Pennyroyal. The triangular beds can be made useful and attractive with a rich variety of herbs.

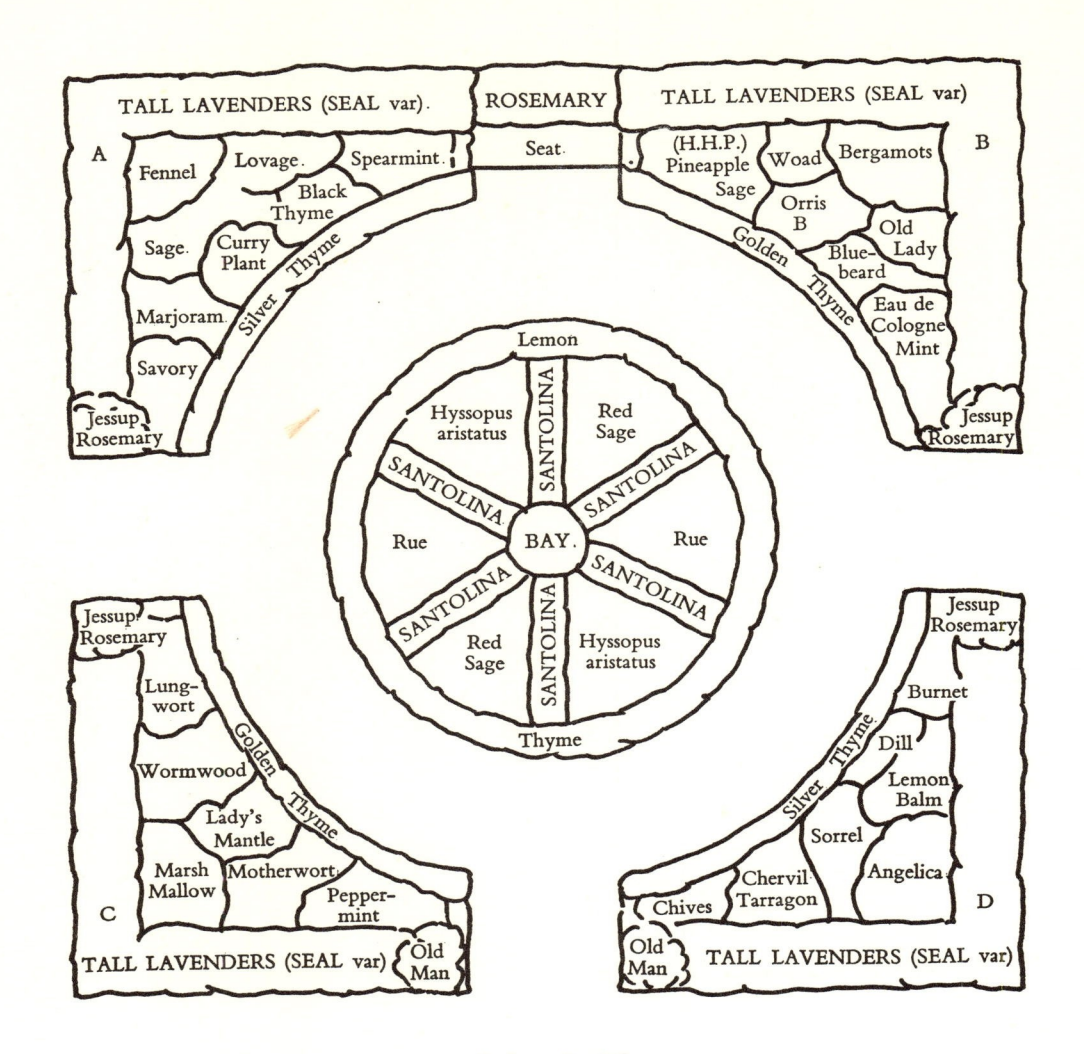

Scale—1 in.-6 ft.

V. This pleasant herb garden is 30 ft. square, but could be modified for smaller dimensions. The garden is edged with Lavender, and the beds edged with decorative Thymes. The "spokes" of the wheel in the central bed are grey *Santolina* (Cotton Lavender), clipped as required. An alternative idea is to have the "spokes" of the very small *Santolina nona*, and fill in the segments with Chamomile. Pennyroyal and creeping and other Thymes in variety. Beds A and D are filled with a valuable range of culinary herbs; bed B with aromatic plants and interesting ones such as Woad and Otris. Bed C has attractive medicinal herbs.

Paths can be grass or paving.

PLATE I LAVENDERS
1. *Lavandula pinnata.*
2. *Lavandula multifida.*
3a. *Lavandula.* lavender Dwf. Munstead, 'a' form.
3b. Lavender, Dwf. Munstead, 'b' form.
4. Grey Hedge Lavender.
5. Old English Lavender, (tall B. group)
6. Bergamot, Rose Queen.
7. Bergamot, Crimson (*Monarda didyma*)
8. Bergamot, Purple.
9. Seal Lavender.
10. Twickle Purple Lavender.
11. Tall White Lavender.
12. Hidcote Purple Lavender.
13. Pink Lavender. (*Lavandula nana rosea*)
14. *Lavandula dentata.*
15. Dwarf White Lavender. (*Lavandula nana alba*)
16. Folgate Blue Lavender.
17. *Lavandula pedunculata.*

PLATE 2 CULINARY HERBS
1. Bronze Fennel.
2. Caraway. (*Carum carvi*)
3. 'Mace'. (*Achillea decolorans*)
4. Angelica. (*Angelica archangelica*)
5. Green Fennel. (*Foeniculum officinale*)
6. Salad Burnet. (*Poterium sanguisorba*)
7. Skirret. (*Sium sisarum*)
8. French Broad-leaf Sorrel. (*Rumex acetosa*)
9. Cumin. (*Cuminum cyminum*)

PLATE 3 CULINARY HERBS
1. Lovage. (*Levisticum officinale*)
2. Dill. (*Anethum graveolens*)
3. Anise. (*Pimpinella anisum*)
4. Alecost. (*Tanacetum balsamita*)
5. Sweet Bay. (*Laurus nobilis*)
6. Purslane. (*Portulaca oleracea*)
7. Good King Henry. (*Chenopodium bonus-henricus*)
8. Chervil. (*Anthriscus cerefolium*)
9. Parsley. (*Petroselinum crispum*)
10. Samphire. (*Crithmum maritimum*)

PLATE 4 CULINARY HERBS
1. Bush Basil. (*Ocimum minimum*)
2. Chicory. (*Cichorium intybus*)
3. Red Orach. (*Atriplex hortensis*)
4. Rampion. (*Campanula rapunculus*)
5. Sweet Basil. (*Ocimum basilicum*)
6. Bistort. (*Polygonum bistorta*)
7. Golden Balm. (*Melissa officinalis var.*)
8. French Shield-Leaf Sorrel. (*Rumex scutatus*)
9. Coriander. (*Coriandrum sativum*)

be stressed is that a herb garden can be both fascinating and decorative as well as purely useful.

Secondly, it may be formal or informal in plan. The herb border outside Dunster Church in Somerset is a pleasing instance of an informal border, planted with a varied collection of scented plants, reminiscent of the way in which the herbs would have been grown in the old monastery gardens.

Again, there may be an irregularly shaped site in your garden, containing one or two shrubs or small flowering trees—not overhanging ones, but perhaps a lilac or cherry-plum—and you would like to turn it into a herb garden. A winding path, or perhaps one curling round the tree in an arc, could be planned, and herbs could be grouped to give a pleasing effect. In such a setting, the large herbs such as angelica, wormwood, elecampane and lovage will have plenty of space to grow naturally and can be arranged in large clumps, to increase and even produce self-sown seedlings (in the case of the first two) as they choose.

In a small garden there is often a strip of bed some 2 feet wide bordering the path leading to the front or side door, or between the front path and garage drive. If you are tired of the half-hardy annual bedding plants, the front could be edged with golden thyme and other herbs, such as golden marjoram, rock hyssop, lemon thyme, savory, and red sage, to give an unusual effect and provide sprigs for cooking. These plants are neat growers, provided that the two latter are 'bobbed back' twice during the course of the summer, and quite colourful.

A well-planned formal herb garden can make a central feature in the garden proper, and give some interest all the year round, where evergreens such as rosemary and evergrey plants, including lavenders, cotton lavender, curry plant and silver thyme, are used.

FEATURES OF THE HERB GARDEN

Lavender Hedges. These give a sense of maturity to the garden, and a vista along a path bordered with lavender to some feature such as a sundial or garden seat is delightful. In smaller gardens dwarf kinds such as Munstead or Folgate Blue may be used. Where there is more space Seal lavender is ideal. If convenient, a double lavender hedge, consisting of a dwarf kind at the front and a taller one, flowering later, at the back, is excellent. The dwarf hedge could consist of alternate bushes of a mauve-purple kind such as Dwarf Munstead or the deep Hidcote Purple and the pink lavender, which is compact in habit. It is always risky to cut back old lavender bushes into the mature wood. We advise cutting the flowers with long stems, to include at least two pairs of basal leaves, in late July–early August, not later. If this is not done, a light clip in March helps compactness. If the flowers are cut long-stalked annually, the bushes will not get 'leggy' for many years.

Rosemary. A 'pointing' feature in design. A bush each end of a lavender hedge or each side of a gateway gives character. The specially upright-growing Miss Jessup is ideal for this purpose.

Low Hedges. To outline beds, southernwood, santolina (cotton lavender, sometimes called French lavender, a name also confusingly applied on occasion to the dwarf true lavenders, such as Munstead), hyssop and rue are pleasing and may be kept clipped back. Rosemary will form an informal hedge some 3–4 feet high.

Edging Herbs. Golden and silver thymes; also the green-foliaged lemon and common thymes are ideal. Chives, golden marjoram, parsley (remembering that this needs sowing annually), may also be used.

All these make a neat line edging. For an informal edging to form a mat on the path, pennyroyal, chamomile and creeping thymes may be used.

Paving Plants. Paved paths form suitable walks for the herb garden, and creeping thymes such as Lemon Curd, *T.serp.*'Coccineus Major', and Pink Chintz may be planted in the interstices. It is labour saving to have the crevices cemented in the main, leaving some pockets leading to the soil beneath at intervals, particularly where two or three stones meet. Pennyroyal, *Mentha requieni*, *Mentha gattefossei* and chamomile are good.

Plants for Paths. To give an aromatic scent when trodden, the plants advised for paving may be planted to form a path, mixed or of one kind only.

Knot-Garden Beds. As a central feature, a bed planted in knot-garden style lends distinction. The simplest form is a wheel with the spokes made of compact herbs such as hyssop, rue, santolina or curry plant (kept clipped) or thymes. The segments between are filled with carpeting herbs such as chamomile, or low-growing kinds such as chives, savory or marjorams.

More elaborate knot-garden effects may be worked out. A friend of ours found two stone panels in her house of Elizabethan date, with fleur-de-lys and crown and circle designs, and these were laid out in front of her house and the outlines planted in dwarf lavender, and cotton lavender principally, with some thymes. The groundwork is in subjects such as golden marjoram and hyssops; also compact flowers such as pansies and pinks, which are in keeping.

Other designs for knot-gardens that we have worked out include a Tudor rose, a cinquefoil for the City of Leicester which appears in their coat-of-arms, and a castle.

The original knot-gardens, as the name suggests, were frequently worked out in formal and elaborate scroll and interwoven patterns. There is an interesting example at Hampton Court.

Herb Seats. At Sissinghurst, *Mentha requieni* forms the 'cushion' to a stone seat. Seats cut out of a bank may be planted with chamomile.

Low 'Dry' Walls. Two low walls constructed informally of stone, without cement and with earth pockets between the stones and with a cavity between the walls about a foot across, are delightful features in the herb garden, or in a garden where space for aromatic plants is limited. They may be used as boundaries to a garden. A low lavender hedge may be planted in the bed formed at the top and creeping thymes planted in the pockets to hang down and clothe the sides of the wall. Other suitable herbs and aromatic plants include the hyssops, calamint, *Artemisia lanata pedimontana, Artemisia rupestris* and in suitable sheltered climates, prostrate rosemary.

Aromatic Shrubs. Many aromatic shrubs are suitable for association with herbs in the garden. These include the allspice, *Calycanthus occidentalis*; winter-sweet, *Chimonanthus praecox*; *Cistus ladanifer* and *C.purpureus*, and others mentioned specifically in the list of aromatic shrubs on p. 93.

If the herb garden is walled, a delightful effect can be obtained by growing fragrant-flowered climbers trained on the walls. Amongst the most pleasing are wistaria, with musky, mysterious-scented mauve chains of flowers; white jasmine, alluring on the air; the homeliness of honeysuckle, *Lonicera periclymenum* and its varieties, and the Japanese honeysuckle, *L.japonica* and its various kinds, including one with gold-netted foliage. The musk hybrid roses, too, have a lovely perfume and usually give a late flowering in autumn.

Chamomile and Thyme Lawns. There is a charming thyme lawn, a carpet of soft purple-crimson and mauve, at Sissinghurst Castle, once the home of Miss V. Sackville-West. Chamomile lawns form an up-to-date as well as traditional feature of the garden, in that many gardeners are planting them now to revive the historical idea. Bacon's Essay *Of Gardens* mentions burnet, wild thyme and watermints for treading—'You are to set whole alleys of them,' he says, 'to have the pleasure when you walk or tread.'

ON KNOWING THE PLANTS

No geometrically correct plan will work out satisfactorily unless the particular tendencies, heights and habits of the herb plants are known. If a special study of the plants is not made, and the vague idea is held that 'herbs grow about the height of sage', then three 5-foot fennels will be made the neighbours of 1-foot-high savory on one side and creeping chamomile on the other. Old lady, which is delightfully smoke-grey, but has a tendency to flop over in late summer, will blanket the creeping thyme, to the latter's distinct disadvantage. Tansy, 4 feet high, will sprawl visibly and creep underground subversively to obliterate the 1-foot-high golden marjoram. It is right to plant *Plumbago capensis*, a toothache cure.

HERB GARDEN DESIGNS

Among the plans illustrated is one we have worked out here at the Herb Farm and elsewhere, that makes a really attractive and unusual plot. A good size for it is 20 feet square, intersected by two paths from the corners. At the centre there can be a small circular piece, with a rosemary bush, bay tree in a small tub or feature such as a sundial, according to disposition. The paths can be bordered with a lavender such as dwarf Munstead or *L.* 'Atropurpurea Nana'; or with santolina or hyssop. The sides of the square are edged with decorative thymes, golden marjoram or similar suitable subjects, and the four triangles planted with a blend of decorative and culinary herbs.

Another herb garden in Wiltshire, of larger dimensions, was based on two circular beds planted wheel-fashion, the surrounding borders being filled with large clumps of a great variety of herbs, with rosemaries each side of paths leading out to the main garden. The owners were surprised to find that herbs could give such a striking effect.

For the City of Leicester herb garden, the central feature was a knot-garden worked out in santolina, variegated rue, and thymes, surrounded by a circle of arc-shaped beds containing the full range of culinary herbs and scented mints, for educational purposes and general interest. There was a triple lavender hedge—tall, Hidcote Purple and pink, and the surrounding borders were planted appropriately with clumps of taller-growing herbs—bergamots, clary sage, wormwood and numerous others, intermingled with scented shrubs—azaleas, choisya, *Eucalyptus gunnii*, lilac, philadelphus and others, with jasmine and honeysuckle trailing over the boundaries.

LONG- OR SHORT-TERM PLANTING

This is always a problem that has to be settled on the one hand by the expense proposed for the garden and, on the other hand, how soon a mature effect is required. For instance, generally reckoning, one plant per square foot will give some interest the first summer after planting, and a mature effect the second summer. After that, those clumps which have spread most will need to be thinned out, and any herbs that have overlapped divided. A thyme edging planted at 9 inches apart will look sparse the first year, reasonable the second and mature the third. But there are other factors. On some strong or rich soils considerably more growth may take place than on others, and this can only certainly be found out by planting to a happy mean and seeing which kinds spread and thrive most robustly. Growth on a light soil will be much more modest; at the other extreme, a lady who had the square design mentioned above had her herb garden on the site of an old hen-run and I found the progress of her plants perfectly startling. The pennyroyal, plants some 3 inches across when inserted, had made a teatray size clump by the end of the season; the alecost had ramped prodigiously; it was fantastic!

SCENTED GARDENS FOR THE BLIND

An understanding and imaginative spirit has led to the planning and planting of scented gardens designed to give pleasure to the blind. Two that I have visited are at Hove and St. Leonards, Sussex, and it is good to see how they are appreciated.

In planning such gardens, the site should be sheltered but not under heavily overhanging trees. Access should be easy, and if steps are necessary in the design, handrails should be provided, continuously with the rails employed to go all round the garden. On these, braille labels are placed in front of the various groups of plants. It might be ideal to have guide-wires from the labels to the middle of the plants themselves. The plants are put on beds raised some 2–3 feet above ground-level, to be more readily enjoyed, where they can be brushed by hand to release their aroma.

Seats in sheltered alcoves are provided, and around these scented flowers are planted, to waft their sweetness on the air. For this, stocks, *Nicotiana*, sweet peas (particularly the old-fashioned ones), briar, sweet and musk roses and pinks are delightful, with hyacinths, narcissus and wallflowers for spring.

The more intriguing aromas amongst plants would give special pleasure; also those with other associations. Amongst the latter, angelica, caraway (or, as more lasting, caraway thyme, *T.herba-barona*), lemon scents such as lemon thyme, lemon balm and lemon pelargonium, *P.crispum*, would be good choices; also eau-de-Cologne mint and peppermint.

Amongst curious and intriguing scents I would put wormwood, hyssop and rue; the minty, balsamic aroma of alecost, the oily scent of tansy and the wide range of rose-scented, nutmeg, true oak-leaf and other pelargoniums. Clary sage and bergamots would be indispensable. Scented plants in paths to be trodden—chamomile, thyme, burnet, pennyroyal—would give interest.

Such gardens would, of course, also give pleasure to sighted people, with reminiscent memories. One gathers from overheard conversation that there is on rare occasions an almost superhuman temptation from the pot-herbs, if visitors are canny cooks and have no gardens themselves!

Of course, quite a number of the 'straight' culinary herbs—mint, 'mace', marjorams in variety, savory, tarragon and even sage are interesting and add variety to such a garden, perhaps with nostalgic reminders of banquets long past, or meals in the 'spacious days'.

THE TOWN GARDEN

It may be possible to have a small herb patch in the town garden. In general, those herbs with smooth but moderately tough leaves, which would not get as choked with grime as very fluffy or felted leaves, should do best. The chief problems that beset plants in towns and cities are the acid-content of the grime deposits; the same effect to make the soil sour; and in many cases poor overworked soils and lack of sun.

Such soils would be benefited by a dressing of lime at $\frac{1}{2}$ lb. to 1 lb. per square yard, preferably a few days before planting; and by the addition of some compost or available organic compound. One realizes that one of the great problems in towns is the difficulty of carting bulky products. 'Bac-peat' or hop manure are both quite useful; leaf mould not to be despised. On clay soils raised beds might be made, brick-contained; or a square yard of clay removed and good compost substituted.

Since foliage-clogging is a great problem, it would help the herb plants if the leaves were powerfully syringed when grimed.

Sunny corners could be planted with marjoram, savory, common and lemon thymes (not too greatly in love with urban conditions but worth trying), sage, tarragon, tree onions and borage (the latter an annual, from seed). For shady spots, mints, fennel, sage (though it does prefer the sun), lemon balm, angelica, also chervil and parsley (the two latter from seed) could be tried, and there is always the sweet bay.

In addition to culinary herbs, such favourites as rosemary, southernwood, lavender and bergamots are well worth trying. As physical conditions and soil vary so much from district to district, it is often wise to plant specimens of each incipient favourite, and more plants can be obtained of those which take kindly to the conditions.

Tubs and Troughs. In paved courtyards and on balconies and roofs, containers such as tubs, large stone jars, and wooden and stone troughs may be used to grow herbs. Some drainage outlet is advisable, an annual change of soil helpful if no actual outlet can be provided. Some rough draining material such as broken clinker, brick or rubble, is best at the bottom, then a layer of rough stuff such as peat. This both helps to conserve moisture at the root and prevents the soil from being washed right down to clog the drainage material.

The ideal soil mixture for filling tubs, troughs and window-boxes is the John Innes potting compost. The basic ingredients are seven parts of loam, three of peat and two of sand, with a fertilizer-blend of hoof-and-horn, sulphate of potash and superphosphate added 'at the stated dose'—which is not a large one. It should be possible to get this whole compost ready mixed from a good sundriesman, and it is good, as it has the right balance of ingredients.

The soil should be firmed and is then ready for planting, which may be done in spring or autumn. The tubs or troughs should, as far as possible, be stood away from all-embracing and repellent draughts, and in as sunny a position as possible away from prevailing winds.

Sweet bay, rosemary and myrtle shrubs could be grown, amongst others, with smaller herbs around their foot; or the receptacles could be devoted entirely to a selection as mentioned in general for town gardens.

Window-boxes. These gallant cameos of country life can well be used for herbs. The sunniest ledges are the best. The boxes should if at all possible be at least 10 inches to 1 foot deep, and filled as outlined for the troughs and tubs. Needless to say, the boxes should be securely fixed on the window-sills and may need an iron bracket to keep them level. They should not be creosoted inside because of the danger of fumes to plant-roots. In a window-box 4 feet long and 9 inches wide the following could be grown—three clumps of chives; one sage; two marjoram; one savory; one tarragon; and, at the further end, a plant of mint. This could be planted in a pot plunged, to keep the soil reasonably moist, in the compost of the window-box, if preferred; it would keep the runners from being *de trop*. The tarragon, which normally grows to some 2 feet (if the true French kind) would need to have its terminal shoots picked at intervals to keep it compact; and the same would be necessary if a fennel, for fish sauce, were to be grown.

When the clumps grew large, pieces could be potted up and presented to co-operative neighbours (including those 'good neighbours' in the flat below who are not allergic to drips when the window-box is watered).

Many will now be asking mentally—parsley, chervil, basil and oregano (knotted annual marjoram)? You have a sporting chance of being able to raise your own seedlings of the two latter, which are half-hardy, sown on the surface of pots filled with a sandy mixture, the seed just covered and kept inside on the kitchen windowledge. Or you might try a control experiment, sowing two pots of each, and having one inside, one out. Why this is suggested is because no two kitchens are the same for airiness, dryness, heat or fumes; nor have any two people quite the same ideas as to watering. To say 'water when necessary' is, practically, about as helpful as saying 'feed dog when necessary'. But watering pot-plants, seeds and window-box has to be learnt by experience, giving much more in warm, sunny growing weather and being least liberal with water during the dead months—autumn till the New Year, and in very cold weather. The soil then needs to feel just moist, but not sodden.

Parsley, dill and chervil seed could either be sown also in pots or attempted in a corner of the window-box, and just covered with fine soil made damp before sowing.

The question is often asked 'Is it better to grow the plants in pots or directly in the window-box soil?' The latter gives a larger root-run and pots are so apt to dry out quickly. At the same time, half-hardy plants such as scented 'geraniums' (so-called oak-leaf pelargoniums, whose leaves can be used to flavour sponge-cakes, the lemon-scented crispum kind, also possible for flavouring), lemon verbena and pineapple sage can be kept indoors on a sunny window-sill for the winter, and plunged out in a window-box or put in the paved yard in tubs or just in their pots for the summer.

(*A list of* flowering times *of scented and aromatic plants through the year appears on pages* 89–91.)

To SIR THOMAS MORE

(Lines begun in Crosby Hall, Chelsea, the site of his garden, on 22nd November 1956)

Green is your memory, for the pungent scent
Of Rosemary, brought for a passing craftsman's show
Stabs with reminder of your dignity, pent
In the grim dungeon walls. Ironic blow
Of hard-mailed fate, many would hold; but you
Met with the lamp of hope, the shield of faith
Fell broods of darkness. Surely your spirit flew
Wing-borne in prayer (no melancholy wraith
But your deep self released) up the silver Thames
To all that you loved at home. You walked, in mind,
Your eden-plot with its Rosemary (soft-blue hems
Of the small Saviour's garment, traditions find)
'Sacred to friendship and to remembrance.' Thrice
Strengthened, my gratitude seeks you in Paradise.

CHAPTER FOUR

Cultivation, Harvesting and Drying and Notes on Herbs in Other Climates

Some culinary herbs such as pot marjorams, salad burnet, fennel, alexanders and creeping (but not bushy) thyme are found as wild plants in this country, but most of the important cooking and aromatic herbs are natives of the Mediterranean regions.

It is suggested that the pungent taste of the essential oils that give the useful characteristics to our herbs may be in part a protection against browsing animals; and, too, when the oils are volatilized in hot weather, provide some cover in the form of vapour against too great radiant heat.

In general, herbs grown on warm slopes, where the soil is light sandy to medium loam, have the best essential oil content, and therefore the strongest flavour or aroma.

Our English climate produces culinary herbs of excellent flavour, and high-quality oil of lavender as well. The constituents making up the scents and flavours of plants are a complicated blend, while the intensity of English summers at their best favours the finest constituents, the fierce heat of more southerly climes seems to cause formation of the more pungent compounds of the turpentine, camphoraceous and other groups, rather than the delicate fruity and flower scents. Most scented leaves have some of the basic compounds such as those of the turpentine group, giving the pleasing scent to pine needles; the eucalyptol or camphoraceous compounds, which give a distinctive tang, with other combinations, to wormwood, tansy, sage amongst others; menthol, a characteristic of mints, as thymol is of thymes; and sulphur-containing compounds give the distinctive taste to garlic, onions and various *Umbelliferae*.

The wonderful range of leaf-aromas is obtained when these constituents are blended with the flower and fruit scents. For instance, a blend of eucalyptol, thymol and a lemon scent gives lemon thyme, while there is a merging of lemon and rose in lemon verbena, and in citrus mint there is the lemon and menthol combination, with other ingredients.

Under violent summer heat, the tendency appears to be for the delicious flower or fruit-scent constituents to diminish, leaving the pungent ingredients to have a dominating effect. Even in our occasional heat-waves, we see something of the same effect. Some mints such as *M.cordifolia* lose the ethereal freshness of scent and flavour and an almost acetylene scent predominates till damper weather comes. This mint, on the other hand, is excellent in spring and autumn. It appears that if our English lemon thyme plants are sent to be grown for instance in Spain, they lose their lemon qualities and smell like common thyme.

Sunshine, then, is, in this country, an asset to quality in herb-growing, and many herbs are used to the parched conditions of hilly country or scrub-land near the sea. When choosing suitable soils for herb-growing, however, it is ideal to strike the balance. A soil that is hot, dry and sandy will produce crops with fine aroma; but crop-weights will be light, unless compost or other organic materials are continually added to the soil; and irrigation allowed for in seasons of drought.

On the other hand, herbs such as thymes, rosemary, lavender and sage do not like damp and waterlogged conditions in winter; and lush growth in summer and autumn, followed by a severe winter causes considerable casualties. A medium soil, therefore, reasonably rich in essential minerals and organic content, should produce good crops without undue danger of winter loss.

One of the greatest causes of damage to herbs (and decorative shrubs also) comes from blistering, cutting March winds after a short thaw following severe weather. In the case of shrubs such as rosemary, the leaves frequently go brown and there is no recovery. With others, such as thymes, sage and phlomis, if the severe cold has killed the leaves and terminal branches, there is often hope of fresh shoots breaking into growth near the base. If these optimistically emerge during the thaw, their enterprise usually meets with disaster, and they are irrevocably nipped by the bitter spring winds.

Therefore, shelter from the north-east winds is an important point when choosing a site for herb-growing. A slope to the south or west is good, and provides a range of sites for different herbs.

While the small-leafed herbs such as thymes, savory and rosemary, the grey-foliaged ones such as lavender, curry plant and santolina, and those with tough foliage, like sage, prefer medium and well-drained sites (though not really dry ones), many of the thin-leafed and lush-leafed herbs can do with moister conditions, if they are not heavily waterlogged in winter; plenty of organic matter in the soil; and while sun is usually beneficial if the soil does not dry out, they are tolerant of some shade. Amongst these are angelica, lovage, lemon balm, parsley, and mints. Amongst aromatics, bergamot and elecampane come in the same group. Tarragon and marjoram are in an intermediate position. They will flourish in quite rich soils provided they are not clammy in winter.

When a site for a herb garden of reasonable size is in question, therefore, type of soil, sun or shade, aspect and shelter are the main considerations. A large garden may provide soil alternatives; or there might be two borders, one in full sun and one in shade, for which it would be welcome to find inhabitants such as the mints and angelica. Most gardens have a boring bed or border which would have point if it could offer a home to some pleasing and useful herbs. For a comprehensive herb garden, however, a sunny position is always advisable; for sun-loving plants usually languish in shade; while those tolerant of shade, given reasonable soil moisture, are generally happy in a sunny spot. If there is no natural shelter such as a wall or hedge, the tactful planting of some robust flowering shrubs may solve the problem; or hurdles are not out of place, at any rate for the beginnings of the garden.

Again, for an average-sized herb garden, it should be possible to improve any existing soil so as to make it suitable for the majority of herbs. On light soils, the addition of organic matter such as garden compost is the prime consideration; other materials that are helpful are well-decayed manure in moderate, not too liberal application; leaf-mould; and peat, if a good dressing of lime is also given (and light soils in general benefit from some lime, applied as chalk, limestone or hydrated lime).

The greatest problem faces the gardener on 'plasticine' clay, fit to mould a masterpiece one day, better, in fact, for anything than the modest culture of a row or two of herb seeds or the reception of the newly arrived box of herb plants; then, after a few days of delectable sunshine, hard as a pavement. Rough digging in early winter, to expose clay soils to the weathering of wind, frost and snow, helps to break up the close crumb-structure. A really heavy dressing of lime, preferably in its hydrated form, also assists 'flocculation', the combining of the small, closely-packed particles into larger crumbs, with air-spaces between them. Again, the addition of all organic matter, particularly in 'long' form—the fibres in the organic matter not yet disintegrated, and the straw in the manure still not broken down—is helpful, as it provides drainage-channels and aeration. Some gardens might well need preliminary draining, but that is rather an enterprise.

For a herb garden say of 10 feet by 5 feet, it might well be worth while, where herbs are valued, to have some of the clay removed, and a load of good loam or of John Innes compost brought in—such a border could be built up with a brick edge, some 9 inches above the ordinary soil-level. An alternative is to take out quite a large spade-hole when planting each herb plant and put some sand at the bottom for drainage; then fill in round the plant with a good mixture of compost and soil.

On very light dry soils it is often helpful to make deep holes with some tool such as a crowbar and put the compost below the plant's roots to hold the moisture and richness where it will be most available, instead of forking the material into the surface-soil and so encouraging a plant's roots to grow nearer the hot and dry surface of the soil.

On the other hand, when choosing a site for the large-scale cultivation of herbs, the general remarks made earlier in the chapter would be relevant, remembering that a balance between quantity and quality of crop is necessary. A sloping site (if the slope is not so great that great loss of rainfall occurs, or erosion) provides suitable situations for plants preferring somewhat drier conditions towards the top; and for the moisture-lovers towards the foot of the hill. A stream at the low level would be valuable and delightful. An informal herb garden running down to a stream or pool would be most pleasing, for the mints, angelicas, elecampane, *Acorus calamus* the sweet flag, musk, balsams and other herbs would be at home.

COMMERCIAL GROWING

Naturally, many different sizes of plot could be eligible for the growing of herbs for crop production on a commercial scale. On the one hand, it might be the aim of a woman with a keen enjoyment of country life and at the same time an interest in a rather personal type of business with individual contacts, to grow some six or eight herbs—perhaps sage, thyme, lemon thyme, culinary mint, marjoram, savory, tarragon and one or two others—and to have perhaps 50-feet-square plots of each—2,500 square yards, using, with paths and shed site, about half an acre of ground; allowing for young plantations coming on and replacements, also propagation beds, some three quarters of an acre.

The herbs may be grown to sell fresh. Some enterprising people would get connections with hotels or restaurants where the chefs wanted a regular fresh supply, and have a standing arrangement with them; or with first-class stores frequented by connoisseurs. Others might offer a regular postal service of fresh herbs to large establishments, domestic science colleges (if these did not, which is best, grow their own herbs), canteens or schools. Butchers might well be glad of a steady source of sage and thyme.

Some part of such crops could be harvested for drying. The drying losses of crops will be discussed in more detail later on, but it has to be realized that the yield from an area of plants is always disappointingly small in the final weight of dried and rubbed culinary herbs. It would be unlikely that the areas mentioned above would yield any profitable return unless a very individual 'pack' was sponsored—a kind of specialist's 'branded' line. But some people have particular gifts in

CULTIVATION, HARVESTING AND DRYING

this type of business; and it is worth consideration. The labour involved would be detailed and considerable.

At the other end of the scale of commercial production is the grower who has half an acre, one acre, three acres or more devoted to one crop; and if mechanization is adopted for as many operations as possible, and the cultivation is carried out as for (and, it may be, in conjunction with) ordinary market garden crops, there is the possibility of useful profit on certain culinary and medicinal crops, and aromatics such as lavender.

During the years since the 1939–45 war, people with no great knowledge of farming conditions have come increasingly to understand that a whole range of factors enters into the vital question of profit or loss from a market garden or herb crop, as with the English fruit market.

In one way, the grower who dries a crop himself is in a much less precarious position than his friend who grows perishables such as lettuces or cut flowers or dessert fruit. The herb grower has a breathing-space, having dried his crop and prepared it, to find a possible market, even to cover expenses; it always seems tragic when growers encounter a glut and it is not economic for them even to market their produce and so to cover output costs.

Foreign imports are the grower's great problem. These, of course, fluctuate, and there seems to be a reasonable demand for English dried mint, sage, marjoram, parsley and lemon thyme. The half-hardy annuals basil and knotted marjoram would not under all normal conditions be a proposition (except fresh-bunched in very limited quantities), and thyme and savory are produced very economically on the Continent. The problem with tarragon lies in the obtaining of sufficient stock of the true French kind for large-scale planting, which would make for considerable initial expense.

Under the individual herbs, notes of commercial cultivation are given for the principal kinds. There is scope for difference of opinion over planting distances, as these vary materially with the type of mechanical cultivation available. The small-scale cultivator with 50-feet-square plots would be likely to plant closely and cultivate intensively, re-planting the bushy subjects such as sage, marjoram and thyme every three years or so. Large-scale growers would favour wider spacing between rows—say up to 30 inches instead of 18 inches.

It is, of course, helpful to have a new young plantation of a particular crop—say marjoram or savory—put in each year or every two years, to grow on to take the place of older ones being scrapped. Naturally, fresh planting material can be obtained from a plantation when it is dug up. It is rather invidious to mention crop yield, as planting distances, age of plantation, soil and weather play so much part.

Our records on a light soil show one-year-old sages at 18 inches by 22 inches yielded 1 ton per acre, at two years 2½ tons per acre. Thyme and marjoram are lighter crops.

HARVESTING

The ideal time to harvest herbs is just before they come into flower; a slight poser is therefore presented by, for example, the non-flowering, broad-leaf sage—also spearmint, which usually condescends to throw the odd blossom in late August.

A sensible middle way has therefore to be adopted. The French narrow-leaf common thyme often bursts into flower in early to mid-May and it needs cutting before its floral chintz is unfolded. Narrow-leaf sage can be cut in May also, as it threatens flower by the end of that month, and broad-leaf sage usually has some 6 inches of suitable growth by then. It is, of course, best to wait until the growth is as advanced as possible, yet before flowering. People ask, 'If my herbs have stolen a march on us and gone to flower while we have been busy elsewhere, does it matter to cut them during or after flowering?' The answer is that to cut before flowering means that one gets the maximum of foliage, and of flavour—strength and material have later gone into the flowers. But, of course, a dried blend of flowers and foliage is perfectly wholesome, but the colour of the dried product cannot be as good as leaf alone. If harvesting is left until after flowering, the seed-heads and dead stems constitute a difficulty.

It is sometimes recommended to cut the herbs in the early morning, before the dew has dried off. The idea is presumably that hot sun later in the day volatilizes some of the essential oil which constitutes the flavour. Actually, with any quantity of a herb, it is most trying to handle if cut wet—it is much better to wait until the day has dried the foliage; and to avoid harvesting in wet weather if possible.

French thyme and the sages, then, are usually ready in May. Summer and autumn-sown parsley will need cutting or pulling from April to May, before it 'bolts'. A spring-sown crop should be ready on good soils by late summer. Marjoram, lemon balm and lemon thyme come in June, followed by tarragon, savory, spearmint and Bowles mint (and all culinary mints) in June or July.

Early July is usually the time to harvest the dwarf lavenders, followed by tall kinds, most grown for drying, from late July to early August. August, too, often sees a second 'cut' for sage and thyme, and there may be a second crop of less bulk than the first cut, of marjoram, savory and other kinds in late August or early September, with the mints coming on again in September, particularly after a damp and lush summer which favours them.

Most of the medicinal herbs—wormwood, marsh mallow, rue, peppermint and others—are cut in July and August, and such aromatic herbs as eau-de-Cologne mint and bergamot for pot-pourri. Chamomile flowers are generally ready for picking in July and August, a busy period for the herb-grower.

Naturally the implement varies with the quantity to be cut. We have favoured the use of curve-bladed linoleum knives, both for culinary herbs and lavender. With a crop such as sage or thyme a robust handful is grasped in one hand and, given skill, severed (without causing mortal injury) with the knife. Sage is sticky with resinous gum but not too difficult to cut, mint easy, thyme tough and requiring slickness and experience. When the art is acquired, a neatly bobbed sage, thyme or savory bush results, the real answer to those who complain about the ancient legginess of their bushes—they do not harvest sufficiently early or frequently. Marjoram, tarragon and other clump plants should be tidily shorn. We always recommend leaving some basal leaves on the plants or bushes to help them to manufacture more food and aid their recuperation, helping them to make ready for a further crop later. A light dressing of a nitrogenous fertilizer such as sulphate of ammonia at 1–2 ounces per square yard sprinkled carefully round the plants when the soil is damp, after harvesting, give a fillip to fresh growth.

Harvesting in quantity is an odd blend of glamour (in the fragrant, traditional crops and on occasion blue skies above) and strain (in one's bent back, dripping cheeks and fingers tense at first in hit-or-miss gestures with the unresponsive knife). Ultimately, there is great satisfaction in the large filled harvest-baskets, containing some 28 lb. or more of fresh sage, or 14 lb. or more of thyme, a lighter crop.

Lavender for drying is normally cut when some flowers are out up each spike. Again, a curved knife is excellent, and large handfuls (some 4–8 ounces in weight) are severed at each stroke and laid on a shorn patch on the bush. A sack is laid at the end of each row, with a strong string underneath it for tying the completed bundle.

The glorious, vibrant, perfumed sheaf, shimmering mauve-blue, is lifted in one arm, then one adds two or three other sheaves from neighbouring bushes. Starting down the 50-feet row to the sack, the vibrancy announces itself as a subversive element of bees (hive and honey), also bees (bumble, striped, plain and fancy) imprisoned in their fragrant cage and announcing their plight with understandable shock or bewilderment.

Dignity and a sense of duty indicate a measured tread to the end of the row; the nervous system signals a rapid dropping of the sheaves on to the nearest bush. Circumstances usually irrevocably indicate the next move. One is profoundly sorry for bees. They only sting in reflex action, in self-defence, not malice, and the hive bees perish—it is a sad story.

Reverting to methods—for larger-scale work a sickle may be used and the crop either bunched as severed (with lavender and other crops when feasible) or left to lie and raked up carefully—this does pose the problem of some proportion of stones, soil and grit getting into the cut material. But mechanical sifters, after drying, can usually cope with the separating—and such cutting methods could only be used for considerable areas of crop.

The side-blade grass-cutters are on occasion used also, particularly for mint where a heavy crop awaits harvesting.

Naturally, harvesting time and labour constitute a considerable portion of the growers' costs and methods must be conditioned to this factor.

DRYING

The general principles involved in this process are that the herbs should be exposed to reasonably steady heat, and sufficient air circulation to remove the moisture-laden air from around them.

In spite of what is said elsewhere, it is not in our considerable experience here wise to attempt to dry flowers or cut herbs in the sun; or relying indirectly on the sun's heat alone. Bleached produce results from such treatment.

Household Drying. An attic trapping much of the sun's heat could be used, provided some other source of heat such as a gas or electric stove was available during the periods of 'deep depressions' centred, not over Iceland, but directly above one's drying facilities. Curtains could be drawn in very sunny weather to shut out direct rays on the herbs.

For quite small quantities dried in the home, a rack over the kitchen stove is useful. Some 2 feet over a stove in an alcove, runners could probably be fixed to the walls and a movable tray inserted—a wooden frame covered with hessian, butter-muslin or (though this is, of course, heavier to handle) perforated zinc. Or such a tray might be fitted with non-combustible 'legs' (ideally hinged to fold away when not in use) to stand when required over the stove—not too close above it or the herbs will tend to scorch on occasion. I am sure that a properly arranged contrivance is a real incentive to the housewife to harvest her herbs regularly—and on such a tray odd handfuls of various things can be spread out after a quick visit to the herb garden. If there has to be the perennial question 'Where shall I hang my herbs?' or 'How shall I dry them?' the psychological odds are against many dried herbs that summer! And regularly cut herbs as gathered are usually too short in stem to hang bunched.

Of course, bunches of herbs or (if driven to it) small amounts in muslin bags can be suspended from the airing-rack over the kitchen stove; but this has practical drawbacks, the greatest being that in any case the stove may not be kept regularly alight during the summer!

In this case, the airing-cupboard is feasible and smaller trays, some 15 inches by 21 inches, might be made to fit, and stack on top of one another, preferably 'staggered' to assist air circulation. Otherwise, the attic, as suggested, may be most practicable.

Some herbs, such as parsley, may be dried in the oven when the heat has been turned off, but some is retained. The door should be left open to prevent charring, for this is a risky process, and even if the results are not damaged, they may be a lovely green colour but devoid of flavour!

Small-scale Commercial Drying. Where quantities between, say, half-hundredweights of several kinds and (stretching the accommodation and facilities to capacity) half a ton of material is to be dried, drying-sheds can be used. These might be adapted from existing stabling or other erections. A moderately steep pitch to the roof is best, and airing-vents should be provided high up, for the moisture-laden air to escape. An electric fan of industrial design and fireproof qualities can be valuable to keep an air circulation. Wooden sheds are best; metal structures present condensation problems unless suitably lined.

During the 1939–45 war we relied on slow-combustion coke-burning Tortoise stoves for heat. These are reasonably safe to use in wooden sheds, and can give out excellent heat, keeping up the temperature of a 20-feet-square shed to 80–90°F. in average weather, during the daytime. But they are temperamental, and need several stokings or some attention during the day, and labour costs have risen so tremendously since that period that careful consideration has to be given to the problem.

Given good-quality fuel, right chimney-height, draught adjustment and other things necessary for maximum efficiency, plus some form of mechanical lighter, such as a gas-poker to save time in relighting if necessary, they have much to recommend them.

Some type of electric convection stove with suitable air circulation such as is now recommended for greenhouses could be used, but research would be necessary into individual costs.

A greenhouse, darkened for the summer with green paint, could be used as a standby and is useful for flower-drying if there is nothing more suitable available—but it is perhaps unnecessary to add that no plants could be grown at the same time because of the dry atmosphere.

A 20-feet-square wooden drying shed could be planned to accommodate from nine to twelve racks, of which it is helpful to have four or six (in pairs) movable, on casters, to bring nearer to stoves to finish drying. Each rack would hold ten trays. A suitable size for these is 32 inches by 46 inches, the framework being of 1½-inch batten-wood—there is no great advantage in heavier frames and great disadvantages in handling full. These trays can be covered with hessian. Such trays will hold from 2 lb. to (when necessity demands) up to 5 lb. of, say, sage.

The racks can be slatted across to hold the trays or (which is quite adequate) equipped with 2-inch runners at each side on which the trays rest. Carpentry must, of course, be accurate or a top tray, slipping down, can cause a trail of chaos contemplating which even Job would have an inner battle for equanimity.

Heavily loading the trays delays drying. With a steady heat and the herbs at 2 lb. per tray, thyme can be ready in five days, being spriggy and small-leafed, sage and marjoram in seven days. Mint is variable and dries badly if close-packed. The trays of herbs should be stirred or shaken up daily when heavily loaded, to prevent the herbs from collecting in dank masses. Aeration right through each layer is important.

The quickest-drying positions are those at the tops of the racks. Fresh material should be put in the top trays. Put underneath drier material it will damp it down. But it is best to keep separate racks for material at different stages, and, ideally, but not always practicably, to fill up the whole shed at once with fresh material.

A wire rack stood over the stoves can be invaluable for finishing parsley and other herbs which could on occasion be sacked loosely; or to re-crisp herbs that have had to be stored after drying, to get them fit for rubbing-down.

When the stems crack as well as the leaves being brittle, the herbs are ready for rubbing-down or storage. A high, slatted rack up in the roof is the driest position for storing sacks of dried herbs on stalk.

Although drying removes almost all the moisture from the herbs in order to preserve them, a small percentage is left, and in any case some moisture from the air is reabsorbed during storage. Herbs, when rubbed-down, should therefore be stored for any considerable length of time in containers such as plywood tubs with lids of 'venesta' type, as these allow for the moisture. Airtight tins are suitable for a matter of weeks or a month or two, but after that the contents are prone to go mouldy on occasion.

Large-scale Drying. I have seen a hop-kiln quite usefully operated with any necessary modifications for the drying of sage and other herbs. Specially designed driers may use hot-air blasts; and dehydration, as used for vegetables, is practised also.

In general, the flavour of many packeted brands of herbs has improved during the last twenty years. It is always frustrating to open a packet of herbs with the bright expectation of adding the notable touch to a ragoût or omelette, only to discover that the herb is anonymous, the name on the label being obviously an alias, as the contents bear closest resemblance to dried lawn-mowings.

Large-scale drying at too high a temperature, producing good colour but driving off the flavour, is responsible for this contradiction in terms, and the qualities vary abysmally. The slow-drying small-scale methods usually produce a product of good colour and natural flavour.

PREPARATION

It is necessary to have an electric sage-grinder if sage is to be ground by the hundredweight to a texture approved by some sausage-makers. On occasion, however, they prefer it rubbed—moderately fine but not pulverized.

For this, and for the first removal of the leaves from the other culinary herbs, large rectangular 'mattress-sieves' of $\frac{1}{4}$-inch mesh are best—the art of removing the leaves, the gentle firmness of the action, is best learnt in practice. Thyme is tricky, as the brittle stems have a knack of fragmenting and coming through with the leaves unless handled with skill. Savory has piercing leaves and stems which leave a deep impression on the operative.

After the initial separation, the leaves need to have the rest of the stalks removed, and a range of sieves, from $\frac{3}{4}$ inch to 1/10th inch should be acquired, the larger meshes, oddly enough, being best, skilfully used. A hair-sieve may be necessary in which the herbs may be shaken to remove grit.

Such methods, of course, only apply satisfactorily to where at least a minimum of 8 ounces to 1 lb., depending on the herb, is available, unless miniature sieves can be obtained or made for the housewife.

The ratio of fresh to finished material has to be faced realistically, as it is distinctly discouraging. Six pounds of fresh sage might produce 1 lb. if smaller stalks were ground up—they also contain the flavour, but woody stems would, of course, have to be eliminated, when the proportion might be 8 to 1. By the time mint and thyme, in common with most of the other herbs, are dried and rubbed down, 1 lb. only usually results from 10 lb. of fresh crop. A sage bush some three years old might yield $\frac{1}{2}$ to $\frac{3}{4}$ lb. of fresh crop, cut twice during the season.

LARGE-SCALE RUBBING

For small-scale work it is rarely worth while to obtain a special herb-rubbing machine, as these are specialized and often best designed for the particular requirement by one with a flair for such things. Firms, however, needing to rub culinary herbs by the ton, have special machines, often operating on a selection or combination of the principles of friction, sifting, winnowing and gravity separation.

HERBS IN OTHER CLIMATES

The foregoing description of herb cultivation has been drawn from experience and contacts under English conditions. These can be applied and adapted to varying climatic situations. The following information is not in any way exhaustive, but designed to show how herbs fare under a variety of conditions.

North America. The Herb Society of America, in Boston, Mass., promotes knowledge and friendly links, and publishes *The Herbarist.* Mrs G. M. Foster publishes *The Herb Grower* from Falls Village, Connecticut; in this area there are several commercial herb enterprises. Miss Woodburn enjoys growing herbs and specializes in herb books at Hopewell, New Jersey. There are commercial herb gardens in the states of Maine, Ohio, New York and Texas, to name a selection.

In general, in the northern and north-eastern areas the directions for growing herbs in England apply, though in favourable seasons April and in late years May planting is recommended, and outside seed-sowing generally takes place in May and the first week of June. There are, however, some differences in hardiness. Rosemary will grow to some 18 inches in a season, and is not hardy; it is sometimes recommended to grow it as an annual, but best to overwinter plants in a greenhouse keeping out the frost. Small pot-grown bays could also pass the winter under glass, as this small tree is not usually found to be hardy. Lemon verbena is treated as half-hardy, as in many English districts. *Mentha requieni* and *Origanum onites* are found to be somewhat tender, and best put under glass for the winter. In exceptionally severe winters damage has been noted to peppermint, chamomile and winter savory, even resulting in complete loss of the first two.

Where temperatures do not go below freezing in the winter, in the south, pelargoniums can be left outside all the year round, as in Cornwall and the British Channel Isles.

From Colorado comes an interesting picture of herb-growing. Here lack of moisture is the problem, in the foothills of the Rockies at over 5,000 feet, and snowfall is often the primary answer when the snow melts. The climate is dry and arid. The English problem of alternating thaw and frost in winter is shared, with the resulting 'winter-kill'. A natural shortage of humus creates a further problem.

However, many herbs flourish. Those found hardy in New England and the mid-west have normally been found hardy in Colorado, apart from exceptionally severe winters. Even thymes have survived such conditions, but *Origanum onites* was a casualty. The leaf growth of herbs is on the whole less luxuriant than in, say, Ohio, but flavour and fragrance are good. Sweet marjoram and basil are the last to be sown in the open ground, when the sun has warmed it in early June. Lavenders grown in this area have a good perfume. Bergamots and mints grow wild in the mountains. Various artemisias and santolinas, savory, rue, fennel, *Nepeta* and dill do well. Rosemary needs winter protection. Sweet Cicely and woodruff grow well, given more shade and moisture. The tendency is to have informal herb gardens or patio herb gardens.

From California comes a fascinating survey of herb-growing experiences. As there is no frost, pelargoniums grow perfectly, given a good soil and plenty of water. Most of the information, however, comes from a garden on a steep hill, and granite soil with a little compost added. Lavenders do very well. Rosemary flourishes. Prostrate rosemary and creeping thymes ramp over the hill. Mints, naturally, need a heavier soil and more water; but the native monardellas, particularly the beautiful *M.macrantha*, grow reasonably—the coastal species, *M.odoratissima*, *crispa* and *undulata*, grow rampantly. *Satureja (Calamintha) chandleri* grows as a weed.

In the kitchen garden, enriched with compost, grow culinary herbs such as tarragon, French sorrel and garden mint, also, amongst medicinal herbs, comfrey.

There are over fifteen native salvias and naturally they flourish. One attractive native salvia is *S.sonomensis*, which is prostrate, silvery leafed, and with purple flowers; *S.mellifera* has a pleasant creeping form; *S.columbariae* is also useful; its seeds are nutritious.

The chief general need is watering, both during the rainless summer and the long dry winter stretches. Under Californian conditions, the drought and sun appear to improve the perfume of scented plants and the flavour also.

Australia. This vast continent has an immense desert in the centre and conditions vary from the tropical north to temperate, cool Tasmania, and the wet eastern coastal area.

Victoria, with a Mediterranean-type climate has, however, the problem of poor rainfall in one area. The growing results about to be described are on a clay soil, 500 feet above sea-level, and with a rainfall of over 30 inches. There are very few frosts. High temperatures are experienced in summer, but watering can be carried out except in drought years. There is usually a fine fragrance to leaves and flowers.

Thymes—common, lemon, and golden flourish and silver thyme does reasonably well, also *T.serp* Coccineus. Mints tend to grow almost too vigorously. These include spearmint, peppermint, applemint, eau-de-cologne mint and pennyroyal. They all grow very well during the damp spring, make little growth during the summer, and begin to grow again in autumn. They do well in light shade, where the sun filters through, and their perfume is excellent.

Lavenders: *L.vera*, *L.dentata* and *L.stoechas* grow quite easily. *L.vera* has a very good scent. Scented pelargoniums are particularly good and stay out in the garden all the year round. Amongst others, the oak-leaf, Lady Plymouth, *P.tomentosum*, *P.crispum* and *P.fragrans* all flourish, and the leaves have been used in pot-pourri. Rosemary is still in bloom at the end of August, the end of the Australian winter. Both upright and prostrate kinds do well. Southernwood flourishes and is easy to propagate at any time. *Salvia rutilans* is still in flower at the end of their winter. *Salvia officinalis* varies in its growth.

In Queensland, *Thymus vulgaris*, *Salvia officinalis*, *Origanum vulgare* and *Mentha spicata* do quite well, especially in the southern part. One problem is that during the hot wet summer months, sage, marjoram and thyme do not have a very good flavour, so are often treated as spring annuals. Parsley is grown, and this completes the list of the common herbs, though a special basil, *Ocimum sanctum*, and all-herb or three-in-one (*Coleus amboinicus, C.aromaticus*) and others are occasionally grown.

New Zealand. In general, growing conditions are much more favourable than in Britain. In fact, the equable and mild conditions of the English Scilly Isles are those most widely experienced in New Zealand. Therefore, the majority of herbs grow really well. In the northern half they may tend to grow rather rampantly. Mint is often found wild as an escape. Lavender is common, but *L.stoechas* is mainly grown, except in the southern, cooler areas. Typical herbs grown are mint, parsley, thyme, sage, garlic, tarragon, bay—the herbs commonly found in England. The flavour and scent appear to be as good as from those grown in the United Kingdom. There is at least one specialist grower in Christchurch.

South Africa. Many of the pelargoniums are native to South Africa. Various species of *Lavandula, Mentha, Thymus* and *Salvia* grow very well indeed, both for decorative use and their kitchen value. The great problem is that of low rainfall. The scent and flavour, where applicable, compare very favourably with the same genera grown in England.

Oil of lavender from *Lavandula vera* produced at Kirstenbosch has been analysed at the Imperial Institute and found to compare very well with French oil, having a high ester content. South Africa has a very rich wild flora, containing many medicinal plants. *Salvia africana* is used in the same way as *S. officinalis*. There are many indigenous salvias and six indigenous *Mentha* species.

CHAPTER FIVE

The Uses of Herbs

Many people who have become acquainted with continental cookery wish that English cooking could be made more interesting. Some housewives, however, have a secret feeling that this also implies that they must make up elaborate dishes, involving an abandoned use of crayfish or oysters, mushrooms, truffles or paté-de-fois-gras; or at any rate the gay tossing-in of dozens of eggs or pounds of butter into the selected dishes; with a prolonged concentration requiring the intuition of a magician's brew, the delicacy of stop-watch timing and the patience of an eastern sage.

There is a second snag. Many housewives feel that husbands or children do not like highly seasoned foods, and prefer (for all their hints about *haute cuisine*) plain flavours. How can these attitudes be reconciled?

To take the second problem first—if we analyse the usual tastes in this country, we shall find that the average household really likes the flavours of mint, parsley, sage (in moderation, traditionally used with pork, goose and such dishes), the onion hint of chives, and lemon thyme. Some are allergic to one or more of these, but in general they are all acceptable. And in passing it should be said that while mint is the classic flavour with new potatoes, green peas and lamb, it is at the same time a valuable digestant with these delightful but slightly upsetting foods. In the same way, sage reduces the richness of pork and goose, for both herbs contain antiseptic ingredients. In Mrs Beeton's time this fact was appreciated! When people say that they cannot take highly seasoned food, it is not usually herbs that cause digestive trouble but the overstimulating spices and condiments.

To resume, the problem is usually that the inexperienced housewife, filled with sudden enthusiasm, piles in the hot-tasting herbs such as common thyme, savory and marjoram, so masking the normal, pleasant taste of the meat or other main ingredient, and incurring the family's disapproval. Herbs should enhance and harmonize with the main flavour, not dominate it; and if the new flavour is appreciated but not fully recognizable that is usually a sign that just sufficient has been added to make the dish a success.

It follows, then, that mint, parsley, chives (with care) and lemon thyme will usually be safe; but common thyme, bay leaves, savory and oregano will need to be used wisely, though, with chervil and tarragon, they are basic continental flavours and make all the difference to dishes.

Regarding the first point, the ordinary housewife can use herbs in the simplest dishes and in this way obtain most interesting and varied results with comparatively little expenditure of energy.

For practical purposes we might group cookery as:

1. *Haute cuisine* and continental cookery.
2. Special occasions for the ordinary housewife.
3. Day-to-day cookery for the ordinary housewife-family cookery.
4. The casual tin-opener.

For deep and sustained initiation into the first class, and for guidance in picking special 'chef-d'oeuvres' for the second group, one can gladly recommend books such as Constance Spry's delightful *Come into the Garden, Cook* and Ethelind Fearon's small but comprehensive book with cosmopolitan recipes, *Herbs, How to Grow, Treat and Use Them*.

In the following pages, some of the continental specialities in the way of flavouring will be mentioned to illustrate the adventurous range of blends available. But really simple ideas will also be given for practical family cookery.

A third point often arises—elementary, but needing a practical reply—'How do I use the herbs?' The answer is, in three main ways—first, fresh when available from the garden or window-box, finely chopped-up with scissors or on a board with a knife (some of the essential flavouring may be lost in this latter way). *Fines herbes*, for example, are chervil, tarragon, chives and parsley used with fish and other dishes, freshly chopped up and sprinkled on.

Enjoying a good February, I have picked and used fennel, parsley, lemon thyme, savory, perennial marjoram, sage, common thyme, rosemary and bay from the garden; forwarded chives, oregano sprigs and scented geranium leaves from pot-plants, and with Florence Craggs and Rosemary Clayton, tried out recipes below.

Secondly, the traditional *bouquet-garni* consists of a fresh or dried bay leaf (only a half-leaf for small dishes), and sprigs of fresh or dried thyme and parsley, tied with thread and suspended in the soup, stew or other appropriate dish—the incriminating evidence is then fished out before the dish is served up. In this way, an ethereal flavour, a bouquet, is obtained, without the fear of overdoing it. The *bouquet-garni* may be varied by the inclusion of lemon thyme, marjoram, savory, basil or other herbs when available. The point is that any enterprising housewife can work out her own variants on the classic culinary directions.

Thirdly, when fresh herbs are not available or time is short, dried herbs, separately or in combination, can be used. Today, we have availed ourselves of dried mint, basil, tarragon, mixed herbs and veal and poultry-stuffing herbs. Dried sage is an excellent standby. When using dried herbs it is wise to powder them as finely as possible to disseminate their flavour throughout the dish. Blends are perhaps harder to make than to use just some two or three herbs. We find that a mixed herbs recipe we have made up for more than twenty years successfully has ordinary thyme, savory and parsley predominating; with some marjoram and lemon thyme also included; while an excellent veal and poultry blend has lemon (lemon thyme or lemon verbena usually) predominating, assisted by parsley and marjoram, with some of the warm flavours also—common thyme and savory.

It is usually wisest to keep sage out of ordinary mixtures and use it separately in partnership with the friendly onion or chives, to keep distinctiveness for the pork and other usual dishes.

SOUPS

Dried mint can be handed separately to sprinkle on pea soup, and parsley in the same way for potato soup. Basil is a good flavour for brown thick meat soups, and is a classic in turtle and tomato soups.

In national cookery, the Hungarian goulash soup is satisfying, and is based on shin of beef, onion and potatoes, with marjoram and, rather surprisingly to our palates, caraway seeds added; in their broths, tarragon, bay leaf and rosemary feature as flavourings.

Chervil is often an ingredient in French soups, and in a fish soup the flavours may range widely from onions and celery to chervil, garlic, fennel and bay.

Italian minestrone is a classic dish, and has a wonderful range of ingredients, including pork, minute marrows, dried pulse, tomato paste and, fittingly, macaroni, and vegetables such as carrots and celery. Amongst herbs, the unusual mixture of sage, tarragon and rosemary is generally appreciated.

When making a straightforward vegetable soup or one based on the stock-pot, some variant of the *bouquet-garni* is invaluable.

MEAT

Dried rosemary may be sprinkled or fresh sprigs laid over the joint of mutton before roasting, to give a distinctive flavour.

Veal is excellent stuffed with a simple stuffing—for instance 3 ounces white breadcrumbs, 1 ounce melted margarine, egg for binding. To this half a teaspoonful of fresh or dried 'veal and poultry herbs' as listed above can be added, also salt and pepper. This mixture could also be made into forcemeat balls and served separately; but tied into the centre of the joint before roasting it permeates the whole with a pleasant flavour. Chopped ham may be added to the stuffing if liked.

To use up left-over slices of veal or other meat, these could be wrapped round portions of the forcemeat and tied up; then cooked in a good gravy; or, for those unmoved by heresy, in an appropriate tinned soup.

Meat in batter. Just tested and proved most satisfactory—lamb cutlets fried in batter to which some herb has been added. With pork, basil and a hint of lemon thyme together are delicious and soften the meat flavour. With a lamb or mutton cutlet, oregano (knotted marjoram) is excellent, again with a dash of lemon thyme, and mellows and enhances the meat. For one person, a lamb cutlet can also be stuffed with veal stuffing, as above, then fried; this is a pleasing change. The chosen herbs are just chopped into the batter mixture before coating the meat.

An open bacon and egg pie is improved if some sage is worked into the pastry before it is finally rolled.

FISH

Stuffed Fish. Ordinary white fish such as cod steaks are transformed if they are stuffed with a simple breadcrumb stuffing, to which chopped fennel, and lemon thyme have been added, and the dish rubbed with a garlic clove (or onion flakings could be added to the stuffing). Bake in the usual way; or steam, having put a nut of butter on the fish and surrounded with milk. Place between fireproof plates over a saucepan of boiling water.

White fish such as whitings or haddock may have sprigs of fennel, lemon thyme and chives laid on them, then butter and milk, and be steamed as in previous recipe. The herbs permeate the whole dish with their flavour.

Plaice, haddock or other filleted fish may be coated with batter to which some chopped herbs such as tarragon, parsley or chervil have been added, and then fried.

The continental flavouring for eels prepared as *anguilles au vert* features chervil, also mint, savory, and sorrel.

HERB BISCUITS

A plain biscuit mixture may be made, using, for instance, 1 lb. of flour, the yolk of one egg, and milk. A pastry mixture may also be used for the same purpose. The mixture is divided into from three to six portions, and into each a different herb blend is sprinkled then, with the pastry mixture, folded over and rolled in. Just tested, basil with lovage (a flavour near to celery) has great distinction (chopped celery leaves could be used instead of the grated lovage root). Tarragon with cheese and a hint of chives is distinctive, too. Rosemary used on its own imparts a ginger flavour. A pinch of the veal-stuffing herbs imparts a lemon taste. Other choices are oregano (knotted marjoram) and mint.

These biscuits are good, plain or buttered, for social occasions when everyone contributes something unusual to the menu; and for picnics. With the variety of flavours, each member of the family will find some special favourite.

PASTRY CASES

Different herbs can be worked into pastry as outlined above, then the cases filled in variety. This gives a new line for those who may find pastry itself boring at times.

Mint-flavoured cases can be filled before baking with mint, brown sugar and sultanas, and covered with pastry these pasties are an unusual sweet. Bowles mint, which has a fruity flavour, is best of all, and dried and reconstituted with hot water is ideal, having a flavour indistinguishable from fresh chopped leaves.

Cases flavoured with sage are good filled with processed cheese with an onion hint, put in before baking. Other successes are the basil flavour, filled with beetroot; parsley, with hard-boiled egg; oregano with watercress; garlic, also lemon thyme, filled with winter salad. Any slices of meat, ham or fish chopped or minced, could also be used, moistened with mayonnaise or other suitable ingredient.

HERB PANCAKES

Savoury pancakes can have a variety of chopped herbs blended into the mixture. Dried sage and grated onion can be tried; and after frying, chopped ham rolled inside the pancake before serving. Oregano is a good choice for a savoury pancake flavour; and minced or chopped beef could be folded inside.

These pancakes can also be eaten cold, like 'scotch pancakes'.

SCRAMBLED EGG HERBS

Mint and parsley chopped and added to scrambled eggs impart a refreshing essence-of-spring flavour. Parsley and chives has a good flavour—the amount of chives needs varying to suit individual taste. Lemon thyme alone is excellent—it is fresh, with also a hint of aromatic warmth. Another interesting variant is to blend in chopped ham, with a pinch of dried sage and chopped chives.

Used cold, these scrambled egg blends make excellent sandwich fillings.

OMELETTE HERBS

A classic blend for this purpose has dried parsley predominating, with common thyme and marjoram added also. The blends suggested for scrambled eggs are suitable for omelettes also.

HERB BUTTERS

Gather sprigs of four to eight herbs—mint, lemon thyme, chives, parsley, marjoram or oregano, salad burnet, pineapple sage and lovage would provide a varied selection. Finely chop each kind then blend separately into dessertspoonfuls of butter. These varied butters may be spread on thin wine or 'symbol savoury' biscuits and make an intriguing and economical tea dish. Or the butters may be used as sandwich fillings or to serve at table with homely baked potatoes in their jackets.

HERB SAVOURIES

More elaborately, on the biscuits spread (as above) with a range of the herb butters, slices of hard-boiled egg, tomato, cucumber and beetroot may be laid, and suitably garnished (and 'labelled') with sprigs of the appropriate herbs, also knobs of processed cheese (chives butter, egg and cheese are good; also tomato over marjoram butter); but the changes can be rung indefinitely.

These are suitable buffet or party snacks.

SALADS

Winter salads can have as basic ingredients some of the following: celery, chopped apple, beetroot (these three are excellent together), grated carrot, shredded chicory or endive, mustard-and-cress, watercress by February, raw cabbage hearts, orange slices. Finely chopped fresh leaves of marjoram, salad burnet (cucumber flavour), winter savory, lemon thyme, parsley, fennel, should be available from the garden during the winter, and a selection, sprinkled over the salad, lends piquancy.

In summer, cold diced new potatoes, lettuce, cresses, tomatoes, cucumber,

PLATE 5 CULINARY AND AROMATIC PLANTS
1. Melilot. (*Melilotus officinalis*)
2. Pink Hyssop. (*Hyssopus officinalis var.*)
3. Lemon Thyme. (*Thymus citriodorus*)
4. Summer Savory. (*Satureia hortensis*)
5. Blue Hyssop. (*Hyssopus officinalis*)
6. Lemon Verbena. (*Lippia citriodora*)
7. Lemon Balm. (*Melissa officinalis*)
8. Tree Onion. (*Allium cepa var.*)
9. Welsh Onion. (*Allium fistulosum*)
10. Garlic. (*Allium sativum*)

PLATE 6 CULINARY, MEDICINAL AND AROMATIC HERBS
1. Blue Comfrey. (*Symphytum caucasicum*)
2. Bluebeard, Annual Clary. (*Salvia horminum*)
3. Russian Tarragon. (*Artemisia dracunculoides*)
4. Rosemary. (*Rosmarinus officinalis*, Miss Jessup)
5. Common Thyme. (*Thymus vulgaris*)
6. Winter Savory. (*Satureia montana*)
7. Rosemary. (*Rosmarinus officinalis*)
8. French Tarragon. (*Artemisia dracunculus*)
9. Lungwort. (*Pulmonaria officinalis*)
10. French Marjoram. (*Origanum onites*)
11. Borage. (*Borago officinalis*)
12. Perennial Marjoram. (*Origanum vulgare*)
13. Knotted Marjoram. (*Origanum marjorana*)
14. Chives. (*Allium schoenoprasum*)
15. Evergreen Alkanet. (*Pentaglottis sempervirens*)

PLATE 7 MEDICINAL HERBS
1. Greater Celandine. (*Chelidonium majus*)
2. *Grindelia robusta*.
3. Elecampane. (*Inula helenium*)
4. Black Bryony. (*Tamus communis*). A. female flowers. B. male flowers.
5. Rue. (*Ruta graveolens*)
6. Eyebright. (*Euphrasia officinalis*)
7. Wall Germander. (*Teucrium chamaedrys*)
8. Sea-Holly. (*Eryngium maritimum*)

PLATE 8 MEDICINAL HERBS
1. Goat's Rue. (*Galega officinalis*)
2. Lady's Mantle. (*Alchemilla vulgaris*)
3. Feverfew. (*Chrysanthemum parthenium*)
4. Motherwort. (*Leonurus cardiaca*)
5. Hound's Tongue. (*Cynoglossum officinale*)
6. Parsley-Piert. (*Alchemilla arvensis*)
7. Chamomile. (*Anthemis nobilis*)
8. Dropwort Meadowsweet. (*Filipendula vulgaris*)

young peas and many other ingredients are available. Mint, chervil, lemon balm, lovage leaves, alecost, chives, tarragon, sorrel and pineapple sage are some summer herbs to use in addition to those available in winter. It is wise to experiment and find the most personally acceptable blends. Many other flavours, such as nasturtium leaves, bergamot, and pineapple mint, can be exciting.

CAKES

A suggestion much recommended recently, that we like very much, is to line a cake tin with scented 'oak-leaf' geranium leaves, and pour in a sponge mixture, then bake as usual. The ethereal fragrance of the leaves imparts a delicious flavour to the sponge cake.

Caraway-seed cake is well known and good for those who like it; and caraway biscuits can also be made.

POT-POURRI

Pot-pourris are of two kinds—the moist and dry recipes. With the moist recipes, fresh or semi-dried rose petals, violets, mock orange, lily-of-the-valley, pinks, and any other suitable flowers are put into layers into a jar, with scented leaves such as sweet geraniums, and covered with alternate layers of common or bay salt. Sprinklings of allspice, cloves and powdered orris-root may be added, and some recipes include a little brandy for preservative purposes. These moist pot-pourris are long-lasting and suitable for pot-pourri jars with perforated lids.

In dry pot-pourris the flowers are dried completely as outlined under drying suggestions. Lavender flowers, chamomile, clove pinks, and carnations, violets, primroses, philadelphus, rosemary, lily-of-the-valley, may be used, with any other pleasantly scented flowers. For a dual-purpose pot-pourri, to look attractive as well, larkspurs, calendula, delphiniums, and other flowers may be dried, for colour. The dry pot-pourris are delightful to arrange in open bowls, but a piece of cellophane, perforated with holes, and held over the bowl with a rubber band to keep it in place, prevents disturbance of the floral design. The dry pot-pourris are most suitable, also, for putting into sachets and bags.

For a natural pot-pourri, scented leaves such as lemon verbena, oak-leaf and lemon-scented geraniums, eau-de-Cologne mint, thymes such as *T. fragrantissimus*, rosemary, southernwood, oregano, marjoram and bay leaves may be added. This type of pot-pourri needs to be stirred and lightly crushed on occasion to bring out the fragrance.

Spicier recipes include as well cinnamon, nutmeg, mace, dried, powdered orange peel, orris and on occasion powdered gums such as benzoin, to give a finish. Many recipes include a few drops of oil of geranium and attar of roses.

It is wise to experiment with different proportions of the various ingredients mentioned, to achieve a scent that is individually liked.

TRADITION

'He hath made everything beautiful in its time,'
The King wrote with flashing insight, 'And He hath set
Eternity deep within our hearts.' In his prime
He knew our crumbling hopes, the high vision met
With the actual dead-sea fruit. So he wrote at length
Of the perfumed garden (envy, the traitor, locked out),
And the springing hyssop, the agelong, spicy strength
Of the Lebanon cedars, shimmering with needles, and stout
With their perching cones. And Solomon passed to his rest.

They wrote with observant eyes, the philosophers then—
Theophrastus and Pliny, their minds on the quest,
Probing the mysteries of herbs, and, with them, the men
'Who drew the likeness of herbs and wrote under them their effects'.

    In the army of Nero the Ruthless a herb-healer served,
Dioscorides, laden with learning. His lore still connects
With materia medica, while the black bryony, curved
To wreathe round the hedges, hangs jewel-burdened with fruit,
Bearing the family name.

                        Bald of the old Saxon race
Wrote a Leech-Book of virtue, containing permissible loot
From the Eastern distilling of medical wisdom, the grace
Of King Alfred being with him.

                        Still the shades strengthen and pass . . .
Green men with the close-clutched inheritance of lore,
Shot through with terrors, sharp outlines of tragedy, farce
Set against smouldering sunsets, in spells, to implore
Aid from the curdling mist-wraiths and gloom; then release
In a prayer, and the healing fingers of light and calm truth
Smoothing the furrows of panic. Cowled figures increase
True knowledge of cures, bringing simples, with mercy and ruth.

              And now by a royal decree the apothecaries stand
Reputed for learning, rich clothed in their secrets' deep green;
Most curious, Culpeper is watching the heavens' far strand
For planets whose influence will govern the plants he can glean.

     Good Gerard is penning his herbal with glowing delight,
His interest enhanced by his garden, hard by Fetter Lane,
Praising the eternal Craftsman.

      In this clear light,
Paradise in the sun, are the gilliflowers, plain
Or striped and marbled, flower de luce and the pompion.
Here, deep in the heart of London, Parkinson flowered
Into his garden's enchantment, where bugloss and rampion,
Arrach and skirrets grew handily, deep embowered
In the weaving of jasmine and clematis; herbs in profusion,
Plaiting a fragrant cord with beguiling names—
Costmary, smallage and succory.

      In conclusion,
Linked by this scented rope that binds the centuries' fames
Lasting or quietly faithful, holders of all we inherit,
Come our own ages' herb-savants, privileged in those they succeed.

Note the lady of Chalfont St. Giles.[1] Inexhaustible merit
Lies in her present-day Herbal. Still sharing her meed
The healer who took as her trade-sign old Culpeper's lure,[2]
Bringing health as her garland, and fame.

     . . . where the sinuous Downs,
Cloud-patterned, flow behind Reigate, and the yews endure
Arching the years, where flower-gemmed turf still crowns
The high hill brow, an author probed the store
Of the long ages, nectar-distilled at last;
Herbs and herb-gardening, strange receipts, and more
She wrote,[3] with the honied secrets of the past.

     Where wine-deep wallflowers first
Flow out in homely, mystic warmth, close held
By walls and shadowed towers, great Sissinghurst
Beacons the Weald with learning, insight-spelled.

Here changeless beauty rests, chaliced to quench the thirst
Of this frustrated, syncope age (the throb
Of engines, diesel breathed, is in our veins).

Here, conquerors of the clay, striped rose and cob
Flourish; and scented pelargonium gains
Glory, cascading scarlet from the urns,
Cooled by the silver garden.

     Fine herbs grace
The patterned acre, where tall bergamot burns,
Rare painted sages glow, with wormwood's place
Stippled with light like a changeful day. Here, spoils
Are won from the temperamental clay by work
Tireless and skilled, but poised by the quieter toils
In wrestling with lovely, haunting phrases (shirk
Her craftsmanship, and all reward is lost).

Perceptively the Land has been revealed,
And the fair Garden, and our gratitude flows.[4]

What would the Ancients think of us? (Concealed
In the mists of time), to know that women chose
To take their heritage, and keep green their name
Then show their knowledge forth? At Seal, deep in the throes
Of visible warfare, our founder worked. Sharp flame
Spat overhead in the conflicts, in the clattering death
With its flying tail of menace and fire; and the sky
Spiralled with silver trails; then the acrid breath
Of rockets, traitors from the blue, far cry
From the dame's violet, sweet rocket of tranquil earth.
In smock of cornflower blue, with kerchiefed head
She grew and gathered herbs[5] to meet the dearth,
And we worked with her; a nation to be fed
Needed the flavourings and the healing herb.

And she was generous with her experience then.
With practical intent she wrote, to curb
The facile theorist; with determined pen
She showed the arduous nature of the life,
To wrest a living from the reluctant ground;

The discipline of knowing plants, the strife
With weather and the organisms that abound
To squander hope.

For thirty years and more
Our herbs have dappled this warm, sandy hill
Mellow in summer, in the strong winter hoar
Frosted and bleak with our lashing winds, but here
The herbs can feel at home in their natural ways,
Informal, as in their country haunts. Austere
And rigid modern treatment? No self-sown strays?
Let them keep their freedom, let mullein candles spill
Ten thousand seeds; while the fennel, sea-green, sways
With blue chicory waves, right up to the house, until
It is met by the walls; let them riot in jostling praise,
Their colour and scent an offering;
        And still
From far and near they come, for our quiet fame—
The men and women who wish for plants to grow—
Whose gardens harbour herbs without a name
And those beguiled by the lore, who long to know
All that they can of the 'mystery and the art'
(To borrow an ancient phrase); and away they go
With a fragrant trophy, an infinitesimal part
Of the stored ages, the perfumed winds that blow
Through the long passage of the centuries' past.

All who have insight must fan the incense-glow
Until we touch the Tree of Life at last.

[1] Mrs. Grieve.
[2] Mrs. Leyel.
[3] Miss Rohde.
[4] Miss Sackville-West.
[5] Miss Hewer.
 (Poem written 1956 by M.E.B.).

REFERENCE SECTION

Flowering Times of Scented and Aromatic Plants through the year

(northern hemisphere)

Evergreen aromatic plants such as rosemary and thymes, and evergrey ones, lavender, curry plant and santolina, give the pleasure of their aromatic properties all the year round; and the deciduous aromatic ones, such as *Rubus odoratus* and sweetbriars, marjorams and scented mints, from spring to autumn.

The list below is of the months in which the shrubs and scented blossoms actually flower, apart from the aromatic qualities of foliage possessed by any of them.

Ar. = aromatic foliage.   A = annual.   B = biennial.
P = perennial.   S = shrub.   H = hardy.   HH = half hardy.

January–February
    (S) *Chimonanthus praecox* (*Calycanthus praecox*) (Winter Sweet)
    (S) *Hamamelis mollis* (Witch Hazel—faint sweetness)
    (HP) *Petasites fragrans* (Winter Heliotrope—for waste spot)

February–March
    (S) *Daphne mezereum* (Purple or white Mezereon)
    (S) *D. laureola* (green flowers)
    (S) *Berberis japonica* (yellow flower—lily-of-the-valley scent)
    (S) *Azara microphylla* (yellow flower—vanilla scent)
    (S) *Corylopsis pauciflora* (yellow flower—cowslip scent)
    (S) *Lonicera fragrantissima* (cream flower)
    (S) *Skimmia japonica*, etc. (white flower—lily-of-the-valley scent)
    (Bulb) *Polyanthus narcissus* (Soleil d'or, etc.)
    (Bulb) *Iris reticulata* (violet scent—evanescent)

April–May
    (Ar.S) Rosemary (soft blue flowers)
    (S) *Sarcococca humilis* (lowly—cream and green scented flowers)
    (S) *Viburnum carlesii, V. burkwoodi*, etc. (white-pink flowers—scented)
    (S) *Daphne japonica* (pale pink flowers—very fragrant)
    (S) *Cytisus praecox* (cream, quietly scented flower)

- (S) *Ulex europaeus* (Gorse—almond-reminiscent scent)
- (S) *Ribes odoratum* (*R.aureum*) (yellow flower—clove scent—good autumn tints)
- (S) *Azaleas* (flaming shades—indefinable warm aroma)
- (S) *Kerria japonica* (Jew's Mallow—yellow flower, sweet scent)
- (S) *Wistarias* (mauve flower—lovely musky scent)
- (S) *Crataegus* (Hawthorn or May—traditional-sweet scent)
- (S) *Osmanthus delavayi* (white scented flower)
- (S) Lilacs (white, mauves and purple-red vary in scent)
- (S) Magnolias, esp. *stellata* (white, fragrant flower)
- (Ar.S) *Choisya ternata* (Mexican Orange—white scented flower)
- (HP) Violets (wild ones are sweetest)
- (HP) Primroses; also *Primula auricula*
- (HP) Lily-of-the-Valley (shady site)
- (HP) Wallflowers (bronze, red, lemon, gold, rose, purple)
- (HB) Brompton Stocks (pastel shades; singles have good scent)
- (Bulbs) Hyacinths and Bluebells
- (Bulbs) Narcissus (in variety, esp. Pheasant's Eye = *Poeticus*)
- (Bulbs) Freesias under glass

June–July

- (S) Roses—Hybrid Teas such as Crimson Glory, Talisman
    Hybrid Perpetuals—George and Hugh Dickson
    Hybrid Musks
- (Ar.S) Penzance Briars (Lord Penzance, Lady P., etc.)
- (Ar.S) *Cistus* (in variety; esp. *C.purpureus*, *C.ladaniferus*)
- (S) *Philadelphus purpureo-maculata* (Mock Orange). *Philadelphus coronarius* and numerous others
- (S) *Genista aetnensis* (Mount Etna broom)
- (S) *Lonicera sp.* (Honeysuckles) *L.periclymenum*, etc.
- (S) *Jasminum off.* (White Jasmine)
- (S) *Staphylea colchica* (white flower—unusual aroma)
- (S) *Veronica salicifolia*
- (HP) Carnations (esp. Clove kinds)
- (HP) *Nymphaea odorata* (Water-Lilies)
- (HP and HHA) *Dianthus* (Pinks, esp. Loveliness)
- (HA) Night-scented Stock
- (HHP) Scented Pelargoniums (in variety)

July–August

- (Ar.S) Lavenders (in variety)
- (Ar.S) *Santolina* (Cotton Lavender)

FLOWERING TIMES OF SCENTED AND AROMATIC PLANTS

(Ar.S) *Rubus odoratus* (purple-pink flower)
(Ar.S) *Perowskia atriplicifolia* (lavender blue flower)
(Ar.S) *Caryopteris clandonensis* (lavender blue flower)
(Ar.S) *Hypericum patulum henryi* (*H.pseudohenryi*)
(S) *Buddleia davidii* (Butterfly Bush—honey-scented flower)
(S) *Ceanothus* Mountain Sweet or red root—faintly sweet)
(HHA) Ten-week Stocks (pastel and rich shades)
(HHA) *Nicotiana* (Tobacco flower)
(HHA) Sweet Scabious (rich shades—soft sweetness)
(HHA) Sweet Sultan (pastel shades—soft sweetness)
(HHA) Sweet Peas (chosen for perfume)
(HB) *Oenothera* (Evening Primrose)
(Bulbous) Lilies—esp. *L.candidum* (Madonna Lily)
          L.regale (Trumpet Lily)
          L.auratum (Gold-Rayed Lily of Japan)
(HP) Bergamots (in jewel shades)
(HP) Clary Sage
(HHP) Heliotrope

August–September
(S) *Elsholtzia stauntonii* (slightly aromatic)
(S) *Clerodendron trichotomum* (white fragrant flower)
(Ar.S) *Myrtus communis* (Myrtle—white flower)
(HP) *Brittonastrum mexicanum* (red flower, aromatic leaf)

October–December
(S) *Viburnum farreri* (*fragrans*)
(S) Roses (often second autumn flower on Musk Hybrids, and H.P.s such as Dicksons; and H.T.s—Talisman)
(HHS) *Salvia grahami* (under glass)
(HHS) *S.rutilans* (Pineapple Sage—under glass)

Classified Lists

AROMATIC SHRUBS (Ar.S.)
Calycanthus macrophyllus, etc. Allspice
Caryopteris clandonensis, etc.
Cistus purpureus, etc. Sun-Roses
Elsholtzia stauntonii
Eucalyptus gunnii, etc.
Gaultheria procumbens. Wintergreen
Hypericum patulum var. henryi
Myrtus communis. Myrtle
Perovskia atriplicifolia, etc. Russian Sage
Rosa primula
Rosa rubiginosa. Sweetbriar
Rubus odoratus
Teucrium fruticans
Umbellularia californica. Californian Laurel

SCENTED SHRUBS (Sc.S)
Azara microphylla
Buddleia. Butterfly Bush
Ceanothus. Mountain Sweet
Chimonanthus fragrans. Winter Sweet
Choisya ternata. Mexican Orange
Clematis flammula
Clerodendron
Corylopsis
Crataegus oxyacantha (= *C.monogyna*). Hawthorn
Cytisus. Broom
Daphne
Erica
Genista aetnensis. Etna Broom
Hamamelis. Witch Hazel
Jasminum officinale. White Jasmine
Kerria japonica. Jew's Mallow
Lonicera. Honeysuckle
Magnolia

Mahonia (Berberis) bealii
Osmanthus delavayi
Philadelphus
Rhododendron
Ribes aureum
Rosa. Rose
Skimmia
Staphylea colchica
Ulex europaeus. Gorse
Viburnum
Wisteria

NORTH AMERICAN HERBS (Amer.)
American Hellebore. *Veratrum viride*
American Liverwort. *Hepatica triloba var. americanum*
American Mandrake. *Podophyllum peltatum*
American Spikenard. *Aralia racemosa*
Asclepias tuberosa. Pleurisy-Root
Bergamots. *Monarda sp.*
Black Cohosh. *Cimicifuga racemosa*
Blood-Root. *Sanguinaria canadensis*
Californian Laurel. *Umbellularia californica*
Ginseng. *Panax quinquefolius*
Golden Seal. *Hydrastis canadensis*
Grindelia
Indian Ginger. *Asarum canadense*
Indian Physic. *Porteranthus trifoliatus*
Labrador Tea. *Ledum groenlandicum*
Lobelia, Scarlet. *Lobelia cardinalis*
Mountain Laurel. *Kalmia latifolia*
Pokeweed. *Phytolacca decandra*
Mountain Sweet or Red-Root. *Ceanothus americanus*
Skunk-Cabbage. *Symplocarpus foetidus*

Alphabetical List of Herbs, and Scented and Aromatic Shrubs

[If an English name does not appear as a principal name at the appropriate alphabetical position, the entry in this list will be under the equivalent Latin name, which may be found after the English name in the index; and *vice versa* for Latin names.]

Ar.S. = aromatic shrub.   Sc.S. = scented shrub.   Amer. = North American herb.

ACONITE   *Aconitum napellus* (Plate 12)   [*Ranunculaceae*]
Aconite also called Monkshood or Wolf's Bane is found wild in the West of England and Wales. Confusion can occur between this poisonous plant with purple spires of hooded flowers and yellow Winter Aconite (*Eranthis hyemalis*).

The medicinal Aconite is propagated by side tubers which form round the original root. A rich soil is necessary for a prolific crop. For medicinal use, the tubers are dug in autumn and sorted, the larger ones washed free from soil, then dried, and the smaller replanted. Homoeopathic chemists use the whole fresh flowering tops. The official tincture is used to keep down the pulse rate in fevers, and to relieve neuralgia.

AGRIMONY   (Church Steeples)   *Agrimonia eupatoria*   [*Rosaceae*]
Growing 2½ ft. high, this wild plant, found in hedgerows and pastures, has pinnate leaves (divided like a feather), and spires of small yellow flowers. Agrimony tea is made from the flowering tops and has value as a gargle for a tired, relaxed throat. Gerard says that 'A decoction of the leaves is good for them that have naughty livers'. It has had a considerable reputation to cure jaundice.

AGRIMONY   (Hemp)   *Eupatorium cannabinum*   [*Compositae*]
A wild English herb found in damp woods and by streams. Growing some 3–4 ft. high, the plant has pinnate leaves and large heads of small pinkish flowers, with a superficial resemblance to the wild medicinal Valerian (not the *Centranthus* of chalk cuttings). A tea is sometimes used to allay influenza. Hemp Agrimony is a hardy perennial, increased by division.

ALECOST *Chrysanthemum balsamita*, formerly *Tanacetum balsamita* (Place 3)
[*Compositae*]

Alecost (Costmary, 'Mace', Allspice) is a pleasant plant for the herb garden, and the scent, reminiscent of mint and with a balsam softness attracts interest. The leaves are ovate, green with greyish bloom, and the flowers are like yellow buttons. Camphor Plant (*Balsamita vulgaris*) is a close relation with similar leaves but the scent is different and the flowers are white daisies. Alecost grows 2–3 ft. high and is a native of Asia, grown for many centuries in this country. Propagation is by division, and small rooted pieces may be severed from the main plant in autumn or spring. Alecost flourishes in a light to rich soil and sunny position. The bruised leaves are soothing rubbed on a bee sting. The young leaves, in spring, finely chopped, give a mint flavour to salads. A little sugar, blended in, reduces the slight bitterness.

An ointment made from Alecost is soothing for burns, bruises and skin troubles. 'Sweete washing water' was formerly made from this plant.

ALEXANDERS (Black Lovage, 3 ft.) *Smyrnium olusatrum* [*Umbelliferae*]

A naturalized plant, growing by the seaside and in waste places. The leaves are deeply divided. The flowers, arranged in umbels, are greenish-yellow. The flowers, when found in quantity, give off a sweet scent. The height is 2½–3 ft.

The large black seeds may be sown outside ½ in. deep in a suitable seedbed in April and early May. The plant was formerly cultivated as celery is grown now. The flavour is pungent, but a leaf may be chopped up in a salad. In ancient times Dioscorides recommended the herb to relieve dropsy.

ALKANETS *Anchusa officinalis. A. sempervirens* (*Pentaglottis semp.*) [*Boraginaceae*]

A. officinalis is, very rarely, found naturalized on ballast-heaps and similar waste places. The typical blue rotate flowers are in scorpioid cymes, and the foliage leaves are long and narrow. This Alkanet grows some 18 in. to 2 ft. high.

Evergreen Alkanet is *A. sempervirens*. This blue-flowered, harsh-leaved herb, growing 2 ft. high, is often mistaken for Borage. It is found naturalized wild on waste ground, usually near inhabited places. The plant flowers from May to August. This herb was formerly prized for a red dye obtained from the bark of the root. This colour is used by dyers and by cabinet-makers for staining wood. (Plate 6).

Anchusa italica.—This intensely blue-flowered plant, often grown in herbaceous borders, is a perennial, growing 3–5 ft. high. The plant yields a red dye, used from earliest Egyptian days as a cosmetic.

PLATE 9 MEDICINAL HERBS
1. Musk Mallow. (*Malva moschata*)
2. Common Mallow. (*Malva sylvestris*)
3. Tansy. (*Tanacetum vulgare*)
4. Marsh Mallow. (*Althaea officinalis*)
5. Acanthus. (*Acanthus spinosus*)
6. Heartsease. (*Viola tricolor*)
7. Poke—Root. (*Phytolacca decandra*)

PLATE 10 MEDICINAL HERBS
1. Liquorice. (*Glycyrrhiza glabra*)
2. Linseed. (*Linum usitatissimum*)
3. Prunella or Self-Heal. (*Prunella vulgaris*)
4. Wood Betony. (*Stachys betonica*)
5. Catmint. (*Nepeta cataria*)
6. Vervain or Wild Verbena. (*Verbena officinalis*)
7. Blessed Thistle. (*Carduus benedictus*)
8. White Horehound. (*Marrubium vulgare*)
9. Mullein. (*Verbascum thapsus*)
10. Our Lady's Milk Thistle. (*Silybum marianum*)
11. Balsam Poplar. (*Populus balsamifera*)

PLATE 11 POISONOUS DRUG HERBS
1. Black Nightshade. (*Solanum nigrum*)
2. Woody Nightshade or Bittersweet. (*Solanum dulcamara*)
3. Opium Poppy. (*Papaver somniferum*)
4. Belladonna or Deadly Nightshade (*Atropa belladonna*)
5. Foxglove. (*Digitalis purpurea*)
6. Fritillary. (*Fritillaria meleagris*)
7. Henbane. (*Hyoscyamus niger*)
8. Thornapple. (*Datura stramonium*)
9. Pasque-Flower. (*Anemone pulsatilla*)

PLATE 12 POISONOUS DRUG HERBS
1. Opium Lettuce. (*Lactuca virosa*)
2. White Bryony. (*Bryonia dioica*). A. male flowers. B. female flowers.
3. Wood Spurge. (*Euphorbia amygdaloides*)
4. Hellebore. (*Helleborus foetidus*)
5. Monkshood. (*Aconitum napellus*)
6. Hemlock. (*Conium maculatum*)
7. Autumn Crocus or Meadow Saffron. (*Colchicum autumnale*)
8. Mandrake. (*Atropa mandragora* or *Mandragora officinarum*)
9. Spurge—Laurel or Green Daphne. (*Daphne laureola*)

ALLSPICE *Calycanthus floridus, C.occidentalis (C.macrophyllus)* (Plate 16) Ar.S.
[*Calycanthaceae*]

These shrubs, growing some 5–7 ft. high, on the average, are not as well known as the Winter Sweet (*Chimonanthus praecox = Calycanthus praecox*) which has ivory-carved, purple-centred, and deliciously fragrant flowers on leafless branches in January and February.

Superficially, the Allspices bear no resemblance to Wintersweet. They flower in August, with rather pleasant terminal carmine, many-petalled flowers, somehow resembling the tuft on a pineapple.

These Allspices are best planted in a sheltered site against a south wall or amongst other shrubs giving some winter protection. Propagation is by layering in July. The leaves, particularly of *C.macrophyllus* have a strong, aromatic scent, pleasing to some, doubtfully reminiscent of roast beef to others.

The wood, however, is delightfully fragrant, with the allspice scent that gives the shrubs their name, although they do not yield the commercial allspice (from a Pimento) and are mainly grown for their aroma and interest.

AMERICAN HELLEBORE, BEARCABBAGE *Veratrum viride*
(Plate 14) Amer. [*Liliaceae*]

The plant is poisonous, and has a perennial rootstock. The inflorescence may be from 2 ft. to 5 ft. or more high. The clasping leaves are much veined. The inflorescence of green flowers is a panicle. This plant is found in swamps and damp woods in parts of Canada and the United States, including New Brunswick and Ontario, south to Georgia and Tennessee. There is a close resemblance to the European *Veratrum album*. The roots and dried rhizome have been used in cases of neuralgia and pneumonia.

AMERICAN LIVERWORT *Hepatica triloba var. americana* (Plate 14)
Amer. [*Ranunculaceae*]

Also called *Anemone hepatica* and *Hepatica americanum*. The leaves have three angular lobes, and are almost evergreen. The delightful flowers, borne in March, are blue, but, mainly in cultivation, there are pink and white forms. The leaves are gathered during flowering time, and used for liver troubles, also in chest and lung complaints.

AMERICAN MANDRAKE *Podophyllum peltatum* (Plate 13) Amer.
[*Berberidaceae*]

This plant, also called May Apple, is found wild in Canada and the eastern United

States. The roots are made up of thick tubers. The handsome leaves are peltate, the white flowers solitary, and followed by a yellow fleshy fruit. The dried rhizome is used medicinally. Both leaves and root contain a poisonous principle. This herb is used in liver complaints, in biliousness and as a purgative. It has been considered on some British evidence unwise for this herb to be taken during pregnancy.

ANGELICA   *Angelica archangelica* (Plate 2)   [*Umbelliferae*]
A relative of this plant with white flowers is found growing wild and was used on occasion during the war but since the members of this family bear great mutual resemblance, to the uninitiated it is usually best to rely on the true garden Angelica, which is, in any case, much preferable for use.

Angelica will grow reasonably in light soils, but prefers slight shade and flourishes most, producing the tenderest leaf stalks, where the soil is reasonably rich and damp to encourage quick growth. The plant is biennial, growing 3–6 ft. high and flowering in May.

Normally, self-sown seedlings are produced if the parent plants are left to shed their seed. Seed may also be sown in a seedbox under glass in March/April or in a seedbed in April and early May. Some prefer to sow the seed as soon as it is ripe in early autumn, but in our experience as long as the seed is not older than the previous summer's harvest, it will germinate reasonably. Older seed quickly loses its viability.

The life of the plant may be prolonged by cutting off the flower spikes before they develop.

The young leaf stems are cut in May and June and there is often the possibility of a second cut in August and early September, particularly from plants set out in late spring.

Angelica has a characteristic flavour. Some like to add a leaf, chopped up, to salads. Angelica jam has an unusual and aromatic taste. The stems may be stewed with rhubarb, which reduces the tartness. The roots and dried leaves are used medicinally as a carminative.

In the herb garden Angelica gives a sculptured dignity of foliage. Plants may be grown in tubs for shady corners of paved yards. The flowers are alluring to queen wasps, owing to the nectar on the open discs of the flowers, and a friend ambushes herself and catches the queens at their banquet.

One method of candying is as follows:

Take stems in April or early May and boil in salt water until tender. Remove and drain it well. Scrape the outside and dry it in a clean cloth. Place it in syrup and allow it to remain there for three or four days, closely covered. The syrup must be made from the same weight of sugar that there is of stems, allowing half a pint of water to a pound of sugar, and must be boiled twice a day, and poured over the stems until nearly absorbed, after which it should be put into a pie-dish and placed near the fire. Time to make, about ten days.

There are, of course, various other methods in circulation.

ANISE *Pimpinella anisum* (Plate 3) [*Umbelliferae*]
Anise is a native of eastern Mediterranean countries. This annual 2 ft. plant is mentioned by Christ, as quoted in St. Matthew's gospel. Seed may be sown outside in April and yields the round aromatic seeds in late summer. The whole plant may be cut off carefully at ground-level when the first umbels of seeds are ripe, and laid on paper in a warm place to finish drying. The Romans offered a cake containing aniseed and cumin at the end of a rich meal to allay indigestion. Anise is used as a flavour in liqueur-making and medicinally against coughs and chest troubles. The seeds are used for flavouring cakes.

ANISE or BLUE GIANT HYSSOP *A. foeniculum* (*Agastache anethiodora, Lopianthus anisatus*) [*Labiatae*]
This plant has long spikes of blue-mauve flowers and a fennel scent, odd in a labiate. It is a hardy perennial, 2½ ft. high, flowering in July and August (Plate 20).

ARNICA *A. montana* (Plate 30) [*Compositae*]
A perennial, found in woods and mountain pastures in Central Europe. The radical leaves form a rosette, from which arises a flower-stem some 1–2 ft. high, and bearing one or more orange-yellow daisies. Both flowers, picked whole and dried, are used, and the dried rhizomes, collected in autumn. The tincture is used as a paint for whole chilblains, and applied to sprains and bruises. A homoeopathic tincture is used internally on occasion, but great care is necessary.

ARTEMISIAS [*Compositae*]
    TARRAGON *A. dracunculus* (Plate 6) (See page 191)
    OLD LADY *A. borealis* (Plate 19)
A perennial plant, growing 18 in. to 2 ft. high, with delightfully fine-cut grey aromatic foliage, attractive in the garden, and particularly so towards autumn,

with a soft smoky effect touched with warm colour. The inconspicuous flowers are yellowish-grey. The foliage and flowers are excellent for harmonizing in floral decorations.

Propagation is by creeping offsets in spring or autumn. This herb flourishes in a light to medium soil and sunny position, and is normally extremely hardy.

LADY'S MAID *A.chamaemelifolia* (18 in.) (Plate 19)
Similar to Old Lady but has green, finely divided leaves and minute yellowish flowers as usual.

OLD WARRIOR (Roman Wormwood) *A.pontica* 18 in. to 2 ft.
A native of southern Europe and very close in appearance to *A.borealis*. It is used in the preparation of 'vermuth', and has an aromatic taste and scent. *A.sericea* and *A.lanata pedemontana* (Plate 19) are miniatures 3 in. high, with shimmering silver feathery leaves. They dislike some English winters, but will pass the worst months peacefully under glass. *A.rupestris* is a prostrate kind also, with green, fine-cut leaves and small yellowish flowers in spikes (Plate 32). These are pleasing for a sheltered sink garden.

A.stellerana $2\frac{1}{2}$–3 ft.
Has whitish-grey, lobed leaves and spikes of greyish-yellow small flowers. It is excellent for the border and in floral decorations, and the foliage is aromatic.

WORMWOOD, OLD WOMAN *A.absinthium* (Plate 19) 3–5 ft.
Wormwood, Mugwort and Sea Wormwood (*A.maritima*) are natives of this country. Wormwood is most decorative during summer in the herb garden, for its shining silver, gracefully cut foliage provides a foil for the richly coloured Bergamots and blue Chicory. Planted in bold groups, the effect is outstanding. The soil should not be too rich, as this tends to diminish the silver quality of the foliage. Wormwood will grow reasonably in poor, light soils, and for its full development likes full sun, but will tolerate slight shade. Propagation is by seed sown outside in April, in drills $\frac{1}{8}$ in. deep. The plants should be put 18 in. to 2 ft. apart to form clumps. *A.*Lambrook Silver has effective foliage.

Mugwort (*A.vulgaris*) is superficially similar at times, but the leaves are silver on the underside only, and green above, the stems are mahogany and the flowers greyish to cream. Mugwort was used to flavour beers and, in Cornwall, as a tea substitute.

Wormwood is still used medicinally, against worms. As a flavour it is used in liqueurs. The whole plant has an extremely bitter taste.

The whole herb may be cut, if grown for cropping purposes, in July and dried in the usual way. Wormwood tea may be made with a handful of fresh leaves, over which a pint of boiling water is poured and after infusing for a few minutes a wineglassful is drunk. This is excellent taken three times a day for indigestion, though the dosage should not be continued for more than a day or two.

The leaves, dried, may be used to keep moths away from woollens, and Old Lady and Southernwood can be used for the same purpose. Wormwood is decorative for cut foliage.

Wormwood is one herb whose name must be familiar as a symbol of bitterness to thousands of people compared with the few who could name the growing plant. Wormwood and gall are mentioned in Lamentations and elsewhere.

SOUTHERNWOOD *A.abrotanum* (Plate 19) [*Compositae*]

Also known as Old Man, Lad's Love, Apple Ringie and, in France, *Garde-Robe*, this is one of the best-known aromatic garden herbs, with a warm fruity scent but a bitter taste.

It is a low shrub, and while it will grow 4 ft. high, it can be kept clipped back to some 2 ft. March is a good time to clip and again in July if a formal appearance is required. The leaves drop in autumn, but the shrub is clothed once again with the finely divided, soft green-grey foliage in April. The spikes of small, brownish-green flowers are produced in favourable summers in August.

Southernwood is a native of southern Europe, but is mentioned in a ninth-century book called *Little Garden*. St. Francis de Sales refers to sprigs of this herb being included in bouquets given by lovers to their lasses as a symbol of sweet fidelity even in bitter circumstances.

Southernwood is delightful as a low hedge planted 1 ft. apart, or as a specimen clipped to a rounded shape, and planted at strategic points in the herb-garden design, such as the end of a line of edging plants at a corner.

Southernwood is very hardy, and flourishes in a light to medium soil to which compost has been added; it will bear light shade but prefers full sun. Propagation is by green cuttings in summer or hardwood cuttings in autumn.

For drying, the tops may be cut in July and August, and the leaves, when rubbed off their stems, can be used in pot-pourri and against moths, as the French name suggests. Some use a very small quantity—one or two leaves—finely chopped in salads.

ASCLEPIAS *A.curassavica* [*Asclepiadaceae*]

A half-hardy perennial plant with gay heads of orange flowers in late summer, flowering on till September, and growing some 2–3 ft. high. In the West Indies this plant is used for emetic purposes.

A. tuberosa, Pleurisy-Root (Plate 30), or Butterfly Weed, is also emetic in large doses, but has been used to cure chest complaints.

AUTUMN CROCUS *Colchicum autumnale* (Plate 12) [*Liliaceae*]

This plant, also called Meadow Saffron, is poisonous, and the corms are used medicinally. The narrow leaves appear in spring, and the graceful rosy lilac to mauve flowers open in August and September, long after the leaves have withered.

The corms are collected in July, and used medicinally, officially prepared, to relieve gout and rheumatism.

It is important not to confuse this plant with true Saffron Crocus, *Crocus sativus*, whose stigmas yield the orange flavour and colour. Saffron crocus also flowers in autumn, but the leaves are slender and grass-like, typical of the real crocuses and appear with the flowers (Plate 32).

AZARA MICROPHYLLA Sc.S. [*Bixaceae*]

This shrub has neat evergreen leaves, an elegant habit and small puffs of yellow, vanilla-scented flowers February to April. It is normally planted against a south wall, or in a similarly protected position, in a light to medium soil, and propagated by cuttings.

BALM, LEMON *Melissa officinalis* (Plate 5) [*Labiatae*]

Lemon Balm is locally naturalized as mainly a garden plant in this country, being a native of central and southern Europe. This plant is often confused with Lemon Verbena and Lemon Thyme. It is the commonest of the lemon-scented plants found in gardens, and often grows prolifically once it is established. It is a hardy perennial, and the leaves are somewhat nettle-like in shape, the flowers small, two-lipped and whitish. Lemon Balm grows 2–3 ft. high.

The leaves keep their pleasant scent reasonably well when dried. They may be used dried and finely rubbed in herb mixtures, particularly for veal and poultry stuffing, and in forcemeat for fish, where a lemon flavour is required.

A fresh leaf or two chopped up adds zest to salads, and one part of balm leaves to two of tea make a refreshing drink. For drying, the foliage should be cut in late July/August.

Lemon Balm grows reasonably in any position, but in light, dry soils it prefers slight shade, and makes most top growth in fairly rich soils. It is propagated by division of roots in spring or autumn.

The name *Melissa* is from the Greek for a bee, and Balm is a good bee plant.

Balm was formerly considered excellent to soothe nervous trouble, to comfort the heart and drive away melancholy.

Variegated Balm, with golden-flecked foliage, is attractive (Plate 4).

BALM OF GILEAD *Cedronella triphylla* (Plate 22) [*Labiatae*]

Not the true Balsam of Gilead, but pleasing for the herb garden. It is somewhat tender, and best treated as a half-hardy perennial, planted out for the summer, propagated by cuttings taken in early autumn, and overwintered under glass. The leaves are three-lobed, with a warm balsamic scent with a hint of citron; the pale pink two-lipped flowers are borne in August and September in terminal heads.

BALSAMS (Plate 29)

The name, applied to several different plants, is confusing. There are various decorative garden Balsams, species of *Impatiens*, which are not of medicinal importance. The wild and naturalized British Balsams, also *Impatiens*, are described under Jewelweed, their herbal name.

The true Balsam of Gilead, yielding Balm of Gilead, has become a stock phrase for healing and comfort since its mention in Jeremiah: 'Is there no balm in Gilead; is there no physician there?'

Balsam of Gilead is a small tree, *Commiphora opobalsamum*, much prized and often closely restricted because of its value, found in the countries on both sides of the Red Sea, and yielding a resinous juice.

Balsam Poplar, *Populus balsamifera* (Plate 10), is often the originator of mysterious and alluring balsamic perfumes wafted down town streets and other unlikely places, for this Poplar can be satisfactorily planted as a specimen tree in city parks and has gummy buds exhaling the lovely aroma, brought out especially by sunshine and brisk breezes after rain.

In America *Populus candicans* is called Balm of Gilead and the buds are used, the resinous coating being separated by immersion in boiling water. The tincture is used for chest and stomach complaints.

BASILS (Plates 4 & 32) [*Labiatae*]

    SWEET BASIL *Ocimum basilicum*
    BUSH BASIL *O. minimum*

Basil has a pleasant, warm, clove-like flavour and is used in many continental recipes. It was used to flavour the special Fetter Lane sausages and is appreciated in tomato dishes, mock-turtle soup and many other blends.

Natives of India, the Basils are grown as half-hardy annuals in this country. It is best to sow seed in pans or boxes in a greenhouse with an average temperature of 60°F. in late March and April. Regrettably the plant is temperamental, and excuses non-appearance with the high-sounding title of 'pre-emergence damping-off'. Sterilizing a small quantity of dust-dry soil by putting it into a bucket with about an inch of water at the bottom, and boiling (with a lid on) until the steam has penetrated to the top of the soil, should be helpful, also watering with Cheshunt compound according to the directions. A reasonably constant temperature is beneficial. Basil can be tried sown outside in warm, sandy soils in late April and May, in drills $\frac{1}{8}$ in. deep, but this is precarious with our weather.

Sown under glass, the seedlings are pricked out and may be planted in a sunny, sheltered spot outside in June.

The leaves of Basil are roughly triangular and irregularly edged, the flowers cream in colour and two-lipped.

The leaves may be used fresh or dried. Owing to the uncertainty of cultivation and the plant's love of a warmer climate, it is not easy to get a worthwhile crop for drying in this country, though sufficient may be raised for a supply of fresh leaves.

Basil was said by Parkinson 'to procure a cheerful and merrie heart,' and was used as a strewing herb, and in washing waters.

Sweet Green Basil is the larger plant, but Bush Basil, seldom above 6 in. in height, has the greater reputation for comparative hardiness. *O. gratissimum* has pale mauve flowers and deliciously-scented foliage, used in India on occasion as a cure for colds.

Purple Basil, sometimes called basilic grand violet, has deep reddish-purple leaves and mauve-pink flowers. Dark Opal is a new variety.

BAY, SWEET *Laurus nobilis* (Plate 3) [*Lauraceae*]

Laurus nobilis is a native of countries bordering the Mediterranean. This tree, which will attain 12 ft. or more after twenty years, should not be confused with the Portugal Laurel, *Prunus lusitanica*, which has terminal spikes of whitish flowers, nor with the ordinary Laurel, *Prunus laurocerasus*, with larger, oval, very glossy leaves.

The Sweet Bay has small axillary, yellow flowers in May, followed by purplish berries if the summer is favourable. There is a variety in which the leaves are more waved at the edges. The foliage scent is characteristic.

Sweet Bay is relatively hard to propagate, though it may be increased by seed sown in the spring, but it is not always easy to obtain viable living seed. The tips of the lower branches may be layered in July and August, or young cuttings taken in late summer and given close conditions and bottom heat.

When purchasing, pot-grown plants should be chosen.

Bays tend to suffer worse frost damage during their early years, and the current season's growth on an older tree may suffer badly while the older branches and foliage survive well. Bays should be given a sheltered situation from biting winds and will stand some shade. When planting, the hole should be part-filled with compost, and sand and drainage material added where the soil is heavy clay. When planting, a large hole some 2½ ft. across and 2 ft. deep should be dug, to allow for the compost. Planting should be firmly done and if the weather is dry the young Bay should be watered copiously when necessary for a month or more after planting, and shaded from drying winds.

The leaves may be used either fresh or dry, in the *bouquet-garni,* to flavour soused herring and mackerel, and in many other savoury dishes. The flavour is, however, potent, and a portion only of a leaf may be sufficient to give a hint of the taste, to avoid its being overwhelming to other ingredients. Bay leaves have often also been used to flavour rice puddings and cornflour moulds.

BELLADONNA *Atropa belladonna* (Plate 11) [*Solanaceae*]

Often called Deadly Nightshade, it is frequently confused with Woody Nightshade, to which, however, it bears little resemblance. Deadly Nightshade is found growing wild in chalky or limestone situations such as the North Downs, in sun or part-shade. It is found too, in the neighbourhood of old ruins. The name Atropa is from the Fate who was said to cut the human life-line. Belladonna refers to the use of the juice by Italian ladies to dilate the pupils of their eyes.

Deadly Nightshade will grow to some 5 or 6 ft. high in semi-shade or under rich cultivation, and forms a handsome bushy clump, dangerously attractive to children when the purplish bell-flowers are followed by black, cherry-like fruits. It is a deadly poison.

Woody Nightshade, the pretty climbing plant of our hedgerows, is much less deadly, and the mauve 'turks-cap' flowers give place to yellow, then red berries.

The whole plants of Belladonna and Woody Nightshade are used by the homoeopathic chemists.

Belladonna, cultivated or collected from the wild state, is particularly valuable in wartime. The leaves and small terminal leafy branches are dried to retain the colour. Medicinally, it is used for the alkaloidal content of Atropine and Hyoscyamine. Atropine is used by oculists to dilate the pupils of the eye. A liniment is used against neuralgia and rheumatism, and internally to keep up the circulation. The root is also used. Belladonna is a herbaceous perennial, and new growths arise from stout purplish buds coming from the woody rootstocks. It may be propagated by seed sown in seedboxes in February and left exposed for two to three weeks to hard frost before bringing into the greenhouse temperature of 55–60°F. When saving one's own seed, the berries may be pulped in a sieve and the seed washed free with running water, or the berries may be dried off and crushed in a sieve to release the seeds.

After pricking out, the young plants are planted out in a medium well-limed soil enriched with decayed manure, compost or leaf-mould.

The next summer, two crops of foliage should be obtained for drying. The plant should not be cut right down but 12 in. of stem and foliage left to supply food-material for further growth. A plantation should last three years in good production after which the roots may be dug and dried.

BERGAMOTS (Plate 1) [Labiatae]
    RED BERGAMOT (*Monarda didyma*), PURPLE BERGAMOT (*M.fistulosa*), and hybrids.

Bergamot, often called Bee-Balm, is a native of woods in America. This delightfully aromatic plant, is one of the most decorative in the herb garden, and large clumps of the jewel-rich, honeysuckle-shaped flowers make the perfect central feature in July and August.

The Crimson is the most fragrant, giving off a delicious perfume all the growing season, particularly when the young shoots are touched in April and May. There is a wide range of modern hybrids in rose-pink, purple, lavender, white and, amongst named kinds, Mahogany (a deep crimson), and Prairie Glow (a salmon kind) are of special interest. The heights vary from $2\frac{1}{2}$ to 5 ft., depending on richness of soil and variety.

In hot, dry soils, Bergamots appreciate slight shade, though, given a cool root-run, and a light to medium soil to which compost has been added, they will flourish in full sun. In a heat wave they are among the first herbs to value copious watering.

In cold soils Bergamots may be hard to establish and the soil sould be lightened with organic matter, and spring planting carried out. Firm planting is essential, with the runners well buried (even though as they grow they come to the surface), but new shoots should be kept above ground-level. The roots may be divided in autumn or spring.

One name for Bergamot is Oswego Tea, and the leaves may be used, fresh or dried, either by the experimental housewife, to impart an aromatic flavour by adding a few Bergamot leaves to the usual brew, or by the happy-go-lucky one who has run out of tea. A herb farm is the ideal surrounding for the latter, who makes use of eau-de-Cologne mint, lemon verbena and other recherche alternatives in a crisis. All these make pleasant brews for which a taste should be cultivated.

A leaf or two of Bergamot, chopped, also the flowers, may be added to salads.

This is an excellent plant for herb gardens for the blind and flowers and leaves may be dried to blend in pot-pourri.

Monarda menthifolia is a distinct kind growing some 2 ft. high, and having mauve flowers.

Oil of Bergamot, characteristic of some eau-de-Cologne blends, comes not from the Monardas, but from the Bergamot Orange.

BETONY, WOOD   *Stachys betonica* (Plate 10)   [*Labiatae*]
Betony, a hardy perennial 18 in. high, is a wayside herb with purple-crimson, two-lipped flowers, in July and August. The herb is used on occasion, medicinally, for nervous headaches; Betony tea, at a pint of boiling water to an ounce of the dried herb, and a wineglassful drunk three times a day being esteemed as a cure, and having a similar taste to ordinary tea. Also to relieve headache, the dried herb may be smoked, blended with other herbs, Eyebright and Coltsfoot being sometimes used also. In former days, Betony was held in high repute for curing many complaints, being cultivated widely in the gardens of apothecaries and monasteries.

BISTORT   *Polygonum bistorta* (Plate 4)   [*Polygonaceae*]
Bistort is a decorative hardy perennial plant with pink spikes of flowers some 18 in. high in late summer, and broad leaves. It is propagated by division. The leaves formed the basis in Easter Puddings (still eaten in Cumberland, where Bistort grows wild plentifully), for which Bistort leaves, young Nettle leaves and a few Black Currant leaves and a sprig of Parsley are used, with barley, oatmeal, condiments and some chives, boiled all together in a bag, and finally having a beaten egg and butter added before serving.

Bistort root is one of the strongest astringents amongst our British plants and is good for staunching wounds and internal haemorrhage. The roots contain a considerable amount of starch and in time of want have been used for food.

BLACK COHOSH   *Cimicifuga racemosa* (Plate 13)   Amer.   [*Ranunculaceae*]
Also called Black Snakeroot, it flowers in June and July. The stems may be 3–5 ft. high. The white flowers have four to eight two-cleft petals and numerous stamens. It is found in woods from Maine to Wisconsin and south to Georgia. The root, collected in autumn, is used. This has astringent properties and has been supposed

to be an antidote against rattlesnake bites and poisons. It has been used in whooping-cough and, as an infusion, against rheumatism.

BLOODROOT *Sanguinaria canadensis* (Plate 13) Amer. [*Papaveraceae*]
Found on shady banks and in woods from Nova Scotia to Manitoba, and south to Florida, and other areas. The attractive white flower, which is wax-like in texture, comes out in April and May. The plant is poisonous. The rootstock exudes a red sap when broken. After the leaves die down, the root is collected in the autumn. The action is purging and emetic. The preparation from the root is used against bronchitis and asthma, also externally to cure ulcers. The American Indians have used the plant as a dye, hence another name, Indian Paint.

BORAGE *Borago officinalis* (Plate 6) [*Boraginaceae*]
This is a most decorative annual herb, with pink buds on stems covered with purplish-grey hairs that glisten in the sun. The flowers are intense blue with a black cone of anthers. The plant usually grows 18 in. to $2\frac{1}{2}$ ft. high. Sown in mid-summer in a sheltered site such as a frame, some plants will pass the winter in rosette form, making especially fine flowering plants by May of the following year. Sown in the soil-bed at the top of a low dry wall, Borage shows to fullest advantage as the flowers are pendulous. It is exciting to encounter the white form in the Oxford Botanic Garden and the pink form in Mrs Salter's garden, at Hassocks, once.

The seeds may be sown in a seedbox in March/April under glass or outside in April/May, in a sunny site and medium soil, in drills $\frac{1}{4}$ in. deep. The peeled stems have a cucumber flavour and may be used in salads, and the flowers put in for decoration.

Leaves, small stems and flowering tops are used in certain drinks.

This herb is an excellent bee-plant. As the plant is rich in potassium nitrate, an infusion of the leaves makes a really cooling drink.

Borago laxiflora (Plate 29) is an attractive relative.

BRYONY, WHITE *Bryonia dioica* (Plate 12) [*Cucurbitae*]
This hardy perennial festoons our hedgerows with its palmate foliage, cream and green flowers and matt-finished berries, ranging from green through chrome yellow and coral to carmine. It is a pleasant subject for decorative designs, with its curving tendrils and is the only wild British member of the valuable *Cucurbitae* family, containing cucumbers, melons, marrows and gourds.

In olden times, a semblance of a man's figure, with arms and legs, was seen in the thick rootstock of the White Byrony. It has therefore been called English Mandrake, and features in country cures. The active principle is bryonine, an irritant poison. It is used on the Continent for its purgative action and has been employed in cases of hysteria and of asthma; also externally the dried root has been used to provide a poultice to relieve lumbago and sciatica.

BRYONY, BLACK *Tamus communis* (Plate 7) [*Dioscoriaceae*]
Black Bryony, with simple, heart-shaped, convolvulus-like leaves, clusters of very small green flowers, and shining yellow to red berries, is the sole British representative of the Yam family. A syrup made from the root was formerly used against asthma.

BUDDLEIAS Butterfly Bush Sc.S. [*Loganiaceae*]
These shrubs give off a honey sweetness and were once known as Honeycomb Trees. *Buddleia alternifolia* has arching sprays of lavender flowers in June. The well-known *B. davidii* has conical spokes of mauve, crimson or purple flowers. Radiant Morn, an exciting chance hybrid, probably between a white form of *B. davidii* and *B. globosa*, has cream, mauve-shaded, orange-centred flowers in clusters. *B. alternifolia* is propagated by semi-ripe cuttings in July, pruned after flowering. A reasonably sheltered site is appreciated. *B. davidii* is pruned in March, and propagated by current season's cuttings in May and June.

BURNET, SALAD *Poterium sanguisorba* (Plate 2) [*Rosaceae*]
Burnet is found growing wild, in a dwarfed form, on our chalk downs. This hardy perennial herb, growing some 18 in. to 2 ft. high in cultivation, has pinnate leaves and heads of greenish flowers, with crimson stigmas and cream anthers. It is good for salads, for the foliage has a flavour of cucumbers with a nutty undertone. It is propagated by seed sown in a seedbed outside in April, and the mature plants put out 1 ft. apart each way.

Salad Burnet is one of the 'Pimpernels' of Continental recipes. It is mentioned by Bacon in his classic essay *Of Gardens* as giving off a refreshing scent when planted in alleyways and paths.

A relative, *Sanguisorba officinalis*, found wild in England, especially in the north, is similar on a larger scale, with decorative reddish heads of flowers. The Latin name refers to a medicinal use, for staunching the flow from wounds.

BURNET SAXIFRAGE *Pimpinella saxifraga* [*Umbelliferae*]
This plant is neither a Burnet nor a Saxifrage, but has leaves somewhat resembling

the former, and umbels of flowers; is related to Anise and used in homoeopathic tinctures and for asthma—also on occasion in salads.

CALAMINT *Calamintha grandiflora* (Plates 20 & 31) [*Labiatae*]

A herbaceous perennial plant, growing some 9–12 in. high, and hardy in reasonable winters.

Some wild Calaminthas, including the Basil-Thyme, are found on the chalk downs and by waysides. They have aromatic foliage varying from pleasantness to pungency, as is the way of Labiates. *C.officinalis* is found wild on waysides and hedge-banks, with flowers in July/August. It has a strong aromatic scent and taste, and a tea made from the herb was used for stomach weaknesses. For garden interest, *C.grandiflora* is a good choice, being suitable for the rock garden or front of the herb border. The foliage is sweetly aromatic. Propagation is by cuttings or division.

CALIFORNIAN LAUREL 'Spice-Tree' *Umbellularia californica* (Plate 22) Ar. S. [*Lauraceae*]

An evergreen tree which rather resembles the *Laurus nobilis*, but the foliage is narrower. The leaves have a pleasantly spicy scent. This tree is hardy in sheltered positions in south-east England, and valuable for gardens in the south and west. The yellowish flowers appear in late spring, followed by purplish fruit. Propagation is by seed and layering.

CAMPHOR-PLANT *Balsamita vulgaris* (= *Chrysanthemum balsamita*) (Plate 23) [*Compositae*]

A hardy herbaceous perennial, growing 3–4 ft. high, it closely resembles Alecost in foliage, but the flowers are white, yellow-centred daisies. The pungent, refreshing scent is characteristic, but the plant is not the true Camphor from which the commercial oil is obtained, the latter, *Cinnamonum camphora*, growing in the warmer climates.

Propagation of the Camphor Plant is by division of rootstocks in spring or autumn. Leaves may be dried and used with other herbs to deter moths.

CAPER SPURGE *Euphorbia lathyrus* (Plate 31) [*Euphorbiaceae*]

This biennial, growing some 3–4 ft. high when fully developed, is sometimes found as an old-established plant in cottage gardens. The rather grim, alien habit of growth, the thin leaves and stiff branching are characteristic. The small green flowers are followed by the fruits, used green as a caper substitute. It is inadvisable for more than a few fruits to be eaten at a time, though they appear to have had this country use for many generations.

The true Capers are the flower-buds of an Eastern plant, *Capparis spinosa*.

CARAWAY *Carum carvi* (Plate 2) [*Umbelliferae*]
At shows where this is exhibited the question is often asked as to whether we have included hedge parsley or a carrot that has bolted! Caraway is a biennial plant 2 ft. high when flowering, grown from seed sown outside in a sandy seedbed in April, in drills some ¼ in. deep, the plants being thinned to 9 in. in the rows.

They will flower the following April/May and the fruits ripen in June and July. As the umbels ripen in succession it is best, when the first fruits approach ripeness, carefully to cut the plants off at ground-level, tie in bunches and hang in a warm, airy place over sheets of paper, to catch the seeds as they dry and fall.

The seeds are then ready to be sprinkled on bread or used in cakes or buns for those who appreciate them, a point on which people are sharply divided; to some caraway cakes being a Victorian anachronism like statice or aspidistras (which former, like caraway, the writer enjoys). Caraway was valued in Shakespearean days and in *Henry IV* Falstaff is invited to 'a pippin and a dish of caraways', which were served together. In Germany caraway seeds are used to flavour soups, cheese and cabbage dishes.

CARYOPTERIS CLANDONENSIS (Plate 15) and *C.mastacanthus* Ar.S.
[*Verbenaceae*]
Surely it is the uncompromising Latin names of these lovely shrubs that are prone to daunt people. Naturally, these technical names are vital and informative, but some popular name such as 'Mountain Mist' or 'Dreaming Waters' would add a descriptive touch. For comprehensiveness and for pleasure, the formal and friendly names of plants should both be in currency. There has been a reference to this shrub as Moustache Plant, but this name does not do it justice and is definitely not one of the more appealing ideas.

These deciduous shrubs normally grow some 3–4 ft. high and their compactness is a great advantage. The warm-scented grey foliage and soft lavender-blue flowers have special charm in August and September, when new-comers are welcome in the garden, bringing freshness to keep at bay the winter threat in the garden and the tattered aftermath of glory in border plants.

Caryopteris clandonensis has greyer foliage and deeper flowers than *C.mastacanthus*, which, however, has great charm to those who appreciate these delicate shades.

A warm, sunny spot, ideally with shelter from north and east, is best, with well-drained soil. Propagation is by half-ripe cuttings in July and August, and as flowers come on the current season's wood, pruning is carried out in March and April, when shoots that bore flowers the previous summer may be shortened by 6–12 in. It is a pity that *Spiraea jap*. A. Waterer is usually past its best when Caryopteris begins to flower, as the rose-crimson heads of the former would associate well; but Red Sage foliage, with its purple 'bloom', and Wall Germander in crimson-purple would make a pleasing group.

CATMINTS *Nepeta faassenii* (*N.mussini*), *N.cataria* (Plate 10) [*Labiatae*]

The popular *Nepeta mussini*, 9 in. high, with its dentate, aromatic grey foliage and two-lipped lavender flowers needs no further introduction. On light soils, in hot, sunny positions, it flourishes, provided compost is added to the soil before planting. The combination of winter damp followed by biting winds seems to be the chief enemy of *N.faassenii* and a position sheltered from the east is helpful. It is not usually advisable to cut the dead growths back in autumn as they help to protect the new buds and when these appear in April the dead ends may be removed.

The variety Six-Hills Giant (Plate 21) grows some 12–18 in. high and is a good form. *N.grandiflora* grows some 2 ft. high and has rich mauve flowers.

Propagation is by division or cuttings and one regrettable use of the plant is to divert cats. More valuably, these catmints are fine bee plants.

Nepeta cataria, Catnep, is the true medicinal Catmint. It often behaves as a biennial, dying away after flowering. It has grey leaves and the small white two-lipped flowers are slightly spotted with red, a description that should not be taken as indicating that the general effect is gaudy. We have been taken to task by some eager gardener (for just such a description) expecting a salvia-like brilliance, whereas the effect is a little shop-soiled. Propagation is by seed sown in spring in a seedbox or the open.

In chi-chi circles the dried foliage has been used to stuff muslin mice made to amuse the cat. One elderly ginger becomes quite wild for a few minutes after biting a leaf of this catmint. Medicinally it is used for Catnep tea, useful in fevers to give quiet sleep and for nervous headaches; it used to be drunk freely before domestic tea became popular.

CEANOTHUS Mountain Sweet Sc.S. [*Rhamnaceae*]

The deciduous *Ceanothus* Gloire de Versailles and the deeper powder blue *C. Topaz* flower delightfully, exhaling a quiet sweetness. They prefer a sheltered position,

PLATE 13 AMERICAN HERBS
1. New Jersey Tea. (*Ceanothus americanus*)
2. American Mandrake. (*Podophyllum peltatum*)
3. Labrador Tea. (*Ledum groenlandicum*)
4. Indian Ginger. (*Asarum canadense*)
5. Bloodroot. (*Sanguinaria canadensis*)
6. Black Cohosh. (*Cimicifuga racemosa*)

PLATE 14 AMERICAN HERBS
1. Mountain Laurel. (*Kalmia latifolia*)
2. Indian Physic. (*Gillenia trifoliata*)
3. Green American Hellebore. (*Veratum viride*)
4. American Liverwort. (*Hepatica triloba var. americana*)
5. Skunk Cabbage. (*Symplocarpus foetidus*)
6. Scarlet Lobelia. (*Lobelia cardinalis*)

PLATE 15 AROMATIC SHRUBS
1. *Cistus ladaniferus.*
2. Myrtle. (*Myrtus communis*)
3. *Rosa primula.*
4. *Caryopteris clandonensis.*
5. Sun-Rose. (*Cistus purpureus*)
6. *Teucrium fruticans.*
7. *Perowskia abrotanifolia.*
8. Sweetbriar, 'Lady Penzance'. (*Rosa rubiginosa var.*)
9. Russian Sage. (*Perowskia atriplicifolia*)
10. *Rubus odoratus.*

PLATE 16 SCENTED AND AROMATIC SHRUBS
1. Mezereon. (*Daphne mezereum*)
2. Witch Hazel. (*Hamamelis japonica*)
3. *Hypericum pseudo henryi.*
4. *Elsholtzia stauntonii.*
5. Allspice. (*Calycanthus occidentalis*)
6. Golden Currant. (*Ribes odoratum*)
7. *Eucalyptus gunnii.*
8. Wintergreen. (*Gaultheria procumbens*)
9. *Skimmia japonica* Foremanii.

and grow pleasantly on a south or west wall. Prune in March or April. Propagation is by cuttings.

CELANDINE, GREATER *Chelidonium majus* (Plate 7) [*Papaveraceae*]
Often found naturalized on waste ground near villages; the stems and leaves, when broken, exude an orange juice. The plant is an interesting illustration of the medieval Doctrine of Signatures by which all plants were said to carry on them some indication of their medicinal use, for those who could read the signs. Hence Greater Celandine was used against jaundice and is good, too, to cure the 'yellows', a similar canine ailment.

The foliage is poppy-like, glaucous grey-green, the flowers yellow. Propagation is by seed, usually prolifically self-sown.

CHAMOMILE *Chamaemelum nobile* (*Anthemis nobilis*) (Plate 8) [*Compositae*]
This English name is used for a number of plants, sometimes with prefixes such as Roman Chamomile (which refers to *A.nobilis*), German Chamomile (*Matricaria chamomilla*), and Scotch Chamomile (the single form of *A.nobilis*). *A.nobilis* and *Matricaria* are the two plants most safely called 'Chamomile', as they have the fruit scent and are valuable medicinally. It is, however, important to know the appropriate Latin name, otherwise an incipient lawn-maker may be confronted with a 3 ft.-high annual (*Matricaria chamomilla*) to clog his mower and finally cool his ardour for aromatic lawns as it withers; or even a charming but impracticable bed of yellow *Anthemis tinctoria*, the herbaceous border plant.

To dispose first of the annual *Matricaria chamomilla* (Plate 21), this has fine-cut foliage, single white daisy flowers with yellow discs; it grows some 2–3 ft. high. The flowers, in contrast to some Mayweeds with unpleasant or inodorous flowers, have a delightfully apple-like fragrance. The flowers may be gathered and dried, for they have the some properties as *Chamaemelum* in fainter degree. The whole fresh flowering plant is used for extraction by homoeopathic chemists.

ANTHEMIS NOBILIS has single and double forms, the latter, the cultivated type, being used for the production of flowers for drying or the whole herb to be cut for distillation for essential oil production. The double kind is also much preferable for lawn-making for its compactness and refined appearance if any patches should elude the shears or mower, and proceed to flower. There is also a non-flowering form, *C.nobil* Treneague.

Chamaemelum nobile grows, naturally, some 6 in. to 9 in. high, with small creeping rootstocks, finely-divided leaves and cream daisy flowers. The whole herb has a delightfully aromatic, fruity scent, reminiscent both of apples and ripe bananas.

Propagation is by detaching the small plantlets and replanting these at distances suitable to the purpose, in autumn in favourable situations, or in exposed ones in late March/May.

For field cultivation, 'islands' of the herb some 3 ft. by 2 ft. are planted, with 2–3 ft. between the islands and between the rows. The crop may be cut with knives or hooks or some may adapt mechanical cutters for the purpose.

On the other hand, to make a close planting for a lawn, the site needs to be deeply dug and all perennial weeds and their runners removed, and compost or other available organic matter added. A good dressing is one barrowload to four square yards.

The area should be well firmed by treading, raked for a preliminary levelling and left for a few weeks to settle. To get a perfect flat surface before planting, a spirit-level on a board poised between two pegs may be used and the levels made up to the board, or to a string stretched between the pegs.

The small plantlets are planted 6 in. apart each way, four (comprising one complete plant) being put per square foot. On light soils, to ensure that the roots have a start in a favourable medium, wide dibber or crowbar holes are made and filled with compost below and around the plantlets' roots, which are thus placed as deep down as possible, but keeping the plants' crown at the surface of the soil. Firm planting is essential and watering till plants begin to grow away is valuable with late planting, and essential in drought.

For a lawn it is advisable not to let the plants flower. Planted even as late as May, they should meet by mid-July and have a first and second cut with shears. Afterwards, when the rootstocks are established, the mower with blades set high may be used. Paths may be similarly planted.

Single Chamomile, grown from seed, may be used if necessary as a second-best for lawn-making. The seed is expensive, and while it is possible to mix with silver sand and sow on the prepared site in showery weather in April and May, it is safer to sow in seedboxes in spring, and prick out the resulting seedlings, then plant out in damp weather in June and July, as outlined above.

A lady writing recently commented on the scent of chamomile on sun-dried dogs who have reposed on her chamomile lawn after a shampoo.

Chamomile flowers are often imported from Belgium, but, particularly in times of emergency, English flowers find a ready market. The natural cream colour can be retained if the flowers are spread thinly on trays and turned daily to prevent the aggregation of lumps of damp flowers. To keep the best colour, the flowers must be picked when really dry, not rain or dew-soaked. The time is when the outside florets are beginning to reflex.

Chamomile tea, a help in sleeplessness, is made by infusing ½–1 oz. of fresh flowers, less if dried, in a pint of boiling water and drinking a cupful of the strained liquid. Chamomile tea is a general and harmless sedative. The flowers are used in shampoos.

CHERVIL *Anthriscus cerefolium* (Plate 3)   [*Umbelliferae*]

A hardy annual, occasionally biennial, growing 1 ft. to 18 in. high, and whose name is familiar in recipes. The French name is Cerfeuil. It is used as a flavouring and garnish, more frequently fresh than dried. The foliage is finely divided and the small white flowers are in umbels.

Chervil prefers a medium but fairly rich soil, not drying out in hot weather, and slight shade. Seed is sown in April and early May, but can be put in later, ⅛ in. deep. The seed leaves are strap-shaped, in contrast to the finely cut foliage leaves. The seedlings are thinned to 6 in. apart.

There is a demand for freshly bunched Chervil, but it is not, except in the most favourable soils, a sufficiently heavy cropper to make cutting and drying profitable.

Chervil is used, for instance, in the French blend of *fines herbes*. Its pungent taste is good in soups, salads and many other dishes. The roots used to be employed medicinally for their warming properties.

CHICORY (Succory) *Cichorium intybus* (Plate 4)   [*Compositae*]

Chicory is a hardy perennial (on occasion it acts as a biennial) and grows 3–5 ft. high. It is an attractive herb with exquisite china-blue flowers which fade by midday in hot weather. The leaves rather resemble Dandelion foliage and the plant is closely related to Endive.

The dried ground root is blended with coffee, and for this Magdebourg or Brunswick Chicory is used. For blanching, Witloof Chicory is a good kind.

The seed is sown in April/May in a moderately rich but sandy soil, ¼ in. deep, in drills 9 in. apart. The roots when lifted may be forced in winter by planting closely in boxes filled with sand, put under the greenhouse staging. Light must be excluded to achieve effective blanching and a fair temperature of 55–60°F. given. The roots need watering as necessary, to keep growth tender.

The young green leaves, finely chopped, may be used from open-ground plants in early spring, but they get bitter as they mature. They can be part-blanched in the open by covering with pots with the drainage hole covered. The blanched tops are excellent in salads.

Chicory, as well as Burnet, is grown as a fodder plant in herb strips for cattle.

CHIMONANTHUS PRAECOX (*C. fragrans, Calycanthus praecox*) Winter Sweet (Plate 18) Sc.S. [*Calycanthaceae*]

Cream flowers with purple-red centres star leafless branches in mid-winter, and emit a lovely fragrance. A sheltered spot near or against a south wall is best. The addition of peat to the soil is helpful. Pruning is done after flowering, and propagation is by layers.

CHIVES *Allium schoenoprasum* (Plate 6) [*Liliaceae*]

Chives has the most refined flavour of the tribe, for the chopped foliage brings a hint of spring onions into the salad or omelette.

There is the small, usual form, preferred by many, and a taller type with slightly thicker foliage, known as Giant Chives. This latter flowers at 9 in. high, while the ordinary Chives is 4–6 in. The plant is a hardy perennial.

Chives makes an excellent edging to the herb bed, planted 6–8 in. apart. Propagation may be by seed, but is usually by division of the clumps in spring, autumn or after flowering, in showery weather in late June.

Chives are good-tempered and will grow under most conditions, many casualties being due to their being dug out, unrecognized, by the casual weeder during the dormant season.

However, a medium loam enriched with compost produces best leaf-growth. If foliage-production is the one criterion, flower buds should be rigorously removed. The mauve-pink, thrift-like flower-heads are, however, very attractive and may be used to decorate salads, thus salving the conscience of aesthetically-minded gardeners who enjoy the flowers.

Plants should not be allowed to seed, but may be cut back after flowering, and if they are then divided, and replanted, will make fresh foliage in late summer, if kept well-watered.

Chives plants should not be completely deprived of their 'grass' when cutting for use, but a few foliage blades should be left on each plant.

Chives 'grass' is used finely chopped in many dishes, to garnish soup, to blend into home-made cream cheese, and for salads. In this case, it is humane and wise to offer the chives separately, from the main salad, to rescue those whose tastes do not lie that way.

Chives will grow in window-boxes, tubs or pots, and the basal bulblets (elongated) may, in an emergency, be used for flavouring.

CHOISYA TERNATA Mexican Orange Blossom (Plate 18) Sc.S. [*Rutaceae*]

This fine evergreen has trifoliate leaves and attractive white flowers, generously produced in April/May, and often again in autumn. The blossoms have a vanilla scent. A sheltered site is best and light to medium soil. Growth may be 6 ft. high. Propagation is by cuttings.

CISTUS   Sun-Roses (Plate 15)   Ar. S. [*Cistaceae*]
These are fascinating shrubs because of the stimulating and evocative nature of their aromatic scents, the variety of foliage and the lovely fragility of the flowers. Cistus are related to Helianthemums or Rock Roses (sometimes also called Sun-Roses), which are not, of course, aromatic.

Cistus ladanifer, the gum Cistus, has deep, pointed evergreen leaves with a resinous 'feel' to the buds and young foliage. White flowers are borne, like a single rose, golden-rayed with stamens and set off by a rich maroon-red blaze at the base of each petal. The Latin name describes the presence of this aromatic gum.

Cistus laurifolius, the hardiest of the group, has ovate green leaves of tough texture, and similar flowers to *C.ladanifer*, while *C.cyprius* has sage-like, wrinkled, green foliage and white flowers.

Cistus purpureus is the most beautiful, with large pink flowers of silken texture, golden-rayed and sprayed with maroon-purple at the centre. Each flower only lasts a day, but they are produced in rich succession from June to August.

The warm incense scent has a penetrating and invigorating effect, more appreciable on the air than when the leaves are touched.

There are forms of *Cistus ladanifer* and of other Cistus without the deep red blaze, but they seem to lack personality, that individual pleasure in a flower that means more than the vague enjoyment of a show of colour.

The Cistus need a warm, well-drained soil, a sheltered site and plenty of sun. They grow 3–4 ft. high on the average, though *C.laurifolius* and others may attain 6 ft. on occasion. They will pass a severe winter happily and unscathed if planted under the south wall of a house, or given the shelter of shrubs to the north and east.

It is frequently not so much frost intensity that kills shrubs and other plants, but biting winds, especially in February and March, following a period of hard frost, when plants are fighting to recover their vitality; and in early April, when they have succeeded in thrusting forth some new and tender green shoots.

Propagation is by cuttings of half-ripe wood. When buying Cistus pot specimens only should be acquired, as they resent root disturbance. Little pruning is necessary, and cutting back into older wood not to be encouraged. Long shoots could if required be cut back in early spring to a fresh new shoot, always a safe principle.

The dried leaves may pleasantly be added to a spicy blend of pot-pourri and these shrubs would give pleasure in scented gardens for the blind.

CLARY SAGES [Labiatae]

PERENNIAL CLARY   *Salvia sclarea* (Plate 24)
ANNUAL BLUEBEARD   *Salvia horminum* (Plates 6 and 25)

The Clary Sages or 'Clear Eye' Sages (so called because of the use of the seeds to clear the eyesight), are interesting members of the delightful and varied Salvia genus, the name coming from the Latin root meaning health or saving or salvation. In this genus, dealt with in more detail further on, are many valuable, aromatic and attractive plants.

Salvia sclarea is a striking plant with mauve-pink bracts and lavender and white, two-lipped flowers in tall spires, 3–5 ft. high, over wrinkled large leaves like those of Foxgloves. The white form appears to be no longer a rarity, and is excellent for floral decoration work.

Salvia sclarea on occasion seems to put all its strength into flowering, then dies away, acting as a biennial.

It is increased by seed sown in boxes under glass in March/April and planted out in July, or outside in a moist, sandy seedbed, in April/May. When planting, it is important not to get the crown buds of the rosettes below ground-level, as the young leaves are woolly and the plants rot away if soil and water are washed into the centre.

S.horminum is sown outside in groups (in the ornamental garden), or in drills $\frac{1}{8}$ in. deep, and thinned to 8 in. apart. If clumps are required, these may be marked out with a stick, and short drills 8 in. apart made across the clumps, as the seeds are more easily covered with soil than if they are broadcast.

S.horminum is often called Bluebeard, from the purple-blue bracts, the flowers being less conspicuous. There is a form with pink bracts which blends in pleasantly; one variety is Pink Sundae.

The perennial Clary, *S.sclarea*, has a scent refreshingly like grape-fruit and the sweet oil, distilled from the plant, is known as Clary Oil or Muscatel Sage, and used as a fixative in perfumery. It was also used to flavour wines.

Medicinally, Clary has been used to help in digestive troubles, and the seeds, soaked in water, to form a thick mucilage, used to remove grit and particles from the eyes, and to soothe their inflammation. This mucilage has also been applied to external swellings, and to draw out thorns.

We have had seed of '*S.turkestanica*' and of Vatican Clary and have found them similar to *S.sclarea* and no apparent improvement upon it.

S.verbenacea the wild English Clary, with small mauve, two-lipped flowers, is found near the sea, by waysides, and on chalky ground. The seeds and leaves have been used as above. (This Latin name is now used for the rare and descriptively named *S.clandestina* while the old *S.verbenacea* is now *S.horminoides*).

The leaves of Clary have been used to flavour soups.

CLEMATIS FLAMMULA   Sc. S.   [*Ranunculaceae*]

A small-flowered Clematis, with white, fragrant blooms in late summer. It is a deciduous climber, suitable for training over a support. Thinning-out may be done in early spring, and propagation by seed.

CLERODENDRON (= *Clerodendrum*) (Plate 17)   Sc. S.   [*Verbenaceae*]

Clerodendron foetidum, a Jekyll and Hyde of the plant world, has a name referring to the curious pungency of the foliage, while the rosy red flowers are fragrant. *C.trichotomum*, grown as a small tree in a sheltered site, or else against a south wall, is outstanding, and reminiscent of spring freshness in September. The leaves are handsome, and the deeply fragrant white flowers have purple calyces. Propagation is by seed or cuttings.

COMFREY   *Symphytum officinale*   [*Boraginaceae*]
RUSSIAN COMFREY   *S.uplandicum*
BLUE COMFREY   *S.caucasicum* (Plate 6)

The wild Comfrey, *S.officinale*, with drooping bell-flowers in purple, pale yellow or white, is found by waysides and stream banks, and is a hardy herbaceous perennial growing some 4–5 ft. high. Russian Comfrey may also be found naturalized as an escape-plant from cultivation and various intermediate forms occur. The flowers of Russian Comfrey are blue to blue-purple, on 4–5 ft. high stems. This Comfrey, and *S.caucasicum* growing 2–3 ft. high, with rich gentian-blue flowers in April/May, and compacter growth, are decorative for the herb garden. All have large, ovate, harsh-haired leaves.

They are accommodating as regards soil and site, growing in sun or semi-shade, but they prefer a fairly rich soil holding the moisture in summer. *S.caucasicum* is excellent for naturalizing among shrubs.

Propagation is by root cuttings, taken in November, or by division of clumps, using a sharp knife to sever the fleshy roots, in spring or autumn.

The Russian Comfrey is sometimes grown as a fodder crop.

In medieval days common wild Comfrey was used as a remedy for broken bones and is still called 'Knit-Bone'. The plant contains abundant mucilage and has similar properties to Marsh Mallow for pulmonary complaints. Externally the leaves can be used as fomentations or poultices to cuts, ulcers and sprains.

CORIANDER *Coriandrum sativum* (Plate 4) [*Umbelliferae*]
A hardy annual herb, growing 18 in.–2 ft. high, and well known for the round 'seeds' (botanically fruits) that are used to flavour curries and in confectionery.

Seed may be sown $\frac{1}{4}$ in. deep in drills outside in an open, sunny seedbed in April and early May. The attractive pale mauve umbels of flowers appear in July and August, and when the first seeds are ripe the plants should be cut off and dried as mentioned for Caraway. A sunny, dry frame can be used for drying if the cut plants are laid on paper. The seeds are beige when ripe. Just before this stage, the plant has for a short time, an unpleasant scent, but the seeds themselves are pleasingly aromatic.

CORYLOPSIS (Plate 18)   Sc. S. [*Hamamelidaceae*]
Corylopsis spicata and *C. pauciflora* have quiet, cowslip-scented pale yellow flowers on leafless branches in March/April; in a late season the foliage may catch up with the flowers. Propagation can be by layering.

CORN SALAD (Lamb's Lettuce) *Valerianella locusta* (= *V. olitoria*)
[*Valerianaceae*]
This relative of the Valerians is a hardy biennial, sown in July and August to give rosette plants that may be used in late autumn as a substitute for lettuce. The seed may be sown in a frame or moist seedbed outside, $\frac{1}{2}$ in. deep, and the seedlings thinned to 5 in. apart.

COTTON LAVENDERS ('French Lavender') [*Compositae*]
SANTOLINA CHAMAECYPARISSUS = *S. incana* (Plate 21)
S. neapolitanica (Plate 21)
S. viridis

These important herbs are low-growing, ever-grey shrubs except for *S. viridis*, which loses most of the foliage in winter. All are decorative and *S. chamaecyparissus* (growing some $2\frac{1}{2}$ ft. high) and its variety nana growing some 9–12 in. high are most valuable for clipping for knot-garden work and low hedges, and have been used since Tudor days for this purpose. Parkinson mentioned this practice in his garden treatise.

The foliage of *S.chamaecyparissus* is like grey coral and the golden-yellow disc flowers in July and August add gaiety to the silver effect. A warm, aromatic scent is given out with sun or after rain.

S.neapolitana has looser, fine-cut foliage, carried fanwise and lemon disc flowers. The foliage is good for flower arrangements. S. Lemon Queen is a compact, pleasing hybrid with grey-green foliage, and a Japanese air about its 1 ft. high growth. It is suitable for a sheltered pocket in the rock garden or consorts well in the herb garden with hyssops and dwarf lavenders. The flowers resemble cream lace doyleys.

S.viridis has green foliage and is covered in July with white or yellow disc flowers.

The foliage of *S.chamaecyparissus* may be used, dried, to ward off moths from woollens. Medicinally, it is said to have stimulant properties as well as some similar qualities to Wormwood.

The Santolinas are hardy and accommodating (S. Lemon Queen requiring the most shelter) and make generous wide bushes in light, well-drained soils and sun-baked sites. When planting, however, they appreciate large holes with some compost to give a good start to the plant.

Clipping may be carried out in March, as soon as new growth begins, and again if foliage rather than flower is the aim, in July. Propagation is by cuttings taken in late spring or autumn, in frames or pans under glass.

COWSLIP ('Paigles')   *Primula veris*   [*Primulaceae*]
This well-known flower and its foliage was used considerably in medieval days for salads. The pendent flowers were said to resemble a bunch of golden keys, giving the names 'Key Flower' and 'Herb Peter'. Cowslip-flower syrup was taken to soothe nervous excitement and restore quietness.

CRATAEGUS MONOGYNA   Sc. S.   [*Rosaceae*]
The well-known wild May or Hawthorn has white flowers with a faintly piscine scent to some, but pleasant and evocative to most of us. Propagation is by seed.

CUMIN   *Cuminum cyminum* (Plate 2)   [*Umbelliferae*]
Although it is mentioned by the prophet Isaiah and by Jesus as quoted in St. Matthew, for thousands who know the name there must be few who have seen the plant. Cumin is a small annual plant, found wild in North Africa, but cultivated from early times in Mediterranean countries.

The leaves are thread-like, like those of Fennel, and the small rose-coloured or white flowers are in umbels. The taste of the seeds rather resembles that of caraway. It seems that smoking the seeds promotes a pale complexion and apparently, according to Pliny, the followers of Porcius Latro, a rhetorician of the time, used to achieve a studious pallor by this means.

In India, Cumin can form an ingredient in curry powder. In this country, the seeds are used on occasion in veterinary medicines, as a carminative.

CYTISUS Broom   Sc. S.   [*Leguminosae*]

Cytisus praecox, with cream-yellow pea-flowers in March and April, enjoys a sunny site. Prune back young shoots only, after flowering, and never cut into the old wood. Propagation is by cuttings.

C. battandieri. This handsome shrub has soft silvery foliage and racemes of yellow, pineapple-scented flowers in summer. The shelter of a south wall is appreciated, and a well-drained soil. Propagation can be by seed.

DANDELION   *Taraxacum officinale*   [*Compositae*]

A homely plant, with the buttercup and daisy, it is probably the best known of our wild plants that stray unappreciated into the garden, but its valuable uses are not always recognized.

Considered objectively, the vivid golden-yellow, strap-shaped florets forming the flowers are striking, and have been likened to a student in his full golden glory, who in due course, following his vocation, becomes the reverend priest of the hoary seedheads and, finally, the shorn receptacle is left. Priest's Crown was a common medieval name.

The name Dandelion is a derivative of Dens leonis, Lion's Tooth, a name possibly given because of the dentate leaves.

Dandelions were included in the bitter Passover herbs. The large leaves are bitter, but small Dandelion leaves, chopped or pulled apart, may be added to salads. If blanched by covering the plants with flower-pots in late winter, the new leaves are valuable for salad use. Seed of a broad-leaf variety can be obtained for culinary use, though the ordinary kind may be employed.

Dandelion wine is made from the flowers, and the roasted roots are used to form Dandelion Coffee. For this the roots are dug in autumn. Dandelion Coffee is said to have good medicinal effects on those who suffer from indigestion and liver troubles, and does not cause insomnia.

Propagation is, notoriously by seed, self-parachuted; or, legitimately, by seed sown in drills in early spring.

Dandelion juice and extract are obtained expressed from the fresh root and used (probably originally by the doctrine of signatures because of the yellow of the flowers), for liver complaints, biliousness, and as a tonic.

DAPHNE (medicinal) [*Thymelaceae*]
    Daphne mezereum   Mezereon (Plate 16)
    D.laureola   Spurge-laurel (Plate 12)

The *Daphne mezereum* is a familiar winter-flowering shrub, opening its fragrant, purple-pink (occasionally white) spikes of flower in February and March, followed by the leaves, and red fruits in late summer. *D.laureola* is found locally growing wild on chalk downs, and has green flowers, with an elusive fragrance, welcome in February. The evergreen leaves are like those of a small laurel. These Daphnes grow as low shrubs, some 3–5 ft. high eventually.

    In large doses, the bark of both Daphnes is regarded as a poison, similarly the berries. The bark has been used as a compress and the official compound of mustard has an extract of Daphne as one ingredient.

    DAPHNE (Plate 18)   Sc. S.   [*Thymelaceae*]
In this delightful group there may be unexpected treasure, in the yellow-green flowers of *D.pontica*, exhaling a lovely scent, and growing well even under trees. Colour and perfume may be allied, in the rose-purple of *D.mezereum*. *D.odora* has rose flowers, and a delicious scent. The variety 'Aureamarginata' is hardier than the type, growing outside in some gardens in the south-east. *D.burkwoodii* has masses of pale pink fragrant flowers, and is reasonably accommodating to grow. 'Somerset' is very similar. The usual methods of propagation are seed (for *D.mezereum*), and layering, but success has been noted with cuttings taken with a heel of the old wood in July.

DILL *Anethum graveolens* (Plate 3)   (= *Peucedanum grav.*)   [*Umbelliferae*]
This hardy annual plant, growing some 18 in.–2 ft. high, is frequently confused with Fennel, which it closely resembles. Fennel, however, is a perennial growing some 3–5 ft. high, and has a somewhat aniseed scent, while Dill has its characteristic cooler, acquired scent.

    Dill may be sown in drills $\frac{1}{4}$ in. deep in a sunny spot in April and May. The yellow umbels of flowers are succeeded by aromatic seeds which were used in wartime as a caraway substitute and can be used steeped in vinegar, and strained, to make Dill vinegar.

    To harvest the seeds, the plant should be treated as described for Caraway. At an earlier stage in the plant's growth the fresh foliage is used in Scandinavia and other continental countries to flavour potatoes and peas during boiling as we use

Mint. Dill leaves are also used to flavour pickled cucumbers and in medicine. Dill water is soothing for children's digestive troubles.

DITTANY-OF-CRETE *Origanum dictamnus* (Plate 19) [*Labiatae*]
FALSE DITTANY *Dictamnus albus* (= *D. fraxinella*) (Plate 19) [*Rutaceae*]

The true Dittany-of-Crete, or 'Hop Plant' as it is sometimes called, is a shrubby perennial, hardy in very favourable situations. It does not, however, find the combination of damp and cold alternating with biting winter winds endearing in our climate. It is therefore safer to overwinter under glass in cold areas.

Dittany-of-Crete has woolly basal leaves, smooth upper ones and delicately fashioned hop-like pink bracts, from which spring pale pink flowers. The height is 18 in.–2 ft.

Dittany-of-Crete was given a great reputation by old writers such as Theophrastus and Virgil, but its real identity only appears to have been established about 400 years ago, and some of its properties were formerly attributed to *Dictamnus fraxinella*.

False Dittany, or Burning Bush, is a true herbaceous perennial hardy in most soils and fairly sheltered sites, once it gets established. It grows some 3 ft. high with ash-like foliage and windswept pink or white flowers. It owes the name Burning Bush (not to be confused with the annual Kochia that turns from green to brilliant red in autumn) to its distinction of exhaling the vapour of an essential oil that may be ignited over the plant on a warm, still summer evening.

ELDER, COMMON *Sambucus nigra* [*Caprifoliaceae*]
E. DANE'S DANEWORT *S. ebulus* (Plate 29)

The ordinary Common Elder is one of the best-known small wild British trees, often found in hedgerows where, being frequently cut back, it keeps a shrubby habit. The leaves are pinnate, the flowers cream with a strong scent, characteristic of the summer countryside, but not always pleasing. The clusters of purplish berries are ripe in autumn, and the leaves often assume soft purplish-pink shades before falling.

The Dane's Elder is a hardy perennial plant, not a shrub, and has a creeping rootstock and annually-ascending stems some 3–5 ft. high. There are more leaflets to a pinnate leaf than with the Common Elder, and the flowers, in terminal corymbs, are cream with purple stamens, and followed by purplish berries. This plant was formerly believed to have been introduced by the Danes, and is found by roadsides and waste places in various parts of Britain, including East Anglia and Worcestershire.

Common Elder is a remarkable plant in that every overground part has numerous uses. The whole tree was formerly considered to have power to ward off witches and country people treated the tree with reverence from various old beliefs, one of which was that Judas hanged himself on an Elder. The tree therefore became the respected symbol of sorrow and death.

Elder pith is used in botanical laboratories to help in cutting plant sections. Elder wood was formerly used for making various musical instruments, as the wood is of a close grain and will polish well. Various dyes have been obtained from the different parts—black from the bark and root, green, with alum, from the leaves, and various shades of blue and mauve from the berries, with alum and on occasion salt.

The fresh or dried flowers, added to ordinary tea, impart a china-tea 'bouquet' and give a muscat-grape flavour to jellies.

The flowers made into an ointment with warm lard are excellent for dressing burns and, a little more elaborately, made into face creams. If the dried flowers are handled (when rubbing through a sieve, for instance) they make the skin deliciously soft. Elder flower tea is a good remedy for colds and throat trouble, and, with Peppermint, is said to be valuable at the onset of influenza.

Elder berries are used for Elderberry wine, which is also considered good against influenza. Various preserves and chutneys using Elderberries were formerly much valued.

Elder flowers are gathered when fully out, in June, and put to dry as quickly as possible to preserve the colour, being laid out thinly on drying trays. When fully dry, the flowers may be rubbed into light balls between the hands to remove the stalks, and then sifted.

ELECAMPANE *Inula helenium* (Plate 7)   [*Compositae*]
This handsome hardy herbaceous perennial is the giant of the herb garden, growing some 6–8 ft. high, with huge leaves and clusters of shaggy yellow daisy flowers in July and August. It is a tolerant plant, growing reasonably on light soils but appreciating a sunny site and fairly rich soil, well drained but moisture-holding in summer.

Propagation is by seed sown under glass in spring or by division of the roots in spring or autumn, spring being the safer time on cold soils.

Elecampane roots were considerably used to make cough candies.

ELSHOLTZIA STAUNTONII (Plate 16)   Ar. S.   [*Labiatae*]
This unusual shrub, some 3–5 ft. high, can be seen flowering pleasantly in the Cambridge Botanic Gardens, in a sheltered border, and commands attentive

interest as it blossoms freely in September. The general effect is rather that of a Veronica, with close whorls of pale pink-purple flowers forming terminal spikes, and foliage with an aromatic scent reminiscent of Calamint. A well-drained soil and sunny site are helpful and pruning takes place in late March and April, as flowering is on the current season's wood. The shoots may be shortened back as convenient.

ERICA Heaths and Heathers (Plate 17)   Sc. S.   [*Ericaceae*]
A honied warmth of sweetness emanates from various Ericas, also *Calluna vulgaris*, the Ling. The tree heath, *E.mediterranea*, has lilac-pink flowers in early spring, and may grow 4–6 ft. or more high. Plant with peat or leaf-mould in the soil. Propagation is by tip-cuttings in early summer.

ERYNGO   *Eryngium maritimum* (Plate 7)   *E.amethystinum*   [*Umbelliferae*]
E.maritimum, the Sea Holly of our coasts, is a beautiful plant, blending silver-grey, turquoise and powder blue in foliage and flower. The roots were candied and valued for restorative properties and for nervous diseases.

A cultivated relative, *E.amethystinum*, can be included in the herb garden both on the basis of affinity and the possibility of its use in the same way. It is also a good bee plant, and the steel-blue bracts and soft blue flowers dry well for indoor winter decoration.

EUCALYPTUS   *E.gunnii* (Plate 16)   Ar. S.   [*Myrtaceae*]
This species of Eucalyptus, with a blue sheen on the roundish foliage, is reasonably hardy outside in this country. The leaves have the characteristic scent of the oil used as an inhalant against colds, catarrh and asthma, also as a local application for sores. The oil, however, is obtained commercially from *E.globulus* (the Australian Blue Gum), *E.smithii* and other species grown in Australia and elsewhere. *E.gunnii* yields Kino or Australian Gum from its bark and leaves.

E.gunnii is an attractive specimen aromatic tree in a sheltered part of the herb garden, but in planning allowance has to be made for eventual growth to tree height. The foliage colour makes a good contrast with ordinary green-leafed subjects amongst trees, such as the Balsam Poplar.

EVENING PRIMROSE   *Oenothera biennis*   [*Onagraceae*]
This biennial, growing 3–4 ft. high, has pale yellow flowers, opening fully to perfume the evening air. The tap-roots have been used as a vegetable.

EYEBRIGHT *Euphrasia officinalis* (Plate 7) [*Scrophulariaceae*]
A small, wiry herb found wild on downs and heaths; it is semi-parasitic. As the name suggests, the plant is used to cure eye troubles, and has also been used against jaundice.

FENNEL *Foeniculum officinale* (= *F.vulgare*) (Plate 2) [*Umbelliferae*]
Fennel may be found growing wild on sea cliffs and downs.

Green Fennel and the elegant bronze variety are indispensable in the herb garden. They are hardy perennials growing 4–6 ft. high, with fine-cut foliage and yellow umbels of flowers followed by aromatic seeds.

The foliage is used, fresh or dried, as a flavouring with salmon, mackerel and other fish. To some people the scent of this plant is warm and pleasing, but to others it is too near to aniseed or liquorice. The flavour, however, is enjoyed by some who do not care for the scent of the plant.

A small leaf may be added to fish boiled in milk with a nut of butter added, and a sprig each of Lemon Thyme and Marjoram blend in well also. Again, the leaves may be finely chopped and used in a sauce in the same way as Parsley.

Florence Fennel, *F.dulce*, is grown particularly on the Continent for the swollen stems, which have a delicate flavour when cooked and eaten as a vegetable.

It is interesting with Fennel and the numerous other Umbelliferous herbs that are relatives to note how the flavours form 'variations on a theme', in which the special tastes we associate with celery, parsley, parsnip, aniseed and angelica are hinted at or combined; and the taste of the root may have a different emphasis from that of the leaf or stem. In Fennel there is a blend of anise and parsley, with a hint of parsnip and chervil.

The green and bronze Fennels are decorative for indoor flower arrangements, but the stems should be plunged deeply into water for some hours before making the arrangement.

Propagation is by seed sown in a sunny seedbed outside in April.

FEVERFEW *Chrysanthemum parthenium* (Plate 8) [*Compositae*]
A $2\frac{1}{2}$ ft. high hardy biennial to perennial plant, with golden-green foliage, white daisy flowers and a pungent fresh smell; often confused with the Chamomiles. It is frequently found growing wild but golden-green foliage forms and semi-double flowers are the forms found in cultivation.

It is propagated by seed or division. Medicinally, it has been used in cold infusion as a general tonic, and a cold infusion of the flowers as a sedative.

FOXGLOVE *Digitalis purpurea* (Plate 11) [*Scrophulariaceae*]

This familiar plant, characteristically gracing our woodlands and copses, contains a poisonous principle, Digitalin, used in the treatment of heart troubles. The plant is usually biennial, sometimes remaining for more than one season in rosette form before flowering, and occasionally plants live on after flowering for another season's blossoming.

In times of emergency the leaves of the wild Foxglove and those from cultivated plants are valuable.

Propagation is by seed sown in the open in April and May in drills $\frac{1}{8}$ in. deep.

FRITILLARY *Fritillaria meleagris* (Plate 11) [*Liliaceae*]

Sometimes called Snake's Head or Chequer-Board Lily, this lovely flower is a choice rarity, growing wild in Oxfordshire and elsewhere, and is often cultivated on rock gardens or naturalized in grass. The pendulous flowers are delicately pencilled and chequered, and while the type is a subtle blend of purple, maroon and chocolate with yellow stamens, white and paler purple forms are also grown.

Propagation is by bulbs planted in the autumn 6–9 in. apart in normal garden soils.

This plant is not ordinarily used for medicinal purposes, but contains a toxic principle, Imperialine, also found in Crown Imperial, *F. imperialis*.

Gerard calls Fritillary also 'Turkie or Ginny Hen Floure, or Chequered Daffodil', and remarks that the root is small, white and of 'the bignesse of half a garden bean'. It is greatly esteemed, he says, 'for the beautifying of our gardens, and the bosoms of the beautifull'.

GARLIC *Allium sativum* (Plate 5) [*Liliaceae*]

Owing to the excessive associations of this odour and flavouring with austere travel and one-track cookery, many will have nothing to do with Garlic, but in moderation it imparts a pleasant taste. It is sufficient to rub a clove round the salad bowl before filling to give the right hint of flavour.

Garlic cloves may be planted 1 in. deep and 6 in. apart in February and March in a well-drained prepared soil and sunny position.

The bulbs ripen in August and comprise from eight to sixteen cloves, which can be stored in a frostproof, cool but reasonably dry place and used as required.

Garlic is used medicinally as a syrup to relieve asthma and has been used externally as an antiseptic for wounds.

Wild Garlic is a different plant and will be found under Onions.

GENISTA AETNENSIS   Etna Broom   Sc.S.   [*Leguminosae*]

A shrub with a graceful habit and bright yellow pea-flowers in July. The Etna Broom may make a small tree 12 ft. or more high. A light, sandy soil is suitable, and propagation may be from seed.

GENTIAN   *Gentiana lutea* (Plate 30)   [*Gentianaceae*]

This plant grows wild in considerable quantities in central and southern Europe. It is a hardy perennial, growing some 4 ft. high. The leaves are conspicuously veined, and the yellow flowers are borne in whorls. A strong, rich soil is best, to encourage the long, stout roots. The rhizomes and roots are dug up in autumn and dried. Yellow Gentian has bitter tonic properties good in cases of jaundice and for toning up the system generally.

GERANIUM, SCENTED (Plate 22)   [*Geraniaceae*]

The name is often used to cover both the aromatic hardy Geraniums such as *G. macrorrhizum* and the half-hardy fragrant Pelargoniums such as the Oak-Leaf Geranium, which will be described under that heading.

G. macrorrhizum has red-purple flowers in June. There are also pink and white varieties. The roundish-lobed foliage has a warm, spicy scent of boiling rhubarb-and-ginger jam.

The flowers provide unusual colour early in the herb-garden season. This plant does not enjoy the worst English winters in exposed spots.

Propagation is by root division in autumn or spring. The herb is valuable as an aromatic plant for the herb border and is a herbaceous perennial.

Various other Geraniums have been valued for their medicinal uses, including *G. dissectum*, for its tannin content which makes the plant styptic (to allay the flow from wounds), astringent and tonic. Herb-Robert, *G. robertianum*, has been used in haemorrhages.

GINSENG   *Panax quinquefolius*   Amer.   [*Araliaceae*]

The name is related to the Greek word for a panacea, and the plant is sometimes called Man's Health. The Chinese Ginseng is a larger plant. The American Ginseng has five-lobed leaves. It has been particularly valued against fatigue and the infirmities of old age, and in nervous disorders. The plant is cultivated for the root, collected in autumn.

GLOBE THISTLE   *Echinops ritro*   [*Compositae*]

This well-known robust and easily grown perennial, 3–4 ft. high, slips in chiefly as a good bee plant. The steel-blue spiky, circular heads of azure flowers are useful to dry, when approaching maturity, for winter decoration. They can be hung in small bunches, head downwards, in a warm place such as on the airing-rack over the kitchen stove. A light to medium soil and sunny site gives good results.

GOAT'S RUE *Galega officinalis* (Plate 8) [*Leguminosae*]
A plant from southern Europe, Goat's Rue is a hardy perennial some 3–5 ft. high, the height varying largely with soil conditions, and the situation in which it is grown. It has pinnate leaves and pale mauve spikes of pea-flowers. Goat's Rue flourishes in light soils and sunny positions. Propagation is by seed sown outside in April and May, but afterwards by self-sown seedlings in astronomical succession. Goat's Rue was formerly used as a cure in malignant fevers and the plague, because the infusion caused sweating.

GOLDEN SEAL *Hydrastis canadensis* Amer. [*Ranunculaceae*]
This plant bears, in its fruit, a resemblance to the genus *Rubus* of the *Rosaceae*, but it belongs to the Buttercup family. It is a native of Canada and the eastern United States, and is also cultivated at times for the root, which is used in digestive disorders, loss of appetite and liver troubles.

GOOD KING HENRY *Chenopodium bonus-henricus* (Plate 3) [*Chenopodiaceae*]
Good King Henry is found wild in waste places near villages. This hardy perennial plant with spearhead-shaped leaves, a frosty bloom on the stems and clusters of minute green flowers has a considerably more intriguing name than appearance. In fact, one finds the plant itself something of an anticlimax. It has been used, however, for many centuries as we use spinach, and being perennial forms an excellent substitute, with a delicate flavour. In coronation year, Good King Henry was much sought after, to provide an appropriate touch at Elizabethan banquets in the Strand. It is also called 'All-good' and 'Mercury'.

Good King Henry is propagated by seed, sown in seedboxes in February. The seeds are hard to germinate unless the boxes are exposed to frost for two to three weeks after sowing, then brought into a greenhouse temperature of 55–60°F., when germination should take place in some three to five weeks.

Sowing outside in February and March before frosts end does not seem to have the same successful effect, as the soil is dank and takes time to warm up after the frosts and the quick contrast of the warm temperature is lacking.

The seedlings are pricked out, hardened off and planted out 9–12 in. apart and the rows 12–15 in. apart, in June or July, preferably in showery weather.

Some foliage and young shoots can be gathered the first autumn and afterwards whenever available, taking care not to strip any plant entirely of leaves.

The young shoots are also sometimes eaten as an asparagus substitute.

When the yield of foliage begins to diminish, the plants can be divided in autumn, using a sharp knife for the purpose. A moderately rich soil, enriched with compost, produces the best growth, and on light, dry soils a semi-shaded position is suitable.

GRINDELIA *Grindelia robusta* (Plate 7)   Amer.   [*Compositae*]
This 2–3 ft. high hardy perennial plant has slightly dandelion-like foliage and yellow daisy flowers with viscid, sticky discs and prickly bracts at the back of the florets. It is an American medicinal plant, propagated by seed sown in spring in seedboxes in the greenhouse. This herb has been used to relieve bronchial catarrh.

HAMAMELIS Witch-Hazel (Plate 16)   Sc. S.   [*Hamamelidaceae*]
The February-flowering Witch-Hazels, *H.mollis* and *H.japonica*, have fine-petalled yellow flowers, with a musky scent, on leafless branches. Leaf-mould and compost in the soil are helpful, and propagation is by grafting.

HEARTSEASE *Viola tricolor* (Plate 9)   [*Violaceae*]
The annual Wild Pansy is fairly common on waste ground and in grassy places throughout England. The flowers are variable, and may have three yellow lower petals and two purple upper ones.

Other English names are Call-me-to-You, Three-Faces-under-a-Hood and Love-in-Idleness, for the plant was used in love-charms, as in the play *A Midsummer Night's Dream*. A more serious name, found in old herbals, is *Herbe Trinitatis*, because there are often three colours in each flower.

This plant was formerly used as a remedy in epilepsy and heart troubles. This herb was officially listed in the Pharmacopoeia of the United States, and used in America as an ointment for eczema.

HELICHRYSUM ANGUSTIFOLIUM (Plate 20)   [*Compositae*]
This delightful shrub besieges the air with a hot and hunger-making, but pleasant scent of curry, and for this reason is sometimes given the name 'Curry Plant'. The Curry Plant is also good tempered in the garden, once it is firmly established in a sunny site, and it likes a light sandy soil but will settle in other types if suitably prepared beforehand.

Further, the slender, gleaming silver foliage, golden-burnished flower-buds, small yellow flowers in July and August, lend real distinction to the herb garden.

The Curry Plant will keep some scent and flavour on drying, but in this instance it is not as pungent as the fresh foliage. It is not the 'curry' of commerce, but sprigs can be used to lend pungency to meat dishes.

In planning the herb garden, Curry Plant makes a 'focal' plant at a corner or as a central feature, where larger plants are to be grouped around. It may be clipped back to a point where new shoots are arising after flowering (but not later than mid-August), or in late March. Hard clipping into old wood showing no new growth-buds is not advisable.

Sprigs of Curry Plant, fresh preferably, or dried, may be floated in curries, as an addition to, rather than a substitute for, the ordinary powder. It can be blended, freshly chopped, into butter as a flavouring for savouries.

HELLEBORE (Plate 12) [Ranunculaceae]
H.niger (Christmas Rose)
H.foetidus (Bears Foot)
H.viridis (Green Hellebore)

Found wild in central and southern Europe and Asia Minor, *H.niger* is the delightful Christmas Rose, with white flowers and yellow stamens, flowering in December and January. The leaves are deep green and divided. Many centuries ago, the root was used in veterinary cures for coughs, as mentioned by Parkinson. The constituents which include Helleborin, are powerful poisons with narcotic effects. It has been used for nervous disorders and hysteria in proper dosage. *Helleborus orientalis* has attractive purple, pink or green flowers in March and April and is called the Lenten Rose. *H.foetidus* has green flowers in February and March and is welcome also for that reason, in the herb garden. All these Hellebores do well planted under trees or amongst shrubs if the soil does not dry out in summer. When planting, a liberal amount of compost is helpful. Propagation is by seed for all species also by division of rootstock for *H.niger* and *H.orientalis*, but the main crowns should be left undisturbed for as many years as they continue flowering well, unless the rhizomes should be required for medicinal purposes.

HELLEBORE, WHITE *Veratrum album* [Liliaceae]

This plant, found wild on the European continent, is no relation of the true botanical Hellebores. Of it, Gerard says with pleasant observation, 'It hath leaves like to a great Gentian but much broader, folded into plaits like a garment plaited to be laid up in a chest; amongst these leaves ariseth up a stalke a cubit long, set towards the top full of little star-like floures of an herby green colour tending to whiteness . . . the root is great and thicke, with many small threads hanging thereat.' 'The root of White Hellebore is good against phrensies.'

This plant is poisonous and is stated to have been one of the chief poisons for weapons such as daggers and arrows. It is used in veterinary medicine.

HELLEBORE, FALSE (also called PHEASANTS' EYE)
Adonis autumnalis [*Ranunculaceae*]

A charming scarlet flowered plant occasionally found as a cornfield weed in South England. The leaves resemble chamomile and the flowers are like a small butter-flowering in spring, with yellow blossoms, contains Adonidin, which has an effect on the heart that is similar to the action of digitalin.

HEMLOCK *Conium maculatum* (Plate 12) [*Umbelliferae*]

Found wild in waste places and stream banks, this biennial poison-drug herb has, historically, sinister associations with the death of Socrates.

It is, practically, advisable to be able to tell it from the various innocuous hedge-parsleys and other members of the family, and the obvious purple blotches (not just vaguely purplish), lower on the stems gives the clue. Hemlock will grow some 6–8 ft. high, has dark green, very finely divided foliage, and white umbels of flowers. The whole fresh plant is, on occasion, used in an extract by the homoeopathic chemists and is valuable in correct prescriptions as an antidote to strychnine poisoning, against tetanus and hydrophobia and as a sedative on the motor-nerve centres.

By streams and in damp places the Hemlock Water Dropwort (*Oenanthe crocata*) is found, and is also on occasion used by the homoeopathic chemists. This plant has as one of its most characteristic features, spindle-shaped tuberous roots giving rise to its name of Dropwort.

This plant does not have purple blotches; the foliage is rather more coarsely divided than Hemlock. It is very poisonous, sometimes accounting for fatalities amongst cattle. The plant usually grows some 2–3 ft. high, with white umbels of flower.

HEMP, INDIAN *Cannabis sativa* [*Cannabinaceae*]

A poisonous plant that is occasionally seen growing in a naturalized state, as it is often found in birdseed. Hemp is a poisonous plant, an annual growing some 3–8 ft. high with longish palmate leaves and yellowish flowers.

HENBANE *Hyoscyamus niger* (Plate 11) [*Solanaceae*]

This poison drug plant, of which there are annual but, more usually, biennial forms, is a relative of the Nightshades and Thornapple, in the diverse and commercially valuable family *Solanaceae*, which contains amongst other plants the Potato, the Tomato, Tobacco, Cape Gooseberries, Aubergines, Capsicums and also a selection of drug-herbs: also, for interest, *Solanum sisymbrifolium* (Plate 32) and *Salpichroa rhomboides* (Plate 32).

Henbane is often considered to look sinister and is described as having a foetid smell, clammy hairs and a lurid flower.

I do not subscribe at all to this view, for I find the flower attractive, with its fine violet pencilling and purple anthers on a primrose ground. The leaves provide the right setting, being soft grey-green, and the elongated, lidded capsules in their spiked calyces (and containing numerous chiselled seeds) are elegant for decoration.

Henbane, too, need not be regarded in a sinister light, but a beneficial one, for, rightly used in correct doses, its Hyoscine forms an ingredient of pills, and powder for avoiding travel sickness by land, sea and air.

Henbane is an unpredictable, sporadic wild flower, arising in a spot, flowering, shedding seed and often not being seen again there for perhaps several years.

Commercially, leaves from the first-year rosettes are used in late summer, and for homoeopathic preparations the whole flowering plant the following May and June. Seed may be sown under glass in February, the seed-pans being exposed to frost for two to three weeks before bringing into the heated greenhouse to accelerate germination. Seedlings are pricked out and finally planted out 1 ft. apart by 18 in. Crowns are very apt to damp off during a variable winter.

HOREHOUND, WHITE *Marrubium vulgare* (Plate 10) [*Labiatae*]
H. BLACK *Ballota nigra*

The name Horehound in cough remedies is often much more familiar to people than the plant concerned. White Horehound, as its name suggests, is a greyish-leafed plant with white and woolly stems, and very small white, two-lipped flowers. It is a hardy perennial, some 18 in.–2½ ft. high and growing satisfactorily in dry, hot sunny situations. The soil should, however, in such sites, have compost put deep in holes around the roots when planting.

Black Horehound, a 2 ft. perennial, has dead-nettle-like leaves, faintly hoary or dusty, and mauve-pink labiate flowers like several other familiar wayside plants.

White Horehound is occasionally found wild also, in waste places.

White Horehound has been used for flavouring beer. The Latin name is from the eastern 'mara', bitter, for Horehound was one of the Passover bitter herbs. It is used in cough cures and in horehound candy.

It is a quietly decorative addition to the herb garden, where grey plants lend attractiveness. Spaniels should be kept away from the ripening fruits, as the hooked calyces are prone to festoon the face and knit the ears together.

The Horehounds are propagated by seed sown in spring in a sandy seedbed in the open air or in a box under glass. As with the other labiates, the first seed-leaves are smooth and roundish and do not resemble the true leaves of the plant.

HORSERADISH   *Cochlearia armoracea.* (= *A.rusticana*)   [*Cruciferae*]
The root of this herb, grated, provides the well-known hot and biting sauce used to accompany roast beef.

The familiar leaves are slightly dock-like, with serrated edges; the flowers, less often seen, white, with four petals.

Horseradish is propagated by root cuttings taken in the winter, for 6 in. pieces with buds will form fresh shoots by spring. The root-cutting may be dibbled-in an inch deep and 8 in. apart, and can be obtained when the main roots are dug for culinary use. Otherwise, roots with buds can be divided from one another with a sharp knife and re-planted.

To get thick, mature roots for use, Horseradish should be planted in a prepared plot enriched with compost. It is, however, an invasive plant and is therefore apt to be relegated to odd corners. If these are isolated, this is excellent, but reasonable soil preparation is advised or the cook will become daunted and bitter when faced with pencil-thin roots to grate.

HOUND'S TONGUE   *Cynoglossum officinale* (Plate 8)   [*Boraginaceae*]
Found wild on downs and waste places, this quietly pleasing biennial herb has grey foliage and small crimson flowers of anchusa shape. It is propagated by the prickly 'seeds' sown outside during spring and early summer. The root used to be used in the form of pills for head colds, coughs and similar ailments.

HOUSELEEK   *Sempervivum tectorum*   [*Crassulaceae*]
A perennial, with fleshy rosettes of leaves, and pink flowers on 9 in. stems, which flourishes in dry places and increases by offsets. Medicinally, the fresh leaves are bruised and laid on burns, scalds and other skin troubles, giving quick relief. According to the 'Flora of the British Isles', its country name is 'welcome home, husband, however drunk you be'.

HYPERICUM PSEUDOHENRYI (H. PATULUM VAR. HENRYI)
(Plate 16)   Ar. S.   [*Hypericaceae*]

This St. John's Wort is not invasive like the Rose of Sharon, but forms a bush some 3–4 ft. high, with typical leaves and yellow sun-like flowers in July and August.

A distinctive feature of this plant is the pleasing scent of tangerine oranges when the twigs and leaves are brushed with the hand.

While a sheltered spot is appreciated this shrub is tolerant of north borders and even draughty places, and is propagated by suckers (severing rooted pieces without uprooting the main plant), by seed or by green cuttings.

HYSSOP   *Hyssopus officinalis* (Plate 5)   [*Labiatae*]

This Hyssop is a native of South Europe to West Asia, including Israel, but it is still questionable whether it was the Biblical Hyssop, which may have been an *Origanum*, which is also found in the Holy Land, six species being represented. Or, according to some, the Caper Plant, *Capparis spinosa*, may have been the correct Hyssop, as it is called by the Arabs 'azaf'.

Hyssopus officinalis has spikes of rich gentian-blue, two-lipped flowers, and the pink, purplish and white kinds are pleasing and decorative. These are all low shrubs, semi-evergreen, growing some 18 in.–2 ft. high, with a warm, aromatic scent. In the herb garden they make valuable low hedges and can be clipped back in late March. Pink Hyssop is restful planted with dwarf lavenders.

H. aristatus, the dwarf Rock Hyssop, is compacter, growing some 12–15 in. in height, with rich blue flowers, and is suitable for a pocket in the rock garden, or dry wall, as well as the herb garden. It flowers a little later than the other kinds, in late August. (*Sideritis hyssopifolius*, like a yellow Hyssop, smells like a gasworks. Plate 32).

Propagation is by seed sown outside in a seedbed in April and May, or in boxes under glass in March/May. Seedlings from the pink kind often yield an interesting range of pinks and purplish shades. Occasionally, a variegated 'sport' occurs in the type. Green cuttings may also be taken in summer.

Medicinally, Hyssop tea is made from dried Hyssop flowers and, with honey, used for chest troubles. The infusion made from the green tops is useful for chronic catarrh and coughs, and is also recommended by some for relieving rheumatism. A sprig may be put into a stew for the warm flavour, but it should not be overdone.

INCENSE PLANT   *Humea elegans* (Plate 23)   [*Compositae*]

Cultivated for the delightfully aromatic foliage, it is a native of south-east

Australia. Here, it is treated as a half-hardy biennial, the seed being sown under glass in May–July, and the plant being kept under glass and potted-on to flower the following summer, when it could be bedded-out in the garden, or enjoyed in the greenhouse.

INDIAN GINGER   *Asarum canadense* (Plate 13)   Amer.   [*Aristolochiaceae*]
Sometimes called Canada Snakeroot, it is a perennial, resembling the European *Asarum* (Asarabacca), but with larger leaves. The solitary flowers appear in April and May. The rootstock is aromatic, and the taste is spicy and like ginger. It is found in woods from New Brunswick to Manitoba and south to North Carolina and in Kansas. The dried rhizome and roots are used, having stimulant and carminative properties.

INDIAN PHYSIC, BOWMAN'S ROOT   *Gillema trifoliata*
(*Porteranthus trifoliatus*) (Plate 14)   Amer.   [*Rosaceae*]
A perennial plant found in woods and thickets in various parts of Canada and the United States, including Ontario, Georgia and Missouri. The flowers are white with reddish calyces. The root-bark is used, and the effect is emetic, tonic and cathartic. The American Indians knew the value of this herb.

INSECT-POWDER PLANT   *Tanacetum cinerarii folium* (= *Pyrethrum cinerariifolium* and *Chrysanthemum cinerariifolium*) (Plate 31)   [*Compositae*]
This plant has elegantly cut grey foliage and white, yellow-centred daisy-flowers on 18 in. high stems. It is a hardy perennial, flowering in July. Large quantities of dried flowers have been imported at one time from Dalmatia, and more recently the plant has been grown in Kenya, as well as in this country. The dried powdered flowers and extracts of the active principle have been valued as insecticides against such pests as certain sucking insects, such as aphis, needing contact washes; and against moths indoors. Domestic animals are unharmed by the use of this preparation. The clumps may be divided in spring or autumn, or seed sown in seedpans in spring.

JACOB'S LADDER   *Polemonium caeruleum* (Plate 30)   [*Polemoniaceae*]
Known also as Greek Valerian, this decorative plant was formerly much grown in borders and the blue flowers above pinnate leaves are pleasing in the herb garden. It is occasionally found wild in northern England.

Jacob's Ladder is a hardy perennial growing some $2\frac{1}{2}$ ft. high and tolerant of any ordinary soil and sun or part-shade. Propagation is by division or seed.

This herb was formerly valued for causing perspiration in fevers and for headaches and nervous complaints.

(COMMON) JASMINE *Jasminum Officinale* Sc. S. [*Oleaceae*]
This Jasmine has constellations of hotly fragrant flowers in the summer. It can be grown on walls and pergola or other supports. Propagation is by layering or cuttings. Weak wood may be cut out in winter.

JERUSALEM SAGE *Phlomis fruticosa* (Plate 21) [*Labiatae*]
A 3–4 ft. high shrub with grey, aromatic foliage and unusual heads of two-lipped yellow flowers in June and July. The foliage keeps its scent quite well on drying, and is useful when aromatic leaves are required for decorative sprays during winter. It is not, however, of culinary value. Propagation is by half-ripe cuttings in summer.

JEWELWEED *Impatiens sp.* (Plate 29) [*Balsaminaceae, formerly Geraniaceae*]
    I. CAPENSIS = *I. fulva*
    I. ROYLEI = *I. glandulifera*
  See also Balsams

The first discovery of *Impatiens capensis* with flowers shining like a hidden treasury of topaz and garnets is an experience to mark a summer. Under the stippled shade of trees overhanging the water, the flowers, by contrast, were translucent flame as they held every piercing ray of sunlight. My second experience of this plant, this summer, was to see it gracing an open stretch of the Thames, orange flowers against silver water. The flower repays close enjoyment, for the curving reflexed spur, the tangerine base and scarlet splashes have a tropical feel, a piquant contrast to our discreet English flora.

    The same jauntiness, almost an air of conquest, clings to *Impatiens roylei* which, with tall rose and carmine flower-heads reflected in our blue or olive water, now paints pictures along our waterways from the Lake District to Devon. The pursuit, some fifteen years ago, of this exotic affair, inaccessibly tantalized me; flaunting its glories it was glimpsed from suburban trains by the Ravensbourne in Lewisham, or the Atlantic Coast Express by the Exe, or deep below a town bridge in Stockport. The plant did not then seem to be considered quite '*comme il faut*' for inclusion in floras or wild flower books. The search ended by stopping a taxi 'somewhere in Devon' where sprays of a single plant of this lovely vagrant, growing by a roadside rivulet, could be picked and examined.

    There are two yellow *Impatiens*. *Impatiens noli-me-tangere* or *noli-tangere* with fairly large flowers, festoons river-banks in South Bucks and elsewhere. Another has become a fairly widespread weed of cultivation, and has small yellow flowers of the characteristic shape, and explosive fruits—this is *I.parviflora*.

The Balsams are more interesting as naturalized flowers than for herbal use, though the yellow-flowered kinds have been used externally to cure warts, corns and similar troubles. Herbals, however, often carry warnings against the internal use of *Impatiens* because of the acrid and irritating effects. *I.noli-me-tangere* provides a rare and pleasant wit in Latin nomenclature, 'Touch-me-Not', describing the explosive fruit mechanism.

JUNIPER *Juniperus communis* (Plate 30) [*Cupressaceae*]
A small tree, often found growing only to shrub height and form, it belongs to the conifers, a relationship disguised by the fruits which superficially resemble (and are called) berries. The shrub has awl-shaped, spiky bluish-grey to green needles, and grows wild in hilly districts, including the North Downs and the Lake District.

Juniper berries are used in Germany as a condiment, in some cases valued to flavour *sauerkraut*. They have been used to flavour some continental gins, and the name is a modification of the word through the French name *genièvre*. Medicinally, Juniper in appropriate forms such as an infusion or the essential oil, has been used for rheumatism, liver troubles and other complaints, with the claim of rejuvenating to youthful vigour.

Juniperus sabina. This is a low wide-spreading shrub. The fresh tops are gathered in spring and dried, being used medicinally as 'Savin', which can be extremely poisonous used in large doses. It is therefore rarely used internally but externally as an ointment for blisters and skin troubles.

KERRIA JAPONICA Jew's Mallow Sc. S. [*Rosaceae*]
This hardy and good-tempered shrub has single or double yellow flowers with a faintly lily-of-the-valley scent. Propagation is by cuttings of semi-ripe wood in July or rooted suckers in the autumn. The oldest wood can be cut out after flowering.

LABRADOR TEA *Ledum groenlandicum* (Plate 13) Amer. [*Ericaceae*]
Grows in marshes, bogs and mountain-tops from Labrador and Greenland to New England and British Columbia. It is an evergreen shrub, growing some 4 ft. high, with woolly branches. The stalkless leaves are oblong and emit a fragrance when crushed. They have brown undersides. The white flowers have long pedicels, and five sepals, petals and stamens. During the American War of Independence the

leaves were often used to make tea, and, for this use, collected before flowering. The leaves have a somewhat spicy taste, and have been used to cure coughs, and ease dyspepsia.

LADY'S MANTLE *Alchemilla vulgaris* (Plate 8) [*Rosaceae*]

This hardy perennial is a quiet member of the Rose family. The 'variations on a theme' that extend through the members of a family can be seen in this genus, for the leaves are simple in *A.vulgaris* most resembling *Rubus odoratus*, but compoundly lobed in *A.alpina*, and more like *Potentilla repens*.

Lady's Mantle grows wild, particularly in the north of England, and is a reminder of the shores of Derwentwater. The leaves are delightfully fan-shaped and pleated, and the pale green flowers open in June. The name *Alchemilla* has the same root as 'alchemy', from the Arabic word, because the plant was formerly thought to have wonderful powers, perhaps due to the diamond effect of 'dew' exuding all round the leaf from the pores.

Lady's Mantle has styptic and astringent properties, and was once considered one of the best herbs for staunching cuts or wounds.

Alchemilla alpina has silken silver hairs over the foliage, with pleasing effect. On the Honister Pass recently this plant was festooning the rocks.

Parsley-Piert (Plate 8) is *Aphanes arvensis* (*Alchemilla arvensis*)—a prevalent annual herb (often a weed of cultivation) of prostrate habit, having small fine-cut leaves and minute green flowers. Parsley-Piert was in great demand during the 1939–45 war, being used medicinally for bladder and kidney trouble; and is valuable in jaundice, and is on occasion used in conjunction with a herb containing soothing mucilage, such as Marsh Mallow, Comfrey or Mullein flowers.

LAVENDER *Lavandula officinalis* (Plates 1 and 20) Ar. S. [*Labiatae*]

Formerly, Lavenders were grouped as *Lavandula vera*, forms of which yielded the best essential oil, and *L.spica*, but both are now considered to be forms of one species which botanists now use the comprehensive name *L.officinalis*. These species grow in a wild state on the mountains of southern France and Spain.

It has been suggested by Fernie in *Herbal Simples* that Nard, and Nardus, being Greek names for Lavender (from Naarda, a city of Syria), near the Euphrates, Spikenard was formed from *Lavandula spica*, Spike Lavender. It appears that in Pliny's time Nardus blossoms sold for a considerable sum. In Parkinson's *Garden of Pleasure* he says that *L.spica* is '. . . called by some Nardus Italica'.

Lavandula stoechas, a native of the Islands of Hyeres, has a scent reminiscent both of lavender and rosemary, and was probably the lavender used in classical days by the Romans for perfuming baths which gave the Latin name *Lavandula* from *lavare*, to wash. *L.stoechas* and dwarf lavenders as a whole are sometimes called French Lavender, which name is also rather confusingly applied to *Santolina*, the Cotton Lavender, which is, of course, no relation to the lavenders, but a member of the daisy family.

L.stoechas was called by our old herbalists 'Sticadore', and the flowers were used medicinally, according to authorities, and were an ingredient in Four Thieves' Vinegar, valued as a protection against plague.

Lavender flowers were also used in conserves to be served at table, for the plant, in common with other labiates, has internally warming and comforting properties.

It is interesting that, while warm sun brings out the essential oil content in many plants, too great heat and drought may make for poor quality. For this reason English Lavender oil has been esteemed for its high aromatic quality, especially in a good summer. Some English varieties exported for experimental purposes to higher and hotter regions, for instance in Africa, lost the distinctive scent, leaving only a kind of 'dusty' perfume residue. This is a similar experience to that of English Lemon Thyme, which loses its fragrance when cultivated in Mediterranean regions.

Oil of Lavender is useful for overcoming faintness. For pleasure, it is surely the typical English perfume, evocative of country gardens and eras when life was lived at a slower tempo.

HARVESTING:

When lavender is harvested for distilling, it must all be cut within a day or so, to give the required bulk for the operation. For general harvesting, the right time is when some flowers are fully open all up the spike, but before fading has occurred. Lavender is best cut with long stems, and a curved-bladed knife is convenient when the technique has been mastered of severing a large handful at a time. Bunches are laid on shorn bushes and gathered into sheaves, wrapped in sacks, keeping the heads all one way, and taken to the drying sheds, where they are laid with the heads outwards on hessian trays. If the stems are shortened before laying-out, two rows can be put to each tray; or numerous bunches can be pushed through the wide mesh of wire-netting trays, and the ends of the stems supported on a hessian tray placed underneath, which catches any loose flowers during drying.

When fully dried, shown by the stems being snappable, the lavender is laid on trays on a table and with one hand on the stems, the other on the heads, the flowers may be rubbed off and finally sifted to remove any short stalks.

PROPAGATION:

While amateurs tend to try using large, woody, torn-off branches on occasion as cuttings, it is in practice best to use small new shoots from 2 in to 5 in. long. April and May are good months for obtaining the right material, or after flowering in late August and September when new growth recommences. Harder cutting can, however, be taken at other times.

The lower leaves should be removed and the cuttings inserted firmly in a sandy bed in a frame or plunge-bed below wind-level, or in pans. A suitable filling can consist of peat for the bottom layer, followed by good loam with some garden compost, and with some 2–3 in. of sand on the top.

In spring, rooting may take place in six to eight weeks; later on, longer time is taken to callus and root.

PLANTING:

If lavender plants are being raised to form a hedge or plantation it will normally be most practicable to plant them out when sufficiently rooted at 9–12 in. between plants and 1 ft. to 18 in. between rows. When the plants have grown to a convenient size for permanent spacing, they may be planted 15 in. apart for dwarf kinds and 18 in. to 21 in. for tall varieties. The distances for field plantation planting depends on the length of time the plantation is reckoned to be economic, which may be up to seven years. Tall kinds intended to be kept for six to seven years may be spaced at 3 ft. apart each way, or even 4 ft., as the possible spread of shab disease in a damp season when the spores are washed from plant to plant is lessened if bushes are well spaced. For plantation work dwarf lavenders could be 2 ft. by 2 ft. or 2 ft. by 3 ft. depending on the type of mechanical cultivation available. Some growers prefer a closer 'plant' in the rows.

For commercial oil production, tall lavenders of the Mitcham class are being in some cases superseded by dwarf kinds of the Munstead, delphinensis and Hidcote range, and selected forms and hybrids from these.

Soil Preparation: Before planting lavender for a hedge or permanent plantation, holes at least 1 ft. in diameter—preferably wider—and 1 ft. or more deep should be dug, and compost or well-decayed manure (preferably the former) put in, with a thin layer of soil on top to prevent the lavender's roots from coming into direct contact with the manure. Some weeks before planting it is advisable to dress the bed with hydrated lime at the rate of 6 oz. per sq. yd. or chalk at 8 oz. per sq. yd.

LAVENDERS—DWARF KINDS

1. **Dwarf Munstead.**—When mature, bushes will grow some 18 in. high, but at eight to ten years may attain 2 ft. or more and a spread of 2 ft. also. Several forms, some legitimate, some not, are sold under this name. The two permissible forms (as illustrated, Plate 1) are:

(*a*) Leaves rather dull grey, very narrow, conspicuously up- and in-curved at tips, sprouting in dense bunches. Flowers are set almost at a right-angle from stems. The blunt spikes are $1-1\frac{1}{2}$ in. long, the calyces deep purplish-violet, flowers paler, of the same shade but with a hint of reddish-purple in colour when the flowers are fully mature. Flowers from 21st June in a good summer, otherwise early July.

(*b*) Foliage a more lively grey, more at right-angles to the stem. Flowers in fairly pointed spikes, deep bluish-violet calyces, flowers paler violet-mauve with a bluish tint. This form has characteristics of *Lavandula delphinensis*, and flowers about a week after (*a*).

Both forms are compact and eminently suitable for hedges, and as edgings to beds where low neat growth is important. At Seal, the (*a*) form has been grown for twenty-three years to my knowledge as Dwarf Munstead. Apart from these one may on occasion get a wide range of varietal forms sold as Dwarf Munstead.

2. **Folgate Blue.**—The flowers are the bluest mauve of the varieties. Foliage is green-grey, leaves at 45 degrees to right-angles to stems, the flowers in $1-1\frac{1}{2}$ in. blunt terminal spikes, the individual flowers standing out at an angle from the stems. The flowers are a pleasing shade, and open in early July, generally a week or ten days later than Dwarf Munstead (*a*). Folgate is a slightly quicker grower than Munstead, getting eventually to 2 ft. or so.

There are various other reasonably attractive dwarf Lavenders, often just sold as 'dwarf', or sometimes as 'early blue', often with mauver flowers than Folgate. Baby Blue, on trial at Wisley, looks very dwarf—some 6 in. high, but is only in its second year of trial (1963).

3. **Dwarf White,** *Lavandula* 'Nana Alba'.—This is a charming miniature shrub, growing some 6–8 in. high, an unusual and diverting choice for the rock garden, for the sink garden where there is time for individual appreciation, or at the front of the herb border. The 'pocket-size' white flowers come out in July and August. This white lavender is moderately hardy, but shelter and care are valued.

4. **Pink Lavender.** *L.* 'Nana Rosea'.—This plant always evokes interested comment. The flower-spikes are somewhat blunt, $1-1\frac{1}{2}$ in. long, with silver calyces and pale flesh-pink flowers. We are now propagating a slightly deeper

form, but were unable to discern deeper colour in Hidcote Pink than the form we were already growing.

Apart from these delicate nuances of shade, Pink Lavender is well worth growing and is delightful to have planted near the deeper kinds, particularly Hidcote Purple. A hedge of this variety could have a Pink Lavender at each end. Pink Lavender grows some 21 in. high eventually and has grey-green foliage. It is a hardy plant under normally suitable conditions for lavenders.

5. LAVANDULA ATROPURPUREA NANA.—Sharing the honours for dwarfness with Munstead, this variety has silver-grey foliage, at right-angles to the main stems, and flower spikes $1-1\frac{1}{2}$ in. long, with violet calyces and purple-violet flowers, giving a deep-rich effect. The growth is neat and compact and this is a good choice for edgings to beds. The flower-spikes are slightly shorter and less dense than those of Hidcote, with flowers of a subtly different shape and tone.

6. SUMMERLAND SUPREME.—A reasonably dwarf variety, of a rather spreading habit laterally. The attractively coloured flower-spikes are carried well above the foliage.

LAVENDERS—SEMI-DWARF KINDS

1. HIDCOTE PURPLE.—This is a lovely lavender.

The bushes grow some $2-2\frac{3}{4}$ ft. high and 2 ft. across after eight to ten years. The calyces are violet, and the flowers, with a more silken sheen, purple-violet, very generously massed on the $1\frac{1}{2}$ in. spikes. The foliage, tending to stand out at right-angles rather precisely from the stems, is silver-grey. The flowers of this kind keep a rich colour when dried carefully on stalk and are valuable for patterns in pot-pourri arrangements.

Hidcote Purple is a charming kind for hedges, as a specimen low shrub for shrub-borders or strategic spots in the herb garden.

2. TWICKLE PURPLE.—This kind has the best scent of all dwarf and semi-dwarf varieties, and is a distinctive variety with much to commend it. The long, graceful flower-spikes, often 6 in. in length, are carried fan-wise over the green-grey foliage. The leaves are sinuous in shape and are set out almost at right-angles to the main stems. The flowers are a good deep mauve, with blue lights with the sun shining through the petals, the calyces being mauve and grey. Twickle makes an excellent hedge, eventually growing up to 2 ft. or more with a $2-2\frac{1}{2}$ ft. spread when eight to twelve years old. The flowers are good to dry for sachets.

Dutch Lavender and Warburton Gem: although these kinds often only attain semi-dwarf stature, they are in origin grouped with the tall kinds and described in due course.

PLATE 17 SCENTED SHRUBS
1. *Magnolia watsonii.*
2. *Magnolia wilsonii.*
3. *Clerodendron trichotomum.*
4. *Philadelphus microphyllus.*
5. Mock Orange. (*Philadelphus* 'Belle Etoile')
6. *Rhododendron augustinii.*
7. *Erica mediterranea superba.*
8. *Mahonia (Berberis) bealii.*
9. *Lonicera fragrantissima.*

PLATE 18 SCENTED SHRUBS
1. *Corylopsis spicata.*
2. *Viburnum carlesii.*
3. *Daphne pontica.*
4. *Viburnum fragrans.*
5. *Choisya ternata.*
6. *Viburnum burkwoodii.*
7. *Osmanthus delavayi.*
8. *Osmarea burkwoodii.*
9. *Chimonanthus praecox.*
10. *Daphne odora.*
11. *Sarcococca humilis.*
12. *Daphne burkwoodii.*

PLATE 19 AROMATIC HERBS
1. Old Lady. (*Artemisia borealis*)
2. Lady's Maid. (*Artemisia chamaemelifolia*)
3. Wormwood. (*Artemisia absinthium*)
4. Southernwood. (*Artemisia abrotanum*)
5. Dittany-of-Crete. (*Origanum dictamnus*)
6. False Dittany. (*Dictamnus fraxinella*)
7. Pelargonium 'Mabel Grey'.
8. *Artemisia lanata pedemontana*.
9. Pelargonium 'Madame Nonon'.

PLATE 20 AROMATIC HERBS
1. *Agastache foeniculum.*
2. Variegated Rue. (*Ruta graveolens variegata*)
3. Lion's Tail. (*Brittonastrum mexicanum*)
4. Golden Marjoram. (*Origanum vulgare*)
5. Curry Plant. (*Helichrysum angustifolium*)
6. Lavender Hidcote Giant.
7. *Pelargonium acetosum.*
8. Calamint. (*Calamintha grandiflora*)
9. *Micromeria corsica.*
10. Lavender Summerland Supreme.

LAVENDERS—TALL VARIETIES

The tall kinds, for the sake of clarity and definition, fall into two main groups.

A. *The Mitcham Types*

Sometimes listed as Old English, when the only course to pursue is to buy from their description. The flower-spikes are thick and close, some 2½–3 in. long with deep bluish-mauve flowers. The foliage tends to be green-grey, and flowering takes place from mid-July to early August, depending on the season, which tends to be late if the first terminal flower-buds were nipped by late frost at their delicate beginnings in May.

1. SEAL.—This kind was selected by Miss D. G. Hewer from Hitchin, and has spikes of delightfully deep rich colour, with an excellent fragrance. The bushes are free-flowering and may produce some 1,200 to 1,400 spikes on mature bushes. The flower-stems are some 12–18 in. long, depending on weather and soil, and are borne in such profusion that those around the sides of the bushes sweep fan-wise. The actual bushes grow to some 2½–3 ft. eventually, and need not get too 'leggy' if the flowers are cut with at least two pairs of basal leaves. Excellent for drying.

2. GRAPPENHALL.—This is a large-growing kind with fine spikes typical of the group.

3. WHITE LAVENDER. *L. alba*.—This White Lavender will grow to 2 ft. or even 2½ ft., but it is not as hardy as the coloured kinds, and is liable to die out in a cold winter. It is wise to plant in a really sheltered place on a light sandy soil, or in a site where the soil has been suitably lightened, and against a south or west wall. In exposed situations it is best to treat White Lavender as a conservatory pot plant, potting on into a 9 in. pot eventually.

The leaves are green-grey, and the flower-stems some 12 in. long. The calyces are grey and the flowers white and fragrant.

B. *The Grey Hedge Types*

In this group the spikes are pointed and pale mauve. They are sweetly fragrant, and suitable for drying. These are the types usually just designated 'Lavender' in the average garden, when the uninitiated have not thought of selecting special kinds. Flowering is in late July and August, in normal seasons about ten days after Seal and similar kinds.

1. GREY HEDGE.—Foliage is silver-grey and fairly narrow. Flowers are soft mauve with silver calyces with a mauve tinge, and the spikes are characteristically very thin and pointed.

2. OLD ENGLISH.—The type we have grown and distributed for over twenty

years under this name has broader, greener leaves than Grey Hedge, but the same pale, pointed, fragrant spikes.

3. DUTCH LAVENDER.—Under different conditions this kind may be semi-dwarf or taller, but it belongs in the Grey Hedge group, and is similar but the foliage typically is broader and even more silver-grey, the best kind where foliage for carpeting or edging is of first importance. The flowers tend to be sparsely produced, and spikes are of the pale, pointed type.

4. WARBURTON GEM.—Pale pointed spikes and grey-green leaves. This kind forms a very squat and rounded bush, which may grow some 18 in. to 2 ft. or more high and 2 ft. or so across.

C. *Hidcote Giant Type*

Lavender HIDCOTE GIANT is different from kinds in both the other classes. The flower-heads are very thick, compact and long-lasting in flower, and of a good, deep mauve-blue. Flowering begins about mid-July. The bush-growth is tall, and the flower-stalks some 2 ft. or more long.

LAVENDER SPECIES

1. LAVANDULA STOECHAS is an unusual lavender for those who appreciate detail in flowers. The flower-heads are surmounted with purple bracts looking rather like a terminal bow, the most outstanding feature. The purple-black flowers, minutely orange-eyed, are arranged in four neat rows on the corn-cob-like green-grey inflorescence.

L.stoechas is hardy in favoured situations and mild winters in the Home Counties, and appreciates a sheltered pocket and light soil. It makes an amusing greenhouse pot-plant and flowers under glass in March and April and in the open is the harbinger of the lavenders, flowering in May.

Propagation is by seed sown in spring in a pan under glass, or by cuttings.

2. L.PEDUNCULATA is similar in general specification to *L.stoechas* but the foliage is softer in texture, slightly greener-grey, and as the name suggests, the flower-heads have longer flower-stalks (or peduncles) above the foliage. The terminal bracts are less violet, more reddish-purple. *L.pedunculata* grows some 18–21 in. high. Propagation is by cuttings in spring or autumn.

This lavender is less hardy than *L.stoechas* and is best grown as a pot-plant for the cool greenhouse, when flowering will take place in spring and summer.

3. L.DENTATA can be grown outside under the most favourable conditions of shelter and warmth, but the vagaries of our weather make this risky. *L.dentata* is a pleasing greenhouse plant with its soft green deeply toothed foliage, most

unusual in this genus, and pale mauve flowers and bracts in short heads. *L.dentata* will flower sporadically under glass through the winter and for this trait and the foliage scent, which is a warm and balsamic blend of lavender and rosemary, suggests the future hope of summer at a bleak time.

The foliage will keep its scent reasonably on drying and may be added to potpourri. *L.dentata* will grow some 3 ft. high and can be potted on into 9 in. pots. Propagation is by green or harder cuttings. If growth becomes too 'leggy' the shrub may be cut back to fresh growing shoots.

4. L.MULTIFIDA was once described by visitors as having an aroma like burning rubber or (as an afterthought) a lion-house.

It is really, however, more like hyssop, warm but with a tang. The leaves are even more startlingly unlike lavender than *L.dentata*, for they are fern-like. *L.multifida* is a half-hardy perennial, dying down to ground-level in winter, and has attractive blue and purple flowers, delicately pencilled and repaying close attention, with deep greyish calyces, in short heads. Propagation is by seed or basal cuttings. This plant makes an uncommon and attractive bedding plant. The seed-heads are ornate, grey to brown, and spirally twisted. Some seedlings can be kept potted-up to flower in the cool greenhouse during spring and early summer.

5. L.PINNATA has rather similar foliage, but of a crisper texture, finer-cut, and the scent is that of cedar pencils. The flowers are very small, pale mauve, and the plant is a half-hardy perennial. *L.pinnata* makes an interesting pot-plant for the connoisseur of this genus.

6. L.VIRIDIS.—This lavender resembles *L.stoechas* in general specification, but the flowers are pale and the terminal bracts pale greenish-yellow. This plant is a native of the Pyrenees.

LETTUCE, OPIUM   *Lactuca virosa* (Plate 12)   [*Compositae*]
The wild or Opium Lettuce is a biennial with glaucous leaves, dandelion-shaped, in the first season, and a tall flower-stem some 3–4 ft. high, bearing small yellow composite flowers the following July.

This plant exudes a milky juice which hardens when exposed to the air, and produces a gum, *Lactucaria*, with narcotic and soporific properties.

The garden Lettuce, *Lactuca sativa*, also contains a milky juice which accounts, with the crisp and cooling texture, for its refreshing and relaxing qualities. Lettuce was served at Roman banquets, for its valuable properties, and there were differences of opinion as to whether it was more useful early on, or at the close, to counteract the effects of wine.

The soothing principle is stronger in unblanched plants.

LIME-FLOWERS *Tilia europea* and other species [*Tiliaceae*]

Lime-flowers consist of the dried flowers and bracts of the Lime-tree. The wonderfully fragrant flowers open in late June and July, and lend enchantment to a grove of trees. The flowers are yellowish green, with a membranaceous bract at the base of each cluster. Lime-flower tea (the French tisane *tilleul*) is valued for headaches and for tonic and soothing properties. Lime-flower honey is universally considered to be the most highly valuable.

LINSEED (Flax) *Linum usitatissimum* (Plate 10) [*Linaceae*]

Flax is a well-known plant, the garden kinds, both annual and perennial, being appreciated for their colours, including red, blue and yellow.

Common Flax has pale blue flowers and is a hardy annual grown from seed sown outside in spring. The seed, when ripe, is Linseed, and when expressed, the oil is obtained. Crushed Linseeds make a useful poultice for abscesses. Linseed tea, made from 1 oz. of the ground or whole seeds to 1 pint of boiling water, contains much mucilage. Wine-glass doses may be taken for colds and coughs. The addition of honey and lemon is valuable. Linseed is used also in veterinary cures.

Flax is grown on occasion as an agricultural crop, doing well on downland, and a field in full flower, rippling silver-blue and green under a brisk July breeze, is an unforgettable sight. Flax is believed to be the plant yielding the fine linen mentioned in Exodus and elsewhere in the Old Testament.

LION'S TAIL *Agastache mexicana* (Plate 20) [*Labiatae*]
Syn. *Brittonastrum mexicanum*

This perennial, growing some 2 ft. high, is valuable because it brings, like the Bergamots, glowing colour into the herb garden, and because the foliage is warmly aromatic, a blend of monarda, balsam and calamint.

The carmine-scarlet flowers are two-lipped, long, thin and tubular, arranged in many whorls round the stem, giving a distinctive effect. The leaves are soft grey-green. A warm, well-drained sheltered spot suits the Lion's Tail, who is not really addicted to our worst winters. Propagation is by division, or by basal cuttings in spring. There is also a purple variety.

A.cana (*Cedronella cana; Brittonastrum canum*) is similar to *B.mexicanum*, but more robust, and is in flower from July to September.

LIQUORICE *Glycyrrhiza glabra* (Plate 10) [*Leguminosae*]

This perennial plant has pinnate leaves, and pale mauve-pink or yellowish pea-shaped flowers, flowering from July to September. Liquorice has been cultivated in Yorkshire from the latter part of the sixteenth century.

The roots are dug when the plants are three years old, and the preparation is used to mask the unpleasant flavour of some medicines. Stick Liquorice is produced, lozenges made, and in these and other forms the herb is used for coughs and pulmonary troubles.

LOBELIA *L.inflata L.syphilitica* (Plate 31) [*Campanulaceae*]
There are two wild British Lobelias, *L.urens* and *L.dortmanna*, with mauvish flowers; the former is a heath plant, the latter makes ones acquaintance growing in Scottish lochs.

Various Lobelias have been used medicinally, for asthma; and, externally, as an application for sprains and bruises. Various other uses are recorded, such as an infusion in ophthalmic troubles. The illustration shows *L.siphilitica*, which is very similar to *L.dresdeniana*. The latter is a plant best treated as a half-hardy perennial, hardy in really sheltered beds, growing some 2 ft. high and blooming in summer.

SCARLET LOBELIA *Lobelia cardinalis* (Plate 14)   Amer.
This handsome perennial plant grows $1\frac{1}{2}$–3 ft. high. The flowers, opening from July to September, have a five-cleft calyx and five-lobed corolla, with two small upper lobes, and three showy lower lobes. The plant is found in wet or low ground, in marshes, damp meadows and stream-banks from New Brunswick to Ontario, west to Colorado and south to Florida. It is used in homoeopathy and is said to have nervine and antispasmodic effects.

LONICERA Honeysuckle (Plate 17)   Sc. S. [*Caprifoliaceae*]
Lonicera fragrantissima lives up to its name, having cream flowers whose perfume far outvies its appearance. The flowers normally come out from February onwards, on leafless branches (the illustration was of very late blooms). Plant in a sunny, sheltered position; prune after flowering. Propagation is by cuttings.

L.periclymenum 'Belgica', the early Dutch Honeysuckle, flowering in late April and May, is followed by *L.periclymenum*, 'Serotina', the late Dutch, flowering in June and July. Both challenge the air with intensely fragrant cream, rose-coral shaded trumpets. They are valuable for walls, pillars and pergolas. Propagate by cuttings from May to August. Pruning: thin out after flowering.

LOVAGE *Levisticum officinale* (Plate 3) [*Umbelliferae*]
This little-known herb has begun to be appreciated, as it brings a celery flavour into soups, stews and salads during the spring and summer, when celery is not in season. The leaves may be used fresh, but can be dried. The flavour is potent and the herb should be used with care.

Lovage is a hardy perennial, dying to the ground in autumn and, in spring, putting up new growths like bronze pennants. The plant will grow 4 ft. or more in height when in flower, and has yellowish flower-umbels in July and August.

Propagation is by seed sown in spring or when ripe in boxes under glass, or by division in spring or autumn. Lovage will do well in semi-shade or sun, and prefers a fairly moist, rich soil, but will also grow reasonably (though not attaining such dimensions) in light soils where manure or compost are added. Formerly Lovage was used medicinally for feverish attacks and colic, in the form of a tea, and having a similar effect to Angelica.

Scotch Lovage, a wild plant, is a coarser-growing herb with whitish umbels of flowers: this is *Ligusticum scoticum*.

Smallage is the wild Celery, *Apium graveolens*, found growing in salt marshes near the sea. Celery seed tea is good for rheumatism, and the whole herb has a valuable effect. It is also a good nervine, giving restful sleep and relaxing the system.

LUNGWORT *Pulmonaria officinalis* (Plate 6) [*Boraginaceae*]
A country plant graced with a variety of names, amongst them Soldiers and Sailors, Adam and Eve, Joseph's Coat, Joseph and Mary, William and Mary, Jerusalem Cowslip and Hundreds and Thousands. The allusion is usually to the flowers, which are pink at first, changing through mauve to blue when fully mature, a characteristic in some degree of many members of the Borage family.

Lungwort foliage is also noteworthy, as it bears pale green spots that were likened to lungs, according to the Doctrine of Signatures. Hence, the plant was taken to be good for pulmonary complaints, and it does contain a soothing mucilage that is of value.

Lungwort is a hardy perennial growing 12–18 in. high, and flourishing in slight shade. It does well planted around low shrubs and is not temperamental as to soil. Compost or other organic matter is helpful, however. Propagation is by division of rootstocks after flowering, in damp weather in late May or in the autumn.

An infusion of the dried herb at one teaspoonful to a cup of boiling water, strained, can be taken several times daily to help pulmonary troubles.

'MACE' *Achillea decolorans* (Plate 2) [*Compositae*]
The true culinary Mace is the outer covering of Myristica fruit, a tropical plant, but the leaves of this plant are used to flavour soups and stews. Sometimes Alecost is also called 'Mace', which is confusing.

Achillea decolorans is a hardy perennial growing some 18 in. high and has cream daisy flowers and narrow toothed leaves. Yarrow is a relation of 'Mace'. Propagation is by division in spring or autumn. 'Mace' does well in moderately rich soils and an open but preferably sheltered position.

MAGNOLIA (Plate 17)   Sc. S. [*Magnoliaceae*]

An impressive genus which comprises a wide range in habit and flowering, and a succession of flowering-season. *M.stellata* has small white fragrant flowers in March. *M.soulangiana* 'Nigra' has purple, tulip-like flowers, with a lemon fragrance, in April and May, *M.wilsonii* and *M.watsonii* have waterlily-shaped flowers with a rich perfume, in June or early July. *M.grandiflora*, an evergreen usually grown against a south wall, has cream, scented flowers in August and September. Add leaf-mould and peat to the soil when planting. Pruning is rarely required. Propagation is often done by seeds and layering. *M.stellata* and *M.soulangeana* will also increase from cuttings taken in June.

MAHONIA (BERBERIS) BEALEI (Plate 17)   Sc. S. [*Berberidaceae*]

This delightful shrub, with handsome pinnate leaves, upholds spires of yellow lily-of-the-valley-scented flowers in February–April. It will grow well in sheltered woodland gardens and other protected situations. There is a lovely specimen in John Sich's pleasant garden at Ivy Hatch; it is 6 ft. high. Propagation may be by seed.

MALLOWS   *Malva sp.* (Plate 9) [*Malvaceae*]

The family contains a number of Mallows and allied plants with a strong resemblance to one another, in the finer points of flower and fruit even if they appear to differ superficially.

M.sylvestris, the Common or Blue Mallow, is a well-known wayside plant with exquisitely pencilled purple-pink flowers with blue shadings in some lights, which can be dried to keep their colour and fragile 'nylon' texture. The leaves are lobed. Unfortunately in the wild state this Mallow is very liable to rust disease. The Common Mallow is a hardy perennial, growing 2–3 ft. high.

M.moschata, the Musk Mallow, has pale pink-mauve or on occasion white flowers, over fine-cut upper foliage, the first leaves more resembling those of Common Mallow. This is a biennial to perennial plant, growing 18 in. to 2 ft. high.

Althaea officinalis is the Marsh Mallow with delightfully velvet-textured grey foliage and very pale mauve-pink flowers. It is sometimes found wild in marshes, especially near the sea, and estuaries. Marsh Mallow grows 3–4 ft. high, and is a hardy perennial with rather fleshy tap-roots. All these Mallows flower in July and August.

Propagation is by seed sown in spring or summer, preferably in seed-pans, or division of rootstocks in spring or autumn.

A sharp knife should be used to divide up the fleshy roots of Marsh Mallow, severing pieces with a bud. An open sunny situation suits these Mallows and even Marsh Mallow will flourish on light soils as well as moister ones, if the roots can be kept cool with compost deep down.

In the herb garden, Marsh Mallow clumps are pleasing towards the back of the herb border, both for foliage and flower. Musk Mallows in the centre consort well with hyssop and dwarf lavenders.

Medicinally, the Marsh Mallow is the most important, and the plant yields a soothing mucilage which is excellent for coughs and inflammation of the digestive tract, the decoction of the root being best for the latter use. In the form of a syrup, Marsh Mallow is used for coughs, bronchitis and other chest complaints.

The leaves are harvested from the plant, or the whole herb cut down just before flowering, and dried in the usual way. The flowers, too, are on occasion used with other ingredients as a gargle.

TREE MALLOWS are found growing naturalized by the sea. The leaves, steeped in hot water, may be laid on sprains to give relief. This plant is *Lavatera arborea*.

HOLLYHOCKS. *Althaea rosea*. Closely related to Mallows, Hollyhock flowers may be used in the same way as those of the Marsh Mallow and are also employed for colouring purposes.

MANDRAKE *Mandragora officinarum* (Plate 12) [Solanaceae]

Legends and romance, as well as practical medicinal use, cling around this plant, which fascinated early writers on herbs, who illustrated the plant as a man sprouting foliage.

Mandrake features in the story of Rachel, Leah and Jacob from its reputedly romantic properties and fertility powers. It is mentioned in Canticles, for the pleasant fragrance of the fruits which, by personal experience, is indeed delicious.

It was considered fatal to a man to dig up a mandrake plant, which was said to shriek when disturbed. The ancients therefore recommended harnessing a dog to the plant, and inciting him to pull it out of the ground, thus diverting the responsibility if it proved lethal.

The name arose owing to a fanciful resemblance of the root to the figure of a man with arms and legs.

There are various species of Mandrake. The true plant, now called *Mandragora officinarum* (var. *vernalis*), or by the synonym *M.vernalis*, is a reasonably hardy perennial with a rosette of radical leaves, springing at ground-level from the rootstock. The leaves are some 6 in. long, deep green and wrinkled. The flowers arise on individual stems, some 4 in. long, coming from the centre of the rosette. The flowers have a subtle beauty in the pencilled blend of cream, pearl grey and soft green on their five petals. They are followed (in this country only in the sunniest seasons) by fruits resembling a small tomato, pale orange to reddish when ripe, and having the delightful perfume appreciated by Solomon. The violet-flowered Mandrake blooming in the autumn is *M.autumnalis*.

The true Mandrake needs to be carefully distinguished from English Mandrake (*Bryonia dioica*) and American Mandrake (*Podophyllum*).

Mandrake root is mentioned by Pliny as providing an ancient form of anaesthetic, a pleasantly humane touch in tough Roman times. A piece of the root was given to be chewed by a patient undergoing an operation. The plant was considered good to procure restful sleep and release from pain, also to be of value in maniacal troubles. In Anglo-Saxon times it was considered to have power against demons.

The leaves are occasionally used today in external ointments, and the roots have emetic properties.

MARIGOLD   *Calendula officinalis*   [*Compositae*]

The old-fashioned single Marigold, orange with or without a dark 'eye', lemon or apricot-striped, is decorative in the herb garden and was used many centuries ago medicinally and for culinary purposes. The flowers were used in salads and, dried, in broths and soups. The whole plant, expressed, makes an excellent soothing ointment for the skin, and for wounds and ulcers.

MARJORAMS   *Origanum sp.* (Plates 6 and 20)   [*Labiatae*]

The name Origanum means 'Joy of the Mountains', from the delightful scent and colour of the plants as they clothe the hillsides. This important genus contains some of the most important and valuable culinary flavourings, the Italian Oregano, which is Sweet or Knotted Marjoram, and the French and English Marjorams.

There are also several forms of Golden Marjoram.

O.onites, French Marjoram, is a hardy perennial, 1 ft. high on average, with rather grass-green foliage and pink-mauve flower-heads. It is more aromatic in flavour than the English perennial or Pot Marjoram, *O.vulgare*, the wild native of chalk downs, which has deeper green leaves, richer purple bracts and mauve-pink flowers. The shades vary, and a selection from some hundreds grown from seed will provide some particularly decorative variants; and there is a white form. This Marjoram makes striking clumps for the front of the herb-border, growing some 18–21 in. high and flowering in July and August.

O.marjorana (= *Marjorana hortensis*), the Oregano or Knotted Marjoram, a native of Portugal, has small grey leaves with a deliciously aromatic scent and flavour. It is a half-hardy perennial usually grown as a half-hardy annual by seed sown in pans under glass in March and April, pricked out when large enough, and planted outside in June. If grown as a pot-plant, in a sandy blend of compost, and kept in the cool greenhouse, the plants will continue for years, and fresh sprigs for flavouring may be picked whenever required. Knotted Marjoram has intriguing knotted grey-green bracts in the characteristically plaited pattern of the genus, from which minute fleur-de-lys-shaped flowers emerge. The same specification, with slight variations in the theme, comes out in Dittany-of-Crete, *Origanum dictamnus*, and all these flowers repay close appreciation.

O.microphyllum very closely resembles *O.marjorana* and may be used for flavouring in the same way. It can be used in the ornamental herb garden during the summer, or as a house pot-plant if it can recuperate in the greenhouse, and grows some 15 in. high.

O.'Aureum' Vulgare is perhaps the most attractive of the Golden Marjorams, with soft pink flower-heads over quiet golden, rounded and very sweetly scented leaves. This is quite a hardy perennial plant for a sunny corner, and it is decorative in the cool greenhouse, growing some 9 in. high.

There is a Golden French Marjoram with leaves that are at their most golden-green in early spring, later on becoming green and gold-dappled and having pinkish flowers in July.

Propagation of Golden Marjorams

All these may be propagated by division in spring or autumn and are invaluable in clumps in the herb border, as edging plants, or for carpeting in the knot garden. Although not primarily for culinary use, sprigs may be abstracted from them when required, especially in an emergency, or if they are more accessible on a wet day than the usual green kinds.

Propagation of French (O.onites) and English Pot (O.vulgare) Marjorams

This may be done by seed in seedboxes in spring under glass or in a frame, which is helpful, as the seeds are minute; but they may, too, be sown in very shallow seed-drills about 1/16 in. deep in April, and just covered with soil. The problem of some small seeds sown outside is that of our uncertain English springs, for the soil should be warmed up and moist but not sticky, so that a friable tilth can be achieved. But cold weather, drying winds and absence of rain after sowing all delay germination, and may cause the seed to decay before emerging. Small seeds are more liable to this kind of loss than large ones, which have a fair food-store to tide them over, and being sown deeper are less aware of fluctuating conditions. Enthusiasm, too, should not be worked off by burying the seeds deeper than mentioned when filling in the seed-drills. Marjoram can therefore be considered something of a chance sown outside.

Sown under glass, seedlings are pricked out, hardened off and planted out in June and early July in showery weather, or watered in.

The surest method of propagation is by division of the rather fibrous rootstocks in spring and autumn.

To give an economic crop for drying, the soil needs to be moderately rich and moist with manure and compost added, but it should be well drained in winter. For garden use, marjoram will grow well in light sandy soils with compost added, in full sun and in exposed positions. But this adaptability does not tend to large cropping and the foliage is not heavy textured like sage.

Plantations can be kept two to three years before replanting, but certain weeds such as sheeps' sorrel, and particularly germander speedwell, whose foliage closely resembles Marjoram, can be tiresome.

Plants can be 1 ft. apart with rows 2 ft. apart. Harvesting is done just before flowering, and as this is fairly late only a light second crop in September is probable.

Marjoram may be used fresh or dried in the *bouquet-garni*, mixed herbs, veal and poultry stuffing, to flavour omelettes or in salads, and the warm flavour is delightful.

Marjoram dries well to keep a good colour, given reasonable conditions, and thin spreading. It is also pleasant and straightforward to rub down for use.

MEADOWSWEET Queen of the Meadows *Spiraea ulmaria* [*Rosaceae*]
Dropwort Meadowsweet *S.filipendula* (= *F.vulgaris*)
(Plate 8)

Ordinary Meadowsweet makes an English summer, as the scent drifts languorously from riversides, marshy places and roadside rills. This herb is a hardy perennial with a basal rhizomatous rootstock, and the leaves are pinnate with broad segments. The elegant panicles of cream flowers open in June and July and the plant grows 2–4 ft. high.

Since the leaves and flowers are aromatic, Meadowsweet was used as a strewing herb, and Gerard says, 'The leaves and floures of Meadowsweet farre excelle all other strowing herbs for to decke up houses . . . for the smell thereof makes the heart merrie and joyful and delighteth the senses.'

This herb was held in veneration by the Druids, and was formerly used in flavouring mead and herb beers.

Owing to the aromatic and astringent properties of the plant, it is used on occasion as an infusion—1 oz. of the dried herb to a pint of water, in wineglassful doses for diarrhoea.

Dropwort has much more finely divided leaves than the ordinary kind, and the flower-buds are red, the cream flowers tinged with red also, which makes this plant decorative in the herb garden or ordinary border. It is a hardy perennial, growing some 3 ft. high. Dropwort Meadowsweet has tuberous roots, hence the name. It is found wild in dry pastures, most frequently on limestone or downland and under such conditions the wild form is often only a few inches high. This plant was recommended by Culpeper for pulmonary troubles, such as shortness of breath, and hoarseness.

MELILOT   *Melilotus officinalis* (Plate 5)   *M.alba*   [*Leguminosae*]
Melilot was formerly much grown as a fodder crop and has become naturalized by waysides and railway banks. The leaves are trifoliate, and there are numerous small pea-shaped yellow or white flowers, in one form in terminal racemes, in summer. Melilot is a biennial, growing some 2–3 ft. high, and when dried smells of new-mown hay, due to the presence of Coumarin, found also in Meadowsweet flowers and Woodruff. Melilot is an excellent bee-plant, with long-flowering qualities and considerable nectar production. The plant has carminative properties and has been used externally for ulcers.

MICROMERIA   *M.corsica* (of gardens) (Plate 20)   *M.piperella*   [*Labiatae*]
A genus closely allied to the Thymes, the plants being miniature evergreen (or evergrey) shrublets some 3–6 in. high, pleasant for the rock-garden or front of the herb garden. *M.corsica* has small, neat foliage, and the flowers are thyme-like. It has a divertingly strong aroma of cod-liver oil and malt, with a peppery undertone, but this need not be a deterrent to growing *Micromeria*, as the scent only emerges when the leaves are pinched. Some cats enjoy this scent.

M.piperella with a peppery scent is said to be irresistible to cats. Micromerias like warm sheltered sunny situations on a lightish soil and, like Thyme, are not always appreciative of our English winters. A cool greenhouse suits them well for the winter and they make pleasing small plants in pots. Propagation is by cuttings.

MINTS *Mentha sp.* (Plate 26) [*Labiatae*]
This fascinating genus ranges from the robust-growing Bowles Mint, 5 ft. high in moist situations, to *Mentha requienii*, smallest of all flowering plants grown in this country, with round leaves no larger than the numerals on a postage stamp, and pinhead-sized flowers. When this plant is on show, comments vary, some likening it to duckweed, others to 'mind-your-own-business' (*Saxifraga sarmentosa* or *Helxine*), till the strong peppermint scent intrigues them and marks the differences.

Mints, too, contribute great diversity of scent, from the straight 'Lamb and green peas' association of Spearmint and *M.cordifolia*, through the fruity undertone and same reminiscent scent that characterizes Bowles Mint. Then there is the russet tang of Apple Mint, the distinctive pungency of Peppermint, and the ethereal, perfumed quality of eau-de-Cologne Mint. After these comes the border-line scent of *Mentha aquatica*, the Water Mint, somewhat like Bergamot with an intangible quality of its own, then that of *M.arvensis*, the Cornmint, which is a little rank, though hinting still of Peppermint; finally to that of *M.longifolia weineriana*, which smells like the exhaust fumes of an old-fashioned car, due to the acetylene content.

Their appearances, too, have quiet charm, from the large, soft grey, deeply veined leaves of Bowles Mint to the white, cream and green dappling of Apple Mint, *M.rotundifolia* 'Variegata'. The purple-bronze of Peppermint, and the twirled leaves of its variety, *M.piperita crispula*, are an unusual contrast to the grey of Horsemint, while eau-de-Cologne Mint is decorative with bronze-green leaves, mauve flowerheads and rich purple overground runners.

There is one curious feature of this genus of which, so far, no really adequate scientific explanation seems forthcoming, their reversion in aroma.

Before the 1939–45 war, some Peppermint runners of excellent pungent scent were sent to St. Helena and there, presumably due to different climatic conditions, deterioration set in, and the aroma began to resemble Cornmint. This is, one assumes, due to a change in some ingredients in the chemical content of the essential oil, but it needs further clarifying.

To some extent, the same effect occurs if Mints are grown for too many years on the same site, especially in light, hot soils, where it is best to transplant or at any rate replant (if no other site is available) with plenty of compost, which seems to avert this trouble.

It is increasingly discovered that many Mints originally thought to be species are hybrids and in some cases, of course, seedlings may arise among a crop which have 'throw-back' qualities. While acknowledging the indebtedness of all botanists to the amended nomenclature in the new *Flora of the British Isles*, (by Clapham, Tutin and Warburg), I have, to avoid further complications in identification, kept to the names under which we have sent out these plants.

CULINARY MINTS

Menthaspicala (M.Viridis). Spearmint, Pea-Mint, Green Lamb Mint.

It is essential to obtain stocks of a strain that has the true Pea-Mint flavour, owing to the problems just mentioned, of flavour deterioration and hybrid throwbacks. In many gardens, and in commerce also, Mints are grown with the cornmint tang which is decidedly unpleasant for culinary use. It is therefore wise to inspect and taste the leaves of stocks if one is buying in any appreciable amount during the growing season before placing an order for the dormant season.

M.suaveolens var. Bowles has a fruity richness as well as the true Pea Mint taste, and is appreciated by connoisseurs of flavours. The large, woolly leaves may appear, superficially, daunting, but they can be chopped fresh, and can be dried most satisfactorily, keeping the green-grey colour.

A well-known essence firm made samples of Mint jelly from these four culinary Mints and several of us preferred that from Bowles because of its aroma. Those from Spearmint and Horsemint were the most orthodox in taste, but that from *M.cordifolia* was less pleasing.

M.cordifolia has very wrinkled, heart-shaped green leaves and a branching habit, with purplish stems. It produces fresh growths earlier in spring than the other Mints, a valuable trait, and holds its foliage well into autumn. In very hot weather, the flavour is not at its best. *M.flongifolia*, Horsemint, has the long foliage of Spearmint, but it is grey and downy. The flavour is good, and the growth moderately robust.

M.cordifolia raripila is an almost smooth-leafed Mint, with cordate leaves and purple stems, the flowers being comparatively large for the genus. The plant is attractive and has a really good Pea-Mint flavour. It is not as widely used as some, but is gaining popularity and is rust free.

Cultivation

The Mints, ideally, enjoy a moderately rich soil and sufficient light to allow free growth of their runners, but moist enough to keep cool in summer, and to give rapid growth.

In the garden, they can be put into a semi-shaded position, where they usually grow well, but, commercially, it is important for the essential oil content, on which the aroma and flavour depend, to be high, and this is developed in a sunny position.

In the garden, also, Mints will grow well in the sun if sufficient compost is added. On light soils deep crowbar or spade-holes may be made and the compost put below and round the roots to ensure a deep, cool root-run.

Propagation is by runners, which can have endless territorial claims. In garden practice, to deal with this problem Mints may be planted in isolated beds, or at least in the corner of a bed, and a corrugated iron sheet buried upright to divide them from the other herbs. Or a robust grower such as Sage or Savory may be planted as a buffer and in normal herb-garden planning this is sufficient.

The runners may be planted in spring or autumn, and laid 6 in. apart in drills 2 in. deep, made on ground that has already been well dug (or ploughed) and dressed with well-decayed manure or compost. For gardens, a barrowload per 4 sq. yd. is a good dressing. In gardens 15 in. between the drills for *M.spicata* and *M.cordifolia* and 18 in. for Bowles would be sufficient. In commercial cultivation, a 2 ft. minimum would be necessary where mechanical cultivation is used. Mints are exceptionally hard to keep clean of weeds, and need to be planted on land free of creeping perennial weeds such as couch.

Mints may be divided during the growing season and rooted pieces planted in deep holes, with the foliage just above ground-level.

M.spicata crispata is a curl-leafed Spearmint, but it is hard to find forms in which the true flavour exists, the usual scent and flavour having a Cornmint tendency.

These culinary mints are grown commercially for marketing in fresh bunches, for drying, and occasionally for distilling, but Peppermint is much more grown for this purpose than culinary Spearmint.

For marketing in bunches, smooth green kinds such as Spearmint are most easily recognized by the public and therefore have the easiest sales; though once educated, they like Bowles Mint and the others. All five kinds mentioned above may be grown for drying. Mint needs a moderately high (80–100°F.) temperature for successful drying, as the leaves pack down (the growth being less spriggy than Thyme), but since the oil is very volatile, a really great heat will drive this off and leave a sample perhaps perfect for colour and minus any flavour. If a mint scent is strong in the drying-place, this usually means that the temperature is too high.

Fresh or dried, leaves of these culinary mints may be used to make mint tea, in a tea-pot. This is good for indigestion and a refreshing drink. Chopped mint is good used fresh in salads and, dried, sprinkled on the tops of soups such as pea-soup.

The use of mint in sauce is widely known, but helpful tips are to add sugar to the mint while it is being chopped, to absorb the oil that exudes during the chopping process, and make this easier; and to 'reconstitute' dried mint by pouring about a tablespoonful of boiling water on top before adding the usual vinegar and sugar.

Chopped mint with sugar and a drop of vinegar makes a delightfully refreshing summer sandwich filling. Mint, sultana (or currant) and brown sugar pasties are a country delicacy.

Mint jelly may be made with apples or plums, particularly in a 'glut' season. If dried mint is used, about 2 oz. would be used for 2 pints of jelly, tied in a muslin bag and simmered for about half an hour. About an equal volume of vinegar is added, and sugar (1 lb. to 1 pint of liquid) together with either about three times the volume of apple juice or a jelly preparation used as directed. (Recipe from *Practical Herb Growing*.)

MEDICINAL MINTS *Mentha piperita* Peppermint

The leaves are longish, toothed and pointed, and the flowers in terminal spikes are mauve. This is the most important medicinal Mint, yielding the universally-known flavour in 'bulls-eyes' and other confectionery infinitely better known than the plant itself. There are two commercial forms, the 'Black' Peppermint, in which the foliage and stems are bronze-purple blended with green (usually darker under drier conditions and less nutriment in the soil) and White Peppermint, which shows less purple, and is said to be less hardy, but yields a finer oil. In practice, there does not seem to be much difference in hardiness. When the term 'Mitcham' Peppermint is used it lacks origin-significance now, since little Peppermint is now grown there; but we take the term to mean a Peppermint having a really true scent, producing oil suitable for distillation to give a product of good flavour. On occasion one comes across 'reverted' Peppermints, in which the flavour is tainted, and reminiscent of Cornmint.

As a crop Peppermint may be grown similarly to *Mentha viridis*, though occasionally growers favour raised beds. The crop should be rotated on to fresh ground every three years, to reduce rust incidence and prevent flavour deterioration, or render its onset less likely. Heavy dressings of compost or manure are necessary for economic crops, and a soil that is both moisture-retaining in summer but not water-logged in winter is best.

Some Peppermint runners are on or close to the surface of the ground, and are liable to frost damage in a hard winter. It is therefore advisable to cover the beds with an extra 3–4 in. of soil in autumn as a protection, or straw could be used.

PLATE 21 AROMATIC HERBS
1. Cotton Lavender. (*Santolina neapolitana*)
2. Jerusalem Sage. (*Phlomis fruticosa*)
3. Cotton Lavender. (*Santolina chamaecy parissus*)
4. Sweet Cicely. (*Myrrhis adorata*)
5. German Chamomile. (*Matricaria chamomilla*)
6. Mauve Catmint. *Nepeta* 'Six-Hills Giant'.
7. Orris. (*Iris florentina*)

PLATE 22 AROMATIC AND MEDICINAL PLANTS
1. Wood Sage. (*Teucrium scorodonia*)
2. Golden Sage. (*Salvia officinalis aurea*)
3. Red-Spurred Valerian. (*Centranthus ruber*)
4. Valerian. (*Valeriana officinalis*)
5. *Hebe cupressoides*.
6. *Geranium macrorrhizum*.
7. Balm of Gilead. (*Cedronella triphylla*)
8. Spice-Tree. (*Umbellularia californica*)
9. Bog Myrtle. (*Myrica gale*)

PLATE 23 AROMATIC AND OTHER PLANTS
1. *Salvia patens.*
2. *Salvia involucrata bethellii.*
3. Incense Plant. (*Humea elegans*)
4. *Salvia glutinosa.*
5. Winter Heliotrope. (*Petasites fragrans*)
6. *Salvia chamaedrioides.*
7. 'Camphor-Plant'. (*Balsamita vulgaris*)

PLATE 24 SALVIAS
1. White Clary Sage. (form of *Salvia sclarea*)
2. Pineapple Sage. (*Salvia rutilans*)
3. Variegated Red Sage. (*Salvia officinalis tricolor*)
4. Non-flowering Red Sage. (*Salvia off. var. purpurea*)
5. *Salvia lavandulifolia*.
6. *Salvia haematodes*.
7. Clary Sage. (*Salvia sclarea*)
8. *Salvia ambigens*.

After cutting, the Peppermint crop is sometimes left for a day or two on the site before despatching to the stills, to reduce the bulk and partially to dry the crop.

Peppermint oil is used in pharmaceutical preparations, its chief constituent being Menthol, which is combined with Wintergreen in an excellent liniment against rheumatism, neuralgia and other complaints. Oil of peppermint is used to disguise the flavour of many drugs, and enters into indigestion compounds. Peppermint tea can be made at home by pouring boiling water on to fresh or dried Peppermint leaves put into an ordinary teapot, and leaving to infuse for five minutes. Elder flowers and Angelica leaves may be mixed with the Peppermint in making the tea, and this mixture is good for colds.

Japanese Mint, *M.arvensis var. piperascens*, has fairly narrow pointed leaves of deep green, sometimes with purplish shading, and the pale mauvish flowers are characteristically in axillary whorls. This is grown in Japan to produce Menthol.

M.piperita crispa is a crisp-leafed form of Peppermint, with reddish-purple stems, bronze-purple foliage unless grown in the shade under lush conditions, and terminal spikes of mauve flowers. It is a decorative plant, and has a 'bull's-eye' scent. Propagation, as usual, is by runners.

Decorative and Fragrant Mints

Apple Mint. *Mentha suaveoleus variegata.*—This form of *M.rotundifolia* is the one most appropriately called Apple Mint as the foliage has a strong scent of russet apples. It is most decorative, with soft green foliage dappled with cream and white, and some shoots are fully albino. Apple Mint grows some 18 in. to $2\frac{1}{2}$ ft. high, and enjoys the usual Mint situations. The leaves can be used in the same way as Bowles Mint, particularly in salads.

Eau-de-Cologne Mint. *M.piperita* 'Citrata' (a variety of the Chartreuse), also Pineapple and Citrus Mints.

The scent of eau-de-Cologne Mint is a 'variation on a theme' from *M.citrata*, the Citrus Mint and its other variety, Pineapple Mint, and their appearance is similar.

The leaves are roundish to heart-shaped, bronze-purple in dry situations and hot summers, and green with a hint of bronze when grown under lusher conditions. The overground runners, produced when the divided plants get re-established, are an attractive metallic purple. The terminal rounded heads of flowers are lilac.

Eau-de-Cologne Mint is one of the most popular and delightfully fragrant herbs. The scent of Citrus Mint is a little sharper, and Pineapple Mint slightly more fruity.

These Mints are accommodating, but enjoy typical mint conditions already mentioned. Beds need to be replanted every two years at the longest, to give the best growth.

For drying these Mints may be cut just before flowering, in July or August. In a cool season, flowering may not begin till September. The dried leaves are valuable to blend in pot-pourris and to use instead of Lavender in sachets, which should be crushed occasionally to bring out the scent.

For recherché taste, these Mints may be used for a change in salads, and Pineapple and Citrus Mints in mint sauce, instead of the usual culinary kinds. Some may find eau-de-Cologne Mint a little too scented in this connection, but it is excellent used to flavour an orange jelly, which is given an 'essence of summer' flavour. Boiling water is poured over fresh eau-de-Cologne Mint leaves, left to steep, then strained and the liquid used to make up the jelly.

Fresh eau-de-Cologne Mint leaves, with Lemon Verbena used fresh or dried, make a useful tea substitute for the adventurous or the improvident housewife, and a taste for such teas should be cultivated.

GINGER MINT. *M.gentilis.*—This mint, growing 18 in. to 2 ft. high, forms a pleasing foil to Apple Mint, as it has golden-variegated foliage. The degree of colouring varies greatly, however. The scent is warm, veering towards that of *M.arvensis*, the Cornmint. Ginger Mint has not been much used for flavouring, but can be used in salads. There is a non-variegated form.

M.longifolia although closely resembling *M.sylvestris* in leaf-shape and hoariness, this has in our experience a tougher leaf-texture and forms usually have a 'reverted' scent, not the true 'Pea-Mint' aroma. The regrettable scent of this variety has been noted already. The habit and spikes of mauve flowers make this kind quite decorative.

PENNYROYAL. *M.pulegium.*—This Mint grows at most some 4–6 in. high and has small oval leaves, and numerous whorls of small mauve flowers. The whole herb has a Peppermint-cum-Cornmint scent. There is an upright form growing some 12 in. high which is best to grow if the herb is being cultivated for harvesting.

Pennyroyal flourishes under the usual Mint conditions, and is a good-tempered plant, useful to plant under the light shade of trees if compost is added.

Pennyroyal may be used to make lawns, as for Chamomile. Divided pieces are put in 6–9 in. apart. Pennyroyal is the best of the carpeters for shaded situations, and exhales its refreshing scent at every step. It is valuable, too, to plant amongst paving. In this case, a deep dibber-hole should be made, with compost or other organic matter around the plant's roots to give a deep root-run.

Pennyroyal has many uses. As a flavouring, particularly in the north, it is included in pig's pudding stuffing. It is sometimes used to deter fleas and, as a tea.

Mentha Gattefossei.—This Mint grows some 6–8 in. high and has small pointed leaves and whorls of white flowers. The scent is pleasantly characteristic and pungent, and this herb is useful for planting between paving and at the front of the herb-border.

Mentha Requienii.—*M.requienii* is a fascinating plant because of its minute size, about ½ in. high, and its terrifically strong Peppermint scent. It is somewhat fussy, liking a damp, warm, sheltered site. In some situations it grows like a weed, but shows temperament in others. At Sissinghurst Castle herb garden, the seat part of a stone bench has been planted with *M.requienii*, which obliges with a green felt of growth.

Propagation is by division, and at times one is favoured with infinitesimal self-sown seedlings, for this plant is reckoned to be the smallest flowering plant grown in this country. The seedlings are recognizable from lower forms of life by their pungency. Ultimately, pinhead-size mauve flowers are produced. For sink gardens this is a gem, or for clothing the surface of a tub under a flowering shrub. *M.requienii* is a native of Corsica, but is sometimes popularly called Spanish Mint. It is often also misidentified as Mother of Thousands or Mind-Your-Own-Business, which, of course, lack the distinctive aroma.

MOLUCCELLA *M.laevis* (Plate 32) [*Labiatae*]
Bells of Ireland or Shell-Flower, as this unusual plant is sometimes called, is of the family to which so many herbs belong, and repays close appreciation, for the white, two-lipped flowers in each green 'bell' calyx look like some minute human figure. The plant, a half-hardy annual grown from seed sown under glass in spring, is mostly useful dried for winter decoration, for the finely-veined calyces are pleasing.

MOTHERWORT Lion's Tail *Leonurus cardiaca* (Plate 8) [*Labiatae*]
This decorative herb is a hardy perennial 2–3 ft. high. The palmately-divided foliage (like a maple) is attractive and uncommon in the family, and the furry, pale mauve-pink, two-lipped flowers in long spires unusual. Motherwort will grow well in an open or slightly tree-shaded site with medium soil, and is a tolerant plant, easily grown from seed or division of rootstocks (i.e. clumps).

Medicinally, Motherwort is considered good for the nervous system, having a soothing effect, also as a mild tonic or in fevers. The infusion may be taken or a conserve made.

MOUNTAIN LAUREL *Kalmia latifolia* (Plate 14) Amer. [*Ericaceae*]
A delightful evergreen shrub found wild in New Brunswick, and Massachusetts, south to Florida and other areas. The pink buds are fluted and the flowers bowl-shaped. They are waxy in texture, and pale pink, opening in June and July. The leaves contain a poisonous principle, and are deadly to stock. They are used in powdered form for neuralgic inflammations and fevers, but care is necessary. This plant was brought to Europe about 1750 by Peter Kalm, a friend of Linnaeus.

MULLEIN *Verbascum thapsus* (Plate 10) [*Scrophulariaceae*]
This distinguished-looking biennial herb with spires of yellow flowers in July–August and felt-textured grey foliage, has many descriptive names, among them High Tapers (from the use of the stem-pith for candles, as well as the stately effect), Our Lady's Flannel and (in France), Herbe de St. Fiacre. St. Fiacre is the little-known Irish patron saint of gardeners, living during the seventh century. Born in Ireland (then called Scotia), he settled finally in France, coming alive for us in Mrs Pond's book *Heaven in a Wildflower*. This herb, with its sanctuary associations, in the making of tapers and for its general utility linked with charm, may well have been appreciated by the saint.

Propagation is by seed sown in late spring or summer. The first year a large rosette of wide, pointed leaves, not unlike those of the Foxglove, appear, and this sends up the flower-spike, some 4–8 ft. high, and frequently branched five or six times towards the top, the second year. The open, lobed flowers are clear yellow, with orange stamens.

Mulleins make lovely groups with blue Chicory, mauve-pink Clary Sage and grey Wormwood amongst tall plants in the herb garden. The individual Mullein flowers have a short life, but open in quick succession, and with characteristic generosity a plethora of seeds is produced.

Medicinally, Mullein leaves and flowers are used for their astringent and emollient properties, against pulmonary disorders, and, smoked in a pipe, to relieve a hacking cough. An infusion of the leaves is given for pulmonary complaints, and a homoeopathic medicine for the relief of migraine prepared from the fresh herb. Numerous other uses for the plant are chronicled.

There are various other British wild species of Mullein, which have similar properties.

MYRTLE *Myrtus communis* (Plate 15) Ar. S. [*Myrtaceae*]
This pleasing evergreen shrub is reasonably hardy in sheltered sites and has small ovate fragrant leaves and white, gold-rayed flowers.

Myrtle is well known in the quotation in the prophet Isaiah: 'Instead of the briar shall come up the myrtle tree,' fulfilled in many ways in the fertility of Israel today.

Propagation is by layering in July, and a soil with compost and leaf-mould is appreciated. A sheltered site, preferably against a south wall, gives best results.

MYRTLE, BOG *Myrica gale* (Plate 22) [*Myricaceae*]
For many people this herb gives the characteristic scent of English adventure in the wilds, of exploring in the Lake District, in Scotland, and in peat-bogs elsewhere.

Bog Myrtle is a low shrub, usually growing some 18 in. to 2 ft. high with lanceolate leaves and inconspicuous greenish flowers. The plant exhales a scent that is a subtle blend of vanilla, incense and allspice, and that is evanescent, fading away from the plucked sprigs. A site near a pond or stream would suit Bog Myrtle, which may be increased by division as it spreads by suckers, but is not always easy to establish.

The leaves have been dried and used as a spice and the berries put in to flavour broths.

NASTURTIUM *Tropaeolum majus* [*Geraniaceae*, formerly *Tropoeolaceae*]
The decorative garden Nasturtium, usually grown from seed as a hardy annual, is really a *Tropaeolum*, while *Nasturtium* is the botanical name for Watercress. Gerard actually calls our decorative Nasturtium Indian Cress, and describes it pleasantly, 'The flowers are dispersed throughout the whole plant, of colour yellow, with a crossed star overthwart the inside of a deeper Orange colour, unto the backpart of the same doth hang a taile or spurre.'

The leaves have a pleasantly fresh but biting flavour in salads; and the seeds, when green, are a useful caper substitute.

Garden Nasturtiums flourish best where the soil is poorish and the site sunny. For the connoisseur of rich and uncommon shades in well-known flowers, there are purple and copper-coloured kinds.

Watercress (*Nasturtium officinale*) is a well-known salad ingredient, excellent because of its vitamin and iron content. There is also the American Land Cress, similar in flavour and useful, as it can conveniently be grown in the garden.

NETTLES *Urtica dioica* (perennial) *U. urens* (annual) [*Urticaceae*]
These touchy plants need little description, as their qualities are self-evident; the annual Nettle, a smaller plant than the perennial, is often regretted as a weed of

cultivation, being more aggressive than the perennial Nettle with its creeping rootstocks and green dangling flowers.

Nettles have many compensating uses. If dark and hirsute caterpillars are encountered on Nettles both should be preserved, as droves of our jewelled butterflies, Peacocks, Red Admirals and Tortoiseshells, browse in their larval stage on the foliage.

Nettles have been used in large quantities for chlorophyll extraction and in former times, and times of emergency, for thread and fibre as an effective cotton substitute in weaving.

Young Nettle tops may be boiled and eaten as a vegetable, but have a curious drying effect on the palate. Nettle tea is a good blood purifier.

NICANDRA *N.physaloides* (Plate 31) [*Solanaceae*]
This plant is decorative in the herb garden and interesting, since its characteristics link up various genera of the family. The leaves are like Thornapple; the inflated calyces resemble *Physalis*, the Cape Gooseberry; and the flowers when fully open come between *Atropa* and Thornapple for shape. They are pale lavender-blue and the plant, growing some 3–4 ft., is a decorative hardy annual, flowering in August and September. This plant has come into prominence as the 'Shoo-Plant', as many believe that it will cause flies to decamp. Practical experiments seem to lead to divided opinions on this point.

NIGHTSHADE, WOODY N. (Plate 11) and Deadly N., see under 'Belladonna'.

NIGHTSHADE, BLACK *Solanum nigrum* (Plate 11) [*Solanaceae*]
A weed of cultivation, with white flowers, black berries, and less poisonous properties than those of the Woody or Deadly Nightshades.
  Solanum sisymbrifolium (Plate 32) is a decorative relative.
  Salpichroa rhomboides (Plate 32) also belongs to the *Solanaceae*.

NIGHTSHADE, ENCHANTER'S *Circaea lutetiana* [*Onagraceae*]
This is a familiar woodland plant, growing some 18 in. high, with Nightshade-shaped leaves but very different flowers. These are small and pale pink, borne in spikes. It is mentioned here to differentiate it from the true Nightshades. The origin of the name for *Circaea* is obscure, but may have been given as the plant haunts dank and overshadowed spots. Circe was a shady enchantress, in mythological circles.

ONIONS *Allium sp.* [*Liliaceae*]

Various relations of the Onion and Chives are useful and interesting in the herb garden.

TREE or EGYPTIAN ONIONS *Allium cepa var. proliferum* (Plate 5)

This intriguing hardy perennial has swollen stem-bases, from which arise leaves, also stems growing some 18 in. high, bearing clusters of small onions the size of a large hazel-nut, often intermingled with small white flowers. A second tier may develop. The bulblets may be separated and planted 8 in. apart to produce new bulb-bearing plants next season. They may also be used for pickling, in salads or stews, or wherever an onion flavour is needed, and are excellent for the emergency cook. Also, the plant's foliage can be chopped up like chives.

Tree Onions thrive in light to rich soils in a sunny position, 8–10 in. apart each way. They may be replanted in spring or autumn.

WELSH ONION *Allium fistulosum* (Plate 5)

This plant is a hardy perennial, rarely producing its white umbels of onion-like flowers. The foliage, too, resembles that of the onion and grows from a basal clump of swollen stem-bases. The leaves and stems may be used instead of spring onions, for which use a clump is dug up and after selecting some pieces for eating, the remainder are divided up and replanted. The foliage, too, may be used as a Chives substitute during the winter, as the leaves remain green. It is sometimes called Ciboul, but this can be confusing, as the same name is applied to other plants.

WILD GARLIC AND RAMSONS *Allium vineale* and *A.ursinum*

Wild Garlic, with narrow foliage and the typical scent, may be found on hedge-banks throughout Great Britain. By contrast, Ramsons (Wood Garlic) grows in damp woods and has starry flowers and lily-of-the-valley-like foliage, unexpectedly revealing to the novice a penetrating odour of garlic. In emergency, the foliage both of Wild Garlic and Ramsons and the small swollen stem-base of the latter may be used with discretion in flavouring. Cows, on the other hand, show indiscretion by browsing on Ramsons. The *Countryman* has a current story from the Camel valley of 'That Ol' Ramsey' ruining a young hostess's tea-party through eggs used in the cake-mixture having become tainted as the hens had dined on Ramsons at flowering-time.

There are numerous delightful and decorative Alliums including *Allium moly*, with golden umbels of flowers and tulip-like leaves. There is nothing against using these in dual-purpose role and chopping up a leaf when needed.

ORACH *Atriplex hortensis* (Plate 4) [*Chenopodiaceae*]
This annual may be sown outside in April and May, or, with more security, under glass in April, and planted out. The leaves are crimson and, seen against the light, the plant glows with a stained-glass window effect that makes it valuable in the herb garden. Given a moderately rich soil, Orach will grow to 5–6 ft. high. Leaves may be used in salads, and the flowering tops, shading in with the leaves, are useful in floral arrangements.

ORRIS *Iris florentina* (Plate 21) [*Iridaceae*]
The Orris powder with a violet scent, used in cosmetic preparations, comes from the dried and pulverized rhizomes of *Iris florentina*, also from *I.pallida* and *I.germanica*. Commercially, this crop frequently comes from Italy, as the name suggests.

The fresh rhizomes are not scented, but the odour develops after preparation.

Iris florentina, a white Iris, shaded with pale mauve and with orange-yellow beards, flowers in late May and June, growing some 2 ft. high. It will grow well in light or moister positions, in sun or part shade. This versatility has earned Irises the name of 'Poor Man's Orchid'. Propagation is by division of rhizomes, preferably after flowering. Each piece with a new bud can be severed and replanted, with the roots going down vertically and the rhizome horizontal, but firmly set in. Orris is welcome in the herb garden to give an early effect.

OSMANTHUS DELAVAYI (Plate 18) Sc. S. [*Oleaceae*]
The small fragrant white flowers set amongst evergreen foliage wreathe the stems. This shrub flourishes in woodland sites, not under dense trees, but where it receives both sunshine and shelter. Other sheltered positions are suitable, and leaf-mould or compost in the soil are helpful. Propagation is by ripe cuttings in late summer, or layering. *O.aquifolium* has holly-like leaves and small white fragrant flowers in late autumn.

OSMAREA BURKWOODII (Plate 18) Sc. S. [*Oleaceae*]
This is an interesting shrub, as it is a generic hybrid between *Osmanthus delavayi* and *Phillyrea decora*. The small white flowers are borne in March and April, having a pleasant fragrance. Propagation may be by layering.

PARSLEY *Petroselinum crispum* (Plate 3) [*Umbelliferae*]
Parsley has collected innumerable sayings, reputed properties and superstitions through the centuries, those notably known in these days being that it is slow in

germinating because it goes to the Devil and back a number of times; that it is unlucky to transplant it; and that where it flourishes the missus is master.

There seems to be a confliction of evidence as to whether the plant used in ancient Greece in funeral wreaths was in fact Parsley or Celery.

Various forms of Parsley are cultivated, French Parsley being broad-leafed and uncrisped, like a large form of Chervil, and has a strong flavour. The curled, crisp-leafed forms are most commonly grown for the table, being more attractive as a garnish and providing more bulk for chopping. Hamburg or Parsnip-rooted Parsley is grown for the fleshy tap-root, which is eaten.

Parsley, with Mint and Sage, are the typically English flavours, and there are few who are allergic to the clean, refreshing taste.

Parsley is a hardy biennial, normally flowering and going to seed the spring after sowing, though in a hot, dry year it may 'bolt' and go to seed in late summer. Many complain of the difficulty of growing Parsley, although it is so popular. Failures may be due to several causes. The seed must be fresh not more than a year after harvesting as older seed, like that of most members of this family, loses its germinating power quickly. Secondly, Parsley resents a cold soil, though it needs to be reasonably moist for germination. It is therefore wise to wait till the soil is really warmed up in spring and water the incipient bed a few hours before sowing. A homely country tip is to pour boiling water down the seed-drills before sowing to provide for warmth and damp. Thirdly, the seed may be sown too deeply—$\frac{1}{8}$ in. covering is sufficient. Seed should germinate in three to four weeks, though occasional delays of eight weeks are known. Compost should be added to the soil before sowing. Drills for sowing may be 10 in. apart and the plants thinned to 6 in. On hot soils a slightly shaded spot is good.

Commercially, reasonably rich soils where growth is rapid are essential for a useful crop, though the soil must be well drained and warm up satisfactorily in spring.

Seed may be sown in April–May for a summer and early autumn crop and a second sowing made in late July–August for the next spring and early summer.

A dressing of nitrogenous fertilizer such as sulphate of ammonia at 2 oz. per sq. yd. is helpful in early summer if the growth is sluggish. Bolting in a hot season is made less likely if the terminal shoots are kept picked out.

Parsley is not easy to dry to retain a good colour, but it requires a higher temperature than Sage or Thyme (some 90–100°F. constantly is best, and direct heat over a stove may be necessary, particularly for finishing). The cut herb should be spread thinly to dry and should not be cut when wet as the crisped leaves hold much moisture and it is almost impossible to produce a bright green colour in the finished product unless it is harvested dry. It is best to sift Parsley when it is crisp, as it re-absorbs moisture from the atmosphere if it is left sacked for a time before rubbing and sifting.

As some Parsley leaves tend to be prostrate there may be grit and sand left clinging to the leaves, splashed up in wet weather, and the finished product may need to be shaken in a hair-sieve to remove the grit.

Some advise pouring boiling water over Parsley before drying to keep the green colour, but this is unnecessary and not recommended if the suitable drying heat can be maintained.

Parsley leaves are rich in iron and, eaten fresh, are good against anaemia.

Parsley jelly, strained and reboiled with sugar, has a honey flavour.

Suitable varieties include Perfection Moss-curled: Dwarf Green.

PASQUE-FLOWER *Anemone pulsatilla* (Plate 11) [*Ranunculaceae*]
[= *Pulsatilla vulgaris*]

This delightful herb is a very rare British plant found on chalk downs. The leaves are very finely divided, and the flowers, borne on silver-silken stems, are mauve-purple, with golden stamens. The flower is surrounded with an involucre of silken floss, and the fruits, too are plumed. Pasque-Flower is a reasonably hardy perennial plant, flowering, as the name suggests, in April, and propagated by division of the rhizomes after flowering or by seed sown in a pan under glass in spring, preferably after exposure to frost.

An open but sheltered position and well-drained soil with compost added are best for success with this plant. Pulsatilla contains an acrid and toxic principle, Aenemonin. Tincture of Pulsatilla is helpful for troubles connected with the digestive and respiratory passages, and for nervous exhaustion.

Hepatica triloba has lobed leaves (with perhaps some resemblance to the lobes of the liver), and usually blue but occasionally rose or white flowers in February and March. This plant was also called *Anenome hepatica* and, in medicinal practice, American Liverwort (not to be confused with the lowly Liverworts, that are nearer allied to the mosses). (See Plate 14.)

Hepatica triloba is welcome for its early flowering. It enjoys a sheltered spot and ordinary garden soil. It is suitable for naturalizing under flowering shrubs. It has been used as a safe remedy for liver and lung troubles, and indigestion. Propagation is by division after flowering.

PELARGONIUMS (Plate 28) [*Geraniaceae*]

The scented Pelargoniums are half-hardy suffruticose (semi-shrubby) plants from the Cape, many having been introduced around 1788. This description does nothing to suggest the allure and charm of entering a greenhouse filled with a varied assortment, and enjoying the aromatic sweetness on the air, as well as the often different impressions when the individual leaves are brushed with the hand.

In Victorian times these plants were largely grown, but they lost popularity and once more became appreciated and fashionable during the last ten years, encouraged, amongst other events, by the interest aroused when they were featured in large iridescent pots and other containers in the Spanish Garden at the Chelsea Flower Show a few years ago, forming a striking feature.

Some of these Pelargoniums, such as the 'Oak-Leaf', are excellent house-plants for a sunny window-ledge, and can have practical uses, for pot-pourri and for flavouring. They are pleasing plants for scented gardens for the blind. It is often noticeable that the general aroma of a Pelargonium on the air may be very different from the scent when the leaves are crushed or brushed over, only the most volatile elements in the aromatic constitution being freely released into the atmosphere.

General Culture of Pelargoniums

Propagation is by green or semi-ripe cuttings. For the so-called 'Oak-Leaf' Geranium it is convenient to make these cuttings some 6 in. long, and to cut them under a joint, but in general cuttings either with or without heels root satisfactorily, given suitable conditions. The soft green cuttings may root in some 6 weeks in the most favourable growing season, March–May, taking three months or more later on. A rooting powder helps the formation of roots, and cuttings should be inserted in pans filled with a sandy mixture, with sand on the top, to trickle into the dibber-holes. The best position is round the edge of the pan, where cuttings usually root first, having had the best combination of aeration and moisture.

Rooted cuttings are potted up singly into $3\frac{1}{2}$–5 in. pots depending on size and time available to re-pot. The John Innes Potting Compost is a suitable medium. Pelargoniums need a reasonable amount of water, but over-watering can cause stem-rot; and during the dank November–December period they need least watering, unless the greenhouse temperature is kept steadily temperate, to encourage active growth.

The 'Oak-Leaf' Pelargoniums flower most during the early spring and summer but sporadically at other seasons, too. If growth becomes long and woody, they may be cut back to a growing bud, having been re-potted, ideally, a week or so before, to give fresh food-material for a new start. This applies, modified by the individual speed of growth, to the other kinds.

PELARGONIUM CAPITATUM

This is popularly known as the 'Oak-Leaf' Geranium, a name properly applied to *P.quercifolium*, which has foliage of real oak shape. *P.capitatum* (closely allied to *P.radula* and *P.graveolens* and over which confusion of naming takes place on occasion) has divided foliage and the one illustrated is often called the rose-scented 'Oak-leaf', as there is a usual, more finely divided form. The basic fragrance is a blend of lemon, rose and a balsamic scent. These geraniums are good house-plants, for sunny window-sills but, if possible, after an annual cut-back, they are improved by a month or two in a temperate greenhouse to get started into fresh growth.

Alternatively, in common with the other Pelargoniums, they may be planted in the open from late May till mid-September, then brought indoors and potted up for the winter. If preferred, they may be plunged in beds or borders in their pots, and the pots completely covered with soil to give a natural effect. The advantage here, where indoor space is limited, is that the root-balls do not grow so large as to require vast pots (9 in. or so) when the plants are lifted for the winter, as can happen when the plants are put potless into the open ground.

Winter can be a hazardous time, and plants should be kept moderately dry, but not dried out, particularly if the temperatures are variable.

These Pelargoniums have clusters of small pinkish flowers. The leaves may be dried for pot-pourri. For variety in culinary operations, when making a sponge cake, the tin may be lined with fresh 'oak-leaf' geranium leaves (not *P.quercifolium*, as the gummy flavour would definitely not be appropriate), before pouring in the mixture, which will be permeated with a pleasant aroma and flavour. The oil of geranium is obtained from various Pelargoniums of this section, and forms of this *Pelargonium capitatum* have been exported to Nyasaland (amongst other places) to standardize the best kinds used and obtain a more constant product.

P.LADY PLYMOUTH has silver-edged, cream-tinged foliage shaped like the 'Oak-leaf' geranium, and with a scent reminiscent of Peppermint and Cinnamon. Pale pink flowers open during the summer. This is a decorative plant for outside bedding during the summer.

P.SCARLET PET has leaves on the same plan as the 'Oak-Leaf', but less finely divided and with a scent having a hint of parsley and of balsam and polish. The flowers are carmine-scarlet, and the effect is delightful if the plants are allowed to trail over the edge of an urn or other garden receptacle.

P.CRISPUM has crisped leaves, with a lemon-juice scent, and *P.crispum minor* has very small, curled foliage, crimped at the edges, and the scent of hot lemon-rind. *P.crispum* 'Variegatum' is most decorative, with foliage edged with silver and cream, and the same refreshing pungency; it is an excellent plant for outside bedding. *P.crispum* and its varieties have comparatively large mauve-pink flowers of the long 'primitive' shape. The foliage may be dried and used in pot-pourri, and to give a lemon flavour in cooking. *P.citriodorum* is close to *P.crispum*.

P.TOMENTOSUM has larger, downy creme-de-menthe-coloured foliage and a pungent peppermint smell. The flowers are small, white and melancholy, but the foliage is striking and of unusual interest for its aroma.

P.ATTAR OF ROSES is probably the gem of the pelargoniums, for the foliage has the most delightful true rose perfume. The leaves are slightly lobed, and the small pink flowers open during the summer. The leaves may be dried for pot-pourri and this plant is always a pleasure to pass in the greenhouse.

P.QUERCIFOLIUM has oak-shaped leaves with maroon markings up the veins, and a characteristic scent, blending gum, incense and musk, fragrant with an almost absurdly exhilarating effect on the air, and releasing the indefinable musky part when the foliage is crushed.

P.FILICIFOLIUM has much the same scent, but the leaves are fern-like in their exceedingly fine dissection, and thin white flowers are borne during summer.

P.ACETOSUM (Plate 20) has fleshy, glaucous blue-green foliage and apricot flowers striped like a *Lewisia*. The foliage is unusual in having a strongly acid taste, like sorrel.

P.MADAME NONON (Plate 19) has sweetly scented lobed and divided foliage and a salmon-pink flower approaching the Show Pelargoniums in size. In this way, it is a valuable intermediate form.

P.FRAGANS, the Nutmeg Geranium, has grey velvet foliage, small white flowers and a scent blending pines and nutmeg. The leaves can be used in the more pungent and spicy pot-pourri recipes.

P.ROSE UNIQUE has pleasantly aromatic foliage and decorative clusters of salmon flowers. Now known also as Paton's Unique.

P.MABEL GREY (Plate 19) has been brought recently from Kenya. The foliage is bold in outline, palmately divided, and has a lovely lemon verbena scent.

P.ODORATISSIMUM resembles *P.fragrans*, the Nutmeg Pelargonium, in appearance, but the leaves have a delicious apple scent. Growth is not as robust as *P.fragrans*.

PELLITORY-OF-THE-WALL *Parietaria officinalis* [*Urticaceae*]
This herb, whose intriguing name is rather belied by the plant itself, is found perched on old walls. Pellitory is a hardy perennial, and has ovate green leaves and clusters of minute green flowers; but in the spring emergence the new young stems are pellucid coral-rose. Pellitory-of-the-Wall, though addicted to heights, will

grow happily on light soils under a wall and provides self-sown seedlings to the *n*th degree.

The plant contains abundant nitre. Gerard mentions its uses to cure coughs, and an infusion of the dried herb or the juice of the fresh herb will stimulate the kidneys.

PERIWINKLES *Vinca major* and *V.minor* (Plate 29) [*Apocynaceae*]
Periwinkles have had a great reputation as herbs, one name being 'Sorcerer's Violet', and the plants were supposed to have power against 'wykked spirytis'. They were used in various charms and potions, and had the pleasant name at some time of 'ye Juy of Grownde', or joy of the ground.

The trailing stems with ovate opposite leaves and mauve to blue wheel-like flowers are well known and Periwinkles are sometimes found wild in woods. *V.minor* has narrower leaves than *V.major* and there is a double wine-purple form that is pleasing. Propagation is by division and tip-layers naturally produced. Periwinkles are excellent for carpeting a bank or place under shrubs, the variegated form being good planted with the plain kinds. Medicinally Periwinkle, particularly *V.major*, has astringent and tonic effects. There is a pleasing variegated form of *V.major*.

PEROVSKIA ATRIPLICIFOLIA (= *Perowskia*) Russian Sage (Plate 15)
Ar. S. [*Labiatae*]
A valuable semi-shrubby plant with silver-grey, warm sage-scented foliage, and almost white felted stems. The lavender-blue, two-lipped flowers come in August and September. Again, being late-flowering, it is refreshing and valuable in the garden.

Perovskia grows some 3–4 ft. high, and, spectacularly, it is at its best near the entrance to the Gardens at Wisley, on a low wall near a flight of steps. Propagation is by division in spring and plants may be cut down almost to ground-level in March and April, for the clean new shoots give a fine effect, terminated by the whorls of flowers. A well-drained sheltered sunny site is needed.

P.ABROTANIFOLIA (Plate 15).
Perovskia abrotanifolia has greenish-grey distinctive foliage, and lavender-blue flowers in August–September.

PHILADELPHUS Mock Orange 'Syringa' (Plate 17) Sc. S. [*Saxifragaceae*]
Some find the perfume of the Mock Orange cloying, but it is richly airborne in the garden. There are many kinds. A gem where space is valuable is *P.microphyllus*,

growing some 3–4 ft. high, with small leaves. The white flowers smell of pineapples. *P.purpureo-maculatus* and *Belle Etoile* are distinguished by a purple blotch at the base of the petals. These varieties are comparatively vigorous. The Mock Oranges are hardy and robust, propagated by cuttings or offsets. Some older wood is cut out after flowering.

POKE-ROOT   *Phytolacca decandra* and *P.octandra* (Plate 9)   [*Phytolaccaceae*]
This plant is also called, from its place of origin, Virginian Poke, Pigeon-berry and Red-ink plant. It is a hardy perennial in sheltered sunny sites, and grows some 3–4 ft. high with spikes of cream flowers followed by decorative purple berries in close spikes. Propagation is by seed.

The plant is poisonous and care is needed. The fruit in proper preparation has been used to help in chronic rheumatism and an ointment has been employed in skin troubles.

POPPIES   OPIUM POPPY   *Papaver somniferum* (Plate 11)   [*Papaveraceae*]
        RED FIELD POPPY   *P.rhoeas*
The Opium Poppy has leaves of typical shape, waved at the edges, but distinguished from most other poppies by being glaucous blue-grey. The flowers are decorative, almost white to soft purple, and large green capsules follow. Decorative Opium Poppies are often grown as hardy annuals, and have flowers of salmon and crimson as well as purple, with a stylish antique feel about the shades.

The whole plant yields a white juice, and the opium of commerce is obtained by making incisions in the capsules. Poppy-heads can be used as a poultice to allay toothache, and even the warmed leaves laid on an aching face will have the same effect. Opium used as a drug is said to produce sharpening of imaginative qualities and to be stimulating for a time, but afterwards depressant.

Poppy seeds are used to decorate and flavour the tops of loaves of bread, giving a pleasant nutty taste. Seeds of the garden poppy may be used for this purpose.

The petals of the Red Poppy, dried, have been used to colour medicines.

PURSLANE   COMMON PURSLANE   *Portulaca oleracea* (Plate 3) [*Portulacaceae*]
         GOLDEN PURSLANE   *P.sativa*
These plants have been grown for many centuries for salad use, and are refreshing in their effects. *P.oleracea* has fleshy green leaves and pinkish-red stems, containing mucilage, and *P.sativa* has golden foliage. They may be sown outside in May, and are annuals in this country, growing some 6 in. high. The leaves and stems are eaten in salads and form an ingredient of *Bonne Femme* soup in France, with

sorrel. The name 'Purslane' is used at times for various plants, including the 'Sea Purslane', a species of *Atriplex*, *A. portulacoides*.

Because of its cooling mucilage, Green Purslane was valued medicinally both internally, with sugar and honey, to allay coughs and thirst, and externally, bruised, laid on to cool the forehead. It was also considered a certain cure for 'Blastings by lightening or planets and burning of gunpowder', and therefore might be considered relevant in these days of discussion of space travel. 'Take 1 space-helmet; 1 pot Purslane...'

RAMPION   *Campanula rapunculus* (Plate 4)   [*Campanulaceae*]
There is some confusion over the English name 'Rampion', as it is given to two plants found wild or naturalized in this country, *Phyteuma orbiculare*, with purple-violet, rather scabious-like flower-heads, and *P. spicatum* with longer flower-spikes in bluish or cream. These are common in alpine districts and sometimes grown on rock-gardens in this country.

The herbs called Rampion, on the other hand, are true bell-flowers. *C. rapunculus* is the more usual, and is a biennial with spoon-shaped pale green lower leaves forming a rosette the first year, and having a tap-root underground; the second season, mauve harebell-like flowers are borne in June on 2–3 ft. stems. This Rampion has established itself as a naturalized native plant in some parts. Rampion was well known as a pot-herb in Shakespeare's day, reference to it being made by Falstaff.

Propagation is by seed sown in a sandy seedbed outside in April and May, a tricky proceeding on any but the stillest days, as the seeds are minute. The plants may be earthed-up in early autumn, and the roots dug in November and stored. For a successful crop, a light sandy soil enriched with compost is essential. Rampion is a decorative plant for the herb garden and if allowed to go to flower usually obliges with countless self-sown seedlings for posterity.

Another Bellflower is also called Rampion—*Campanula rapunculoides*, a perennial with creeping rootstocks, spindle-shaped swollen roots, formerly used also for culinary purposes, and more heart-shaped leaves than *C. rapunculus*. The flowering stems are some 18 in. high and the bellflowers look down, not up. This Rampion does well in shady spots under trees and can be very invasive.

RED-ROOT, NEW JERSEY TEA   *Ceanothus americanus* (Plate 13)
Amer.   [*Rhamnaceae*]
This shrub has downy leaves and stems and white flower-clusters. The leaves were used as a tea substitute during the American War of Independence, hence the name

PLATE 25 SAGES AND DECORATIVE SALVIAS
1. Meadow Sage, rose var. (*Salvia pratensis var.*)
2. *Salvia grahamii.*
3. Annual Clary Sage, pink var. (*Salvia horminum var.*)
4. Narrow-Leaf Sage, white var. (*Salvia off. var.*)
5. Narrow-Leaf Sage, orchid-pink var. (*Salvia off. var.*)
6. *Salvia superba.* (*Salvia nemorosa*)
7. Flowering Red Sage. (*Salvia off. var. purpurea*)
8. Narrow-Leaf Sage. (*Salvia off.*)
9. Meadow Sage. (*Salvia pratensis*)
10. *Salvia verticillata.*
11. *Salvia uliginosa.*
12. Broad-Leaf non-flowering Sage. (*Salvia off.*)

PLATE 26 MINTS
1. Ginger Mint. (*Mentha gentilis*)
2. Crisped Peppermint. (*Mentha piperita crispula*)
3. Bowles Mint, Apple Mint. (*M. Suaveolens var.* Bowles)
4. Black Peppermint. (*Mentha piperita*)
5. Apple Mint, variegated. (*Mentha Suaveolens var.*)
6. *Mentha cardifolia raripila.*
7. Cordifolia Mint. (*Mentha cordifolia*)
8. Spearmint. (*Mentha spicata*)
9. Pennyroyal. (*Mentha pulegium*)
10. Eau de Cologne Mint. (*Mentha citrata*, Chartreuse var.)
11. Horsemint. (*Mentha longifolia*)
12. *Mentha requienii.*
13. Japanese Mint. (*Mentha arvensis var. piperascens*)
14. *Mentha gattefossei.*

PLATE 27 THYMES
1. *Thymus caespititius.*
2. *T. membranaceus.*
3. *T. mastachinus.*
4. *T. erectus.*
5. *T. zygis.*
6. *T. ericifolius.*
7. *T. citriodorus aureus.*
8. *T. vulgaris,* Golden.
9. *T. vulgaris,* Silver Posie.
10. *T. fragrantissimus.*
11. *T. citriodorus,* Silver Queen.
12. *T. hyemalis.*
13. *T. serpyllum minus.*
14. *T. serpyllum,* Lemon Curd.
15. *T. herba-barona.*
16. *T. serpyllum coccineus.*
17. *T. serpyllum,* Annie Hall.
18. *T. serpyllum coccineus major.*

PLATE 28 PELARGONIUMS (SCENTED GERANIUMS)
1. *Pelargonium* Paton's Unique.
2. *P. filicifolium*.
3. *P.* Attar of Roses.
4. *P. citriodorum*.
5. *P. crispum*.
6. *P.* Lady Plymouth.
7. *P. crispum variegatum*.
8. *P.* Scarlet Pet.
9. *P. capitatum*. ('Oak-Leaf')
10. *P. fragrans*. (Nutmeg Geranium)
11. *P. tomentosum*.
12. *P. quercifolium*. (True Oak-Leaf Geranium)

New Jersey Tea. The large red roots have been used as a dye for wool. The flowers have five sepals, petals and stamens, and are borne from May to July. This shrub is found from Maine to Ontario, west to Manitoba and south to Florida. The root or root-bark have been used as a gargle and mouth-wash, and in asthma and chronic bronchitis, in suitable preparations.

RHODODENDRON (Plate 17)   Sc. S.   [*Ericaceae*]
Rhododendrons and Azaleas are peat-lovers. The use of sequestrene can help when growing these shrubs on chalk soils. Many Azaleas, including the *Ghent* and *rustica* types, with flamboyant colourings, give off a challenging, balsamic scent. The lavender-blue *R.augustinii* has a sweet fragrance, and *R.fragrans*, a late-flowering lilac kind, is described by its name. There are many other scented rhododendrons. In general, propagation is by grafting and layering. It helps growth to remove seedheads after flowering.

RIBES ODORATUM   Golden Currant (Plate 16)   Sc. S.   [*Saxifragaceae*]
A faintly feline aura haunts *R.sanguineum*, of which *R.odoratum* is innocent. The yellow flowers have a pleasant clove scent, and the foliage shows fine autumn tints. Propagation is by cuttings, and the bush may be thinned after flowering. *R.odoratum* grows to some 5–6 ft., and is hardy.

ROSEMARY   *Rosmarinus officinalis* (Plate 6)   Ar. S.   [*Labiatae*]
This is one of the best-known herbs, and the legends surrounding it are innumerable. It is mentioned in the Saxon *Leech Book* of Bald and again as having been introduced to this country by Queen Philippa of Hainault, in the middle of the fourteenth century.

Rosemary was greatly favoured in Tudor days. Sir Thomas More wrote that he let it run over his garden walls, because his bees liked it, and because it is the herb of remembrance and friendship.

There is an old legend that the flowers were originally white but that during the flight to Egypt Mary spread out the Christ-child's clothes to dry on a bush and the flowers were blue ever after.

Rosemary has had varied traditional uses and has played a part in various ceremonies, including that of bringing in the Boar's Head, garnished with Rosemary, at the Christmas banquet at Queen's College, Oxford. To Gerard, Rosemary was one of the herbs that 'comforteth the hart and maketh it merrie, quickeneth the spirits and maketh them more lively'.

The type has narrow, deep-green leaves, silver underneath, and elegantly fluted mist-blue flowers in April and May, on last year's wood. The scent is refreshingly pungent with more than a hint of ginger. Mature bushes may live twenty years or more, and grow 6 ft. or more in height in sheltered situations. There are also white and pink forms. In our experience the latter is rather mauve-pink.

Miss Jessup's variety (introduced by the late Mr E. A. Bowles) has a more upright, fastigiate growth than the type, and the foliage is a more golden-green, the flowers being smaller and paler blue. In bad winters Miss Jessup is less hardy and the foliage is liable to look rusty brown after the biting March winds, but often makes a complete recovery later. Apart from this, Miss Jessup is a desirable variety, as the 'Irish Yew' habit of growth makes an attractive focal point in garden design. The varieties Seven Seas and Tuscan Blue have attractive blue flowers.

Prostrate Rosemary *R.lavandulaceus* grows some 6–12 in. high, spreading laterally, with a 'japanese' style of growth, and has mist-blue flowers, like the type. It needs a really warm, dry and sheltered spot outside and is a risky investment, but makes a delightful cool greenhouse plant, with the flowers coming out in February and March, an encouraging harbinger of spring. Prostrate Rosemary is also suitable as a specimen for a sheltered sink garden.

The Rosemaries are propagated by cuttings taken in late spring and summer, of the young current season's growth, or in autumn and winter, of the mature shoots. Cuttings are inserted in pans or in sheltered sandy sites outside.

Rosemarinus officinalis forms a pleasant 3 ft. evergreen hedge outside, planted 15–18 in. apart. To achieve both flowers and compactness, the bushes should be clipped back in late May and June, after flowering, allowing the new shoots to grow for flowering the next year. The clippings may be dried, and afterwards the leaves can be stripped off their stems for use.

A sandy, well-drained soil and sunny sheltered position are ideal for growing Rosemary. Growth is slow at first, but steady once the bushes are established.

While he mentions a custom of gilding Rosemary branches for decoration as we gild fir and pine cones and branches on occasion now, Parkinson also speaks of a variety called the gilded Rosemary, with golden-touched foliage. If this is still growing in some obscure garden, it would be valuable for its continued existence to be put on record.

Rosemary leaves may be used in spicy pot-pourri blends and the dried leaves, heated on a shovel permeates a room with a pungent fragrance. Rosemary is coming into favour as a culinary herb. A fresh sprig may be stuck into a joint of lamb before roasting, or dried leaves sprinkled on top to impart the characteristic flavour.

An infusion of dried or fresh Rosemary leaves makes a good rinse for brunette hair.

ROSA   Sc. S.   [*Rosaceae*]
Amongst Hybrid Tea roses, one can make a selection of sweetly scented kinds, the very personality of the flower revealed. Shot Silk, pink shot gold; Talisman, flame-orange, with pointed buds, Betty Uprichard, pink with a deeper pink reverse, and Crimson Glory and Charles Mallerin, both crimsons, are all perfumed. Many of the older roses, such as the hybrid perpetuals, Hugh Dickson, carmine-crimson and George Dickson, velvet crimson, are deliciously scented. The small carmine rose Grüss an Teplitz has a perfumed flower with an aroma of Russian leather. Many of the Musk Hybrids, excellent for pillars, waft their scent over a wide area.

RUBUS ODORATUS (Plate 15)   Ar. S.   [*Rosaceae*]
This is not a gaudy plant, but appreciated by the connoisseur of delicate points, and needs to be better known.

In contrast to those already described, *Rubus odoratus* is a lover of semi-shade, a valuable trait in town or wild gardens. Good growth will often be made in odd sunless corners, provided they are not exposed to blasting or furtive winds.

The large sycamore-like leaves are handsome and the soft rose-purple, chalice-shaped flowers pleasing to meet year by year from late June to August, succeeded by attractive raspberry-like fruits of no great edible value. There is a pale pink-flowering form, less fine than the type.

As with the Sweetbriars, the aromatic principle is carried in glandular hairs around the calyces and the young stems, and a warm, slightly leathery fragrance given off, particularly when the plant is rubbed.

Growth is individualist for a flowering shrub, being carried on in the raspberry-cane manner, the shoots growing 4–6 ft. high. Propagation is carried out by taking and replanting suckers in spring or autumn, giving organic matter such as compost under the roots for moisture and coolness.

RUE   *Ruta graveolens* (Plate 7)   [*Rutaceae*]
'Rue, sour herb of grace' and 'Herb a grace a Sundays' is famous as the symbol of regret and repentance. It is still carried by judges at the Assizes, traditionally to ward off gaol fever and presumably also as a penetrating hint or symbol.

The scent affects people very differently. To some, it is pleasant, and reminiscent of 'gorse scent blown to sea off the Cornish coast', as a naval officer put it; or it suggests coconuts. To others, the smell is odd, with a hint of washing-day, and to more people, frankly disagreeable, reminding them variously of musty churches, gorgonzola cheese or Aden.

Rue is a hardy perennial shrub growing some 2–3 ft. high. In a severe winter older bushes are liable to lose most of their leaves but otherwise the colour is pleasing in the dull days on young plants. The blue form, rather more metallic than the softer sea-blue-green of the type, is striking and good in the mixed shrub border.

Rue foliage is finely cut and the four-petalled flowers are soft yellow with an emerald centre, and followed by chiselled seed-capsules.

Variegated Rue (Plate 20) is unusual, and the creamy plumes of young foliage, breaking into yellow flowers, decorative in foliage arrangements. The seed of this variegated form has the uncommon property of coming true to the variegation, presumably because the colour-change applies to the flowers as well as the foliage, therefore the chromosome differentiation remains constant in the ovules.

Rue may be propagated by seed sown in a seed-pan or outside in April, or by cuttings of the new shoots taken during the summer in a frame or pan in a greenhouse. Rue prefers an open, sunny site, but is not fussy as to soil, though a light to medium loam is suitable.

A very small amount of chopped leaf may be used to give a piquant flavour to a salad dish containing tomatoes.

Rue tea is a tonic drink, boiled in treacle, with stimulating properties. A leaf of Rue, chewed, is said to be good for dispelling nervous headaches. Rue is given to poultry to help in curing croup.

SAFFRON CROCUS (true)—see under Autumn Crocus.

SAGES *Salvia sp.* (Plates 22, 23, 24, 25) [*Labiatae*]

The name *Salvia* has its Latin origin from a word signifying to save, the same root as our 'salvation', from the high opinion in which sages were held, bringing health to the whole man.

This group is one of the most varied and fascinating amongst herbs and aromatic plants and their relatives. To many, the name *Salvia* conveys only the scarlet blaze of *Salvia splendens* and its varieties, used in formal park bedding. The name, of course, applies to a whole genus whose flowers range from the intense blues of *S. ambigens* and *S. patens*, the azure and kingfisher of *S. uliginosa*, the purples and violet of *S. officinalis* (the type) merging into pale pink and white in some varieties, to the yellow of *S.glutinosa* and scarlet of *S.grahami*, a veritable palette of colour.

The scents range from the characteristically 'sage' class to the delicious fruit scent of *S.rutilans*, the Pineapple Sage, and Clary Sage with a hint of grapefruit and black currants.

Often, as in *S.horminum* and *S.virgata nemorosa*, bracts provide the fine colour and make for lasting effect in the herb garden or border. In Red and Golden Sages the foliage provides the outstanding colour.

The two-lipped flowers are gaily curved and fluted, flicked out from the calyces and small bracts with characteristic effect. Once Salvias are enjoyed, the first encounter with a new species or variety holds a curious pleasure, as one appraises yet another 'variation on a theme'.

In duration, Salvias, again, vary from the hardy annual habit of *S.horminum*, through the hardy perennials such as *S.glutinosa*, with *S.patens* a half-hardy perennial and *S.officinalis*, a low shrub.

There are two wild British representatives. *Salvia verbenacea*, with samll mauve flowers, is found growing wild by the seaside and in waste places. There is an historically evocative and nostalgic passage in Gerard's *Herbal* where he says: 'Wild Clarie or Oculus Christi. groweth wilde in divers barren places, almost in every country, especially in the fields of Holborne neere unto Graye's Inn, on the highway by the end of a brickewall.'

Salvia pratensis is an increasingly rare and therefore exciting find on chalk downs.

S.OFFICINALIS SAGE

Sage is well known as a flavour and is often linked in our senses with Christmas or other special festivals when duck, goose or perhaps pork are the *pièce de résistance*. In the everyday cuisine, pork sausages are characteristically sage-flavoured.

There are numerous varieties of the common Sage. The Broad-Leaved variety very rarely flowers and is valuable on this account, as all the strength goes into foliage. The flavour is good, with less of a 'tang' than Narrow-Leaved Sage, of which there are pale orchid-pink and white-flowered forms, both decorative in the garden; and it is amusing to sort out good blue-violet, larger-flowered forms from a large batch of seedlings, while some are the usual purple.

S.officinalis var. purpurea usually called Purple Sage, is a purple-leafed variety, and has a soft appearance like the bloom of a plum. There is a fine purple-flowering form and one that does not flower. Red Sage is valuable for carpet-planting for knot-garden work, as it can be kept clipped low.

Red Variegated Sage has purple flowers, but the chief beauty lies in the purple foliage, which is inconsequently splashed, particularly on the new young leaves, with carmine, cream and green, Gerard's 'painted Sage'. The variegation is variable seasonally and from plant to plant.

Golden Sage rarely flowers, but the blending of yellow, gold and green in the foliage is pleasant, and gives a bright colour off-season in the herb border. Golden and Red Variegated Sage are both good for planting between the spokes of a cart-wheel for a small 'carpet arrangement'.

S. lavandulifolia is very close to *S. officinalis*, but as the name suggests the leaves are long and narrower, with a very faint suggestion of lavender combined with sage in the scent. The flowers are mauve-purple and sparse.

Propagation.—Narrow-Leafed culinary Sage is grown from seed. To complicate matters, some seedsmen sell seed of what they call Broad-Leafed Sage which is a wide-leafed form of Narrow-Leaf Sage but not the true Broad-Leafed Sage which, as it does not flower, seldom produces seeds.

Sage seed is sown in drills outside in late March–May. As the seedcoats are hard the seed may take some weeks to germinate in a dry spring. The drills are ½ in. deep and may be 8 in. apart if the seedlings are to be planted out, or 2 ft. or so if they are merely to be thinned out in the rows in large-scale field practice.

Narrow-Leaf Sage can also be increased by cuttings taken in summer or division in spring or autumn.

Broad-Leafed Sage, Red Sage and the variegated forms are propagated by cuttings of fresh shoots taken in late spring or summer, or in late summer, of shoots that have hardened. The cuttings may be inserted in frames or pans under glass, or in prepared sandy beds, suitably protected, in the open.

General Cultivation.—When sufficiently developed, the young Broad-Leafed and Narrow-Leafed Sage plants can be planted in the open, leaving at least 15 in. between the plants and 21 in. between the rows, the distances apart being determined by the length of time it is proposed to leave the plantations. These can be undisturbed for three to four years, but the crop carried does diminish and many growers, particularly with the Narrow-Leafed Sage, leave for two to three years only.

To grow economic crops, well-drained but rich soils are necessary. On light soils, organic matter needs to be added, by a heavy dressing to the soil or in the individual planting holes.

Sage is one of the earliest crops to be harvested, a first cut being obtained in May, a second one in August and often a third later. Some growers recommend a first cut from spring-sown seed in November, saying that 'bleeding' after cutting is least then.

Sage is a straightforward crop to dry, and can be piled fairly heavily on trays, provided that it is stirred up daily to prevent its going into a solid mass, when the foliage will go black and have an unpleasant dank smell. If there is sufficient space for the trays to be moderately filled, given a steady temperature of 70°F. or so, Sage should dry crisp in six to seven days.

Sage is reasonably hardy but really severe winters may cause some casualties. Narrow-Leafed Sage is hardier than the non-flowering Broad-Leafed kind.

Verticillium Wilt, a disease of hops and other plants, caused trouble and received resultant notice during the 1940–45 period, and can cause the yellowing and collapse of Sage plants. The outer bark of the roots peels off easily in rings, and the inner part of the stems has black markings. If this disease is suspected in a large commercial crop advisory biological examination is recommended. Propagation should be carried out from obviously healthy plants.

Uses of Sage

Purple Sage, Golden Sage and Red Variegated Sage all enjoy a well-drained but good soil, a sunny situation and shelter from winter winds. They are reasonably hardy but resent exceptionally severe winters.

In the herb garden they are attractive planted in groups of three to five plants. Purple and Red Variegated Sage harmonize well with pink- and blue-flowered Hyssops and with Lavenders.

There is nothing against using the foliage of Purple Sage for ordinary culinary purposes, and some butchers prefer it. The flavour is mild. However, it is regarded more for medicinal uses, and has been employed for toothpowders and as a gargle for sore throats.

Salvia Species

These Salvias like light to rich well-drained soil well prepared with organic matter. In general, the hardy perennials are suitable for the herbaceous border and appropriate at the approach to the herb garden; or a selection would make an unusual 'species bed'.

S.ambigens is a hardy perennial growing some 3 ft. high, with a warm aromatic scent and elegant royal blue flowers in whorls. Propagation is by division.

S.chamaedrioides (Plate 23) is another unusual pleasure, with a semi-prostrate Wall Germander habit and foliage, as the name suggests, but a plentiful supply of ultramarine flowers as late as September. It is half-hardy.

S.glutinosa (Plate 23) is a rather strange hardy perennial *Salvia*, uncommon in having pale primrose flowers pencilled with greenish black that are almost luminous at dusk. This is given on excellent authority, though not yet personally observed, as plants need to be in the right setting. The young shoots and flower calyces are covered with sticky, aromatic gum giving rise to the Latin name.

S.grahamii (= *S.neurepia*) is a deciduous shrub, hardy in the south-west and favoured situations in the Home Counties, against a south or west wall. Otherwise, it is best grown in 9 in. pots under glass and plunged outside for the summer, or grown in a movable tub. *S.grahami* will attain 5 ft. or more and flowers with gay generosity for nine to ten months if overwintered under glass, throwing out a succession of glowing carmine-scarlet flowers with a wavy and broad lower lip.

Propagation is by green cuttings during the summer, or severing rooted pieces from an established plant. Pruning an outside plant is done in late March–April by cutting some older shoots to their new basal growths when these are showing, unless the frost has clean-pruned the plant to ground-level, as with fuchsias on occasion. *S.greggei* has pinkish flowers.

S.haematodes is usually considered a hardy perennial, but may not be very long-lived. The leaves are wrinkled and casually lobed, and the attractive lavender-blue flowers are in typical whorls, the stems growing some 2–4 ft. high, depending on general conditions.

S.involucrata bethellii (Plate 23)—it grows with distinction in the Oxford Botanic Gardens—causes a shock of appreciation when first encountered, for the whole set-up is unusual, from the bright carmine-magenta flowers, a little inflated and hairy on the upper lips, to the tightly folded terminal bunches of rose-carmine involucral bracts. There is a slight hint of aroma from these, but the smooth, purple-veined leaves seem entirely scentless. *S.bethelli* is hardy in really favourable winters, but it is best to have cuttings under glass in case casualties occur. Flowering continues well into September.

S.patens (Plate 23) is used in bedding schemes, and has special distinction in the large and significant flowers equally elegant in deep or Cambridge blue. This *Salvia* is a half-hardy perennial, needing to be lifted and potted-up under glass for the winter, and being planted out in late May and early June. Flowering is from late July till mid-October.

S.pratensis has value in the border or herb garden. It is a short-lived perennial, with royal blue and violet flowers, translucent like a stained-glass window at the right angle in sunlight, and suggesting the lower alpine meadows. *S.pratensis rosea* is a good mauve-pink form. *S.pratensis* can be planted appropriately in the herb garden proper.

S.rutilans, the Pineapple Sage, has a real pineapple scent and flavour. The fresh leaves can be used in salads or in flavouring herb butter. This is a half-hardy shrub, growing some 2–3 ft. high eventually, but the plant can be kept compact by being pinched back or cut to a growing shoot. This herb needs to be kept under glass or on a sunny window-ledge with a temperature of 50°F. or more during the winter, and planted or plunged outside for the summer. Propagation is by green cuttings, whenever available. The J.I. Potting Compost is a suitable mixture for culture. From late autumn onwards spikes of velvet-textured, slender scarlet flowers are produced, a heartening sight in the dark months.

S.superba (*S.virgata nemorosa*) is an essential plant in the herbaceous border, as the crimson-purple bracts and violet flowers make a show for July and August. Propagation can be by basal cuttings in spring or autumn.

S.uliginosa has turquoise to kingfisher blue flowers at an appreciated period, from August till early October. It is a moderately hardy perennial, a little thin in growth, going up to some 3–5 ft. high, and needs to be planted behind some bushy subject.

S.verticillata is perennial, with purple furry calyces and mauve flowers. It is occasionally a naturalized escape and a friend, perceiving plants in flower on a railway bank and being immured in a train with botany an insufficient reason for pulling the communication cord, resourcefully counted the number of railway beats and bridges to the nearest station to identify the spot for an expedition on foot.

Other agreeable Salvias include *S.farinacea*, in lavender-blue, *S.coccinea*, scarlet, and *S.jurisicii*, blue.

S.argentea has densely silvery white woolly leaves in basal clumps. In summer, it shoots up with a flower-stem some 3 ft. high, with mauvish-white, clary-like flowers.

SAMPHIRE *Crithmum maritimum* (Plate 3) [Umbelliferae]
This is a well-known plant of cliffs and rocks near the sea, and has fleshy green leaves and umbels of cream flowers. Samphire has been used for centuries as a salad herb and as a pickle, prepared in vinegar. Samphire is mentioned as being gathered on the cliffs of Dover in Shakespeare's *King Lear*. The name is said to be from *Saint Pierre*, or, in Italian, *Herba di San Pietro*.

Golden Samphire is an entirely different plant with large golden-yellow daisy flowers, and is found wild in the Isle of Sheppey. In former days it was sold to the gullible as Samphire, to the horror of connoisseurs, since it lacked the warm aromatic flavour of true Samphire. Golden Samphire is *Inula crithmoides*.

Gerard's description cannot be bettered for detailed portraiture. He says of 'Sampier', 'It has a stalk divided into many small spraies or sprigs on the top whereof grow spoky tufts of white floures, like the tufts of Fennel.'

SARCOCOCCA HUMILIS (Plate 18)   Sc. S. [*Euphorbiaceae*]

A lowly shrub, some 1–3 ft. high, often growing with great good temper in the shade of trees. The foliage is evergreen and the small white fragrant flowers appear in early spring. Propagation may be by division or cuttings in late summer.

SAVORY   WINTER—*Satureja montana* (Plate 6)   (= *Satureia*)   [*Labiatae*]
SUMMER—*S.hortensis* (Plate 5)

A native of the Mediterranean region, these useful kitchen herbs generally resemble long-leafed Thymes. *S.montana* is a low shrub, growing 12–18 in. high, with white and pale pinkish flowers in August and September. The foliage has a warm, almost pungent, scent and taste.

According to Mrs. Grieve, the use of Savory dates back into remote ages, the herb because of its pungency being used instead of spices, and it is known that the Romans made a sauce with it in the manner of our mint sauce. Savory was supposed to have connections with the Satyrs, hence *Satureia*. The flowers are most attractive to bees.

Summer Savory is sown outside in a suitable sandy seedbed in April, and used from July onwards, a sprig being put with broad beans when cooking or used in the *bouquet-garni*.

Winter Savory, being a low perennial shrub, is more enduring, and therefore more popular than Summer Savory. It is propagated by cuttings taken in a sandy pan in spring, or division of roots in spring or autumn or, if preferred, by seed sown in a seedpan under glass in April. A light to medium soil is suitable.

Plants can be put towards the front of the herb border 1 ft. apart each way; or in a plantation, 1 ft. by 18 in. or 2 ft. Harvesting takes place in July, before flowering. Savory bushes can be neatly 'bobbed', and the cut material is comparatively easy to dry to a good colour, but not so straightforward to rub through sieves, as the leaves are long, and the stalks sharp. As well as its uses with broad beans, Savory is an important constituent of mixed herbs, and older writers recommended its use in dressing trout. Like other labiates, it is useful also medicinally, having carminative properties. Savory is the *Benekraut* of the Continent. There is a plant in commerce called *S.montana* with deeper pink flowers but almost no scent, therefore valueless for flavouring.

SCULLCAP *Scutellaria lateriflora* (Plate 30) [*Labiatae*]
This Virginian Scullcap has ovate to cordate leaves and one-sided racemes of two-lipped blue flowers, with the 'hall-mark' of the cap-like calyces. It is a hardy perennial, growing some 2 ft. high and flowering in June and July, a decorative plant in a quiet way for the herb garden, for the flowers have character and repay close inspection.

Propagation is by division in spring or by seed; and medium to sandy soil suits this Scullcap (which may also be spelt Skullcap).

Scullcap is an excellent nervine, and may be taken as an infusion, 1 oz. of the dried powdered herb to a pint of boiling water, and half a cupful taken at a time. Scullcap has been reputed of value against hydrophobia.

The English Scullcap, *S.galericulata*, also blue-flowered, grows wild by streams and is an interesting plant to encounter. There is also *S.minor*, frequenting damp spots in woods, and having paler mauve flowers. These Scullcaps share the valuable properties of the Virginian Scullcap. There is an alpine, *S.alpina*.

SELF-HEAL *Prunella vulgaris* (Plate 10) [*Labiatae*]
Prunella is one of those mauve two-lipped wild flowers that are dimly accepted as being part of the wayside scene (or, more personally, an ornament or menace in lawns, depending on the point of view) without being truly recognized. *Prunella* is normally annual or biennial, and the ovate leaves and violet-mauve flowers with bronze bracts in oval heads are attractive. This plant, as the name suggests, was formerly much esteemed for healing wounds. Gerard recommends making a paste or salve by bruising the herb with a knife on a plate, and applying to the wound. Bugle, he considers, has a similarly good effect. Bugle has rich royal-blue two-lipped flowers in terminal spires in spring, and frequents woods, and is an *Ajuga*, *A.reptans*.

SKIMMIA (Plate 16) Sc. S. [*Rutaceae*]
The starry white flowers of *S.japonica* and *S.foremanii* welcome in the spring with a lily-of-the-valley fragrance. They are evergreen shrubs, growing 3–5 ft. high, and happily tolerant of shade. To produce berries, male and female plants of *S.japonica* are needed. *S.foremanii* is normally self-fertile. Propagation is by cuttings.

SHRUBS, AROMATIC—see list on p. 93, and individual entries
Flowering shrubs are taking their true place in the garden, and it is increasingly realized that they bring permanent colour and charm and, an important point, that

many are compact growers, suited to the small site and consorting cheerfully with the lower-growing border plants.

Added to these qualities, there are some pleasantly aromatic shrubs which also lend colour, and are appropriate for the scented garden as well as for ordinary planting.

SKIRRET *Sium sisarum* (Plate 2) [*Umbelliferae*]
This little-known herb has clusters of tuberous roots, formerly cooked and eaten. For good development, they need a soil enriched with compost. Propagation is by division in spring. The basal leaves may be round to ovate and the flowers whitish, in characteristic umbels, on stems some 12–18 in. high. Skirret is a hardy perennial.

SKUNK-CABBAGE *Symplocarpus foetidus* (*Spathyema foetida*) (Plate 14)
Amer. [*Araceae*]
This plant lives up to its popular and specific names. It is usually the first plant to flower in the spring, but a posy would, one thinks, lack the self-effacing charm of the gift of a bunch of snowdrops. The ovate, heart-shaped leaves appear after the intriguing flowers, and are 1–2 ft. or more long. This plant is well known in damp woods, marshes and meadows, and is a relative of the arums. The seeds and root have been used in cases of chronic catarrh, asthma and rheumatism. Large doses have a harmful effect.

SOAPWORT *Saponaria officinalis* (Plate 29) [*Caryophyllaceae*]
Soapwort is a hardy (inordinately hardy) perennial with creeping rhizomes, and the flowering stems, with opposite leaves, grow some 3 ft. high, with pale pink flowers, sometimes double. Soapwort has been called Bouncing Bet and Wild Sweet William. It is propagated by its own territorial claims, but in a suitable site is attractive in the herb garden. This plant has come into valuable prominence as, carefully handled, a solution may be used to clean and restore the original colours to old tapestry without damaging the precious fabric.

SORREL *Rumex acetosa* (Plate 2) [*Polygonaceae*]
The cultivated broad-leafed form of the ordinary wild Sorrel has large, pale, slightly fleshy green leaves with an acid flavour. If allowed to bolt, the flowers produced are in the characteristic reddish spikes. Propagation is by seed sown in drills ¼ in. deep in April and May. A moderately rich soil is suitable. Plants may be thinned out to 8 in. apart in the seedrows or preferably planted out 8 in. apart in June in damp weather in crowbar holes filled with compost. This encourages quick, lush growth. The foliage is used in salads, sparingly; and made into Sorrel

soup. Some cooks wrap a rather tough joint of meat in Sorrel leaves tied securely round before boiling, and the acidity given off helps to make the meat tender while cooking.

French Sorrel, *R.scutatus* (Plate 4), has smaller, often grey-green shield-like leaves on a partly-trailing stem. This is used for cooking in the same way as the above.

Wood Sorrel, *Oxalis acetosella* (*Oxalidaceae*), with trefoil leaves and fragile, pale mauve flowers, may be used in salads.

SPIKENARD, AMERICAN *Aralia racemosa* (Plate 32) [*Araliaceae*]

This reasonably hardy perennial has creeping rootstocks, from which arise 3–6 ft. high stems bearing pinnate leaves, small greenish flowers in numerous clusters, and dark purplish berries, in September. There is little scent to the foliage, but the rootstock exudes a gummy substance, and is aromatic. Medicinally, this plant has been used for pulmonary affections.

The American Sarsaparilla is another *Aralia*, and is also used for pulmonary troubles.

In the herb garden, American Spikenard is decorative for its fine foliage, and will flourish in a semi-shaded spot.

SPURGES *Euphorbia sp.* (Plate 12) [*Euphorbiaceae*]

Some Spurges are found as wild plants in this country, *E.amygdaloides* being one of the most familiar, as it often frequents bluebell woods, and opens its pale yellow-green flower-clusters at the same time. *Euphorbia polychroma*, a cultivated Spurge, is most decorative for May-flowering, with striking yellow bracts surrounding the small flowers. It is a hardy perennial growing 18 in. to 2 ft. high.

The Spurges contain an acrid milky juice that can act internally as an irritant poison. Applied externally, the juice has been used to remove warts.

Euphorbia lathyrus, the Caper-Spurge, is described on page 110.

STAPHYLEA COLCHICA Sc. S. [*Staphylaceae*]

This is a hardy shrub, enjoying a semi-shaded site and well-drained deep soil. The white flowers have a scent of oiled leather, odd and intriguing. Propagation is by cuttings or layering.

SWEETBRIAR, EGLANTINE *Rosa rubiginosa* (*R.eglanteria*) (Plate 15)
Ar. S. [*Rosaceae*]

One of the most exquisite and elusive scents comes from the Sweetbriar shoots, pervading the garden on a warm April day after rain. The spicy fruit fragrance, sweet yet subtle, is exhaled to add individual pleasure to the promise of a summer morning.

The type has pale pink single, five-petalled flowers and leaf-stalks, the receptacle and calyx are reddish pin-headed hairs containing the fragrant essential oil.

The type, crossed with the Austrian Copper Briar and others, has given the Penzance Briars, and of these, a hedge of Lady Penzance as at Denman College, is a glowing sight. The flowers are a blend of apricot, flame and copper-rose. Other Penzance briars are pink, cream and red, and all of them carry the characteristic fragrance, and are of great garden value.

A Sweetbriar hedge may be planted according to taste and kept either naturally or clipped back, when flowering will still be reasonably profuse, for the blossoms are carried on shoots arising from the older wood.

For a free-growing effect Sweetbriars can be planted 5–6 ft. apart. They can be trained on wires for more formal effect. Alternatively, to make a close, thick-set hedge, 2 ft. apart would be a suitable distance.

Propagation is by half-ripe cuttings from shoots that have flowered in August, or by layers. In soils that will grow rose bushes Sweetbriars should flourish, but a light soil suits them well, suitably prepared with garden compost before planting, incorporated in large planting-holes.

Sweetbriar flowers and foliage, when dried, will blend in pot-pourris.

Rosa primula has dainty foliage, with numerous leaflets, with a pleasantly aromatic scent, and single yellow flowers (Plate 15).

SWEET CICELY *Myrrhis odorata* (Plate 21) [*Umbelliferae*]

This herb has an engaging name and is one of the most attractive members of the *Umbelliferae*, having very large, soft-textured and lacy foliage, described by Parkinson as 'divers faire and great winged leaves'. They have a characteristic whitish flecking, and a distinctly anise scent. Sweet Cicely has white umbels of flowers in May, followed by very large black seeds. This plant is a hardy perennial, with a thick taproot, found on occasion wild in woods, and in the herb garden, appreciating a shady but sheltered dampish spot. Propagation is by root-division in early spring, or seed sown in early spring outside in a cool seedbed.

The roots used to be boiled as a vegetable and roots and leaves put into salads, for the quiet aniseed flavour.

SWEET FLAG *Acorus calamus* (Plate 31) [*Araceae*]

All parts of this plant (also called Sweet Rush and sometimes *Calamus aromaticus*) have a delicious cinnamon-like scent. It is found wild in various parts, including

East Anglia, and grows in ditches, the margins of lakes and marshy places. It is said to have been employed as a strewing-herb. The Sweet Flag has been used for many purposes, including the flavouring of wines and spirits, to scent French snuff and, medicinally, in cases of dyspepsia and headaches coming from the same cause.

TANSY *Tanacetum vulgare* (= *Chrysanthemum vulgare*) (Plate 9) [*Compositae*]
A well-known hardy perennial plant of water-brinks and waysides, with pinnate green leaves with a slightly oily aromatic scent, and yellow button flowers. On account of these Tansy is frequently confused with the shrub *Santolina* (Cotton Lavender), but the foliage of the latter is encrusted like coral, and grey, and it grows 3 ft. high at most, while Tansy grows to some 3–5 ft.

Tansy was formerly much used as a flavouring herb. Dried and powdered, a very small pinch can be added to mint, sultana and brown sugar pasties to give a special tang.

Tansy cakes used to be eaten after Lent, to purge the 'bad-humours' of the body after the restricted diet and the winter.

Tansy will grow happily under most garden conditions, and as it is an invasive herb, with extending underground rootstocks, it needs a fair space in which to grow. Propagation is by division in autumn or spring.

Tansy puddings were elaborate affairs, using eggs, cream, tansy juice, white wine, and biscuit.

Tansy has been employed medicinally against fevers, taken as Tansy tea; and for nervous affections.

TARRAGON *Artemisia dracunculus* (True French) (Plate 6) [*Compositae*]
A. dracunculoides (Russian)
French: *Estragon*

This herb, singularly enough, is an *Artemisia*, a close relative of the Southernwood and Wormwood. The name is a household word in connection with Tarragon vinegar, but the plant is often unrecognized when it is seen growing. True Tarragon is a native of South Europe.

The true French Tarragon flavour is both warmly aromatic and slightly biting, with taste compounded of anise, balsam and a hint of pepper. There are various graduations in flavour between the true French Tarragon flavour and the much less pungent and distinctive taste of the all-too-common Russian kind. Frequently, after some years, a French strain appears to deteriorate to nearer the other type. In some cases it may be due to self-sown seedlings arising, but in practical experience, French and Russian do not act as though they were two distinct species.

In appearance, true French Tarragon is a stockier plant than the Russian, growing some 2–3 ft. high, with more glossy, deeper green leaves. Russian Tarragon, which may grow 3–5 ft. high, has rather pale green willowy leaves.

To thrive and produce the richest flavour, Tarragon needs a really sunny position, ideally sheltered from cold winds, and a well-drained soil to which compost has been liberally added. Tarragon is a hardy perennial under the right conditions, but the brittle, fleshy rootstocks will rot in damp winter situations.

Propagation is by division, preferably when the new shoots are showing, in May, and pieces with root and a shoot are severed with a sharp knife. Commercially, divisions would be planted 1 ft. to 18 in. apart in the rows and 2 ft. between the rows.

Harvesting takes place before the small, greenish flowers appear in late July and August, and there is often a smaller second cut in September. Tarragon is not hard to dry, a steady moderate temperature of 70–80°F. being sufficient to keep the colour and flavour unimpaired if the herb is spread out reasonably thinly.

To make Tarragon vinegar, fresh Tarragon leaves, picked when very dry or slightly dried before use, are put, after stripping them from their stalks, into wide-mouthed glass bottles, and covered with white wine vinegar. After leaving for some days, the flavoured vinegar is strained off and corked down in suitable bottles.

Tarragon is an ingredient in chicken stuffings and many other dishes and is one of the herbs most featured in continental recipes.

In France, mustard is often mixed with Tarragon vinegar, which is also the proper flavouring for Sauce Tartare.

'TEA PLANT' *Lycium barbarum* (= *L.halimifolium*) (Plate 29) [*Solanaceae*]
This plant is one of those referred to (if observed at all) as 'Oh, that . . . er . . . thing', for it is naturalized in places in England and Wales, occurring on railway cuttings and in roadside hedges. The small mauve and cream flowers appear sparsely on the woody stems which bear long, narrow leaves, and decorative orange fruits are borne later, in September. *Lycium* is a relative of the Nightshades. It is closely allied to *S.chinense* and sometimes called the Duke of Argyll's Tea Tree.

TEUCRIUM FRUTICANS (Plate 15)   Ar. S.   [*Labiatae*]
This shrub (abbreviated in nursery-garden parlance on occasion to Tutti-Frutti) has pleasingly silver-grey leaves and stems. The foliage has a scent reminiscent of cod-liver oil and malt but with a *je ne sais quoi* that redeems the association and

PLATE 29 VARIOUS PLANTS
1. Lesser Periwinkle. (*Vinca minor*)
2. Duke of Argyll's Tea-Plant. (*Lycium halimifolium*)
3. *Borago laxiflora.*
4. Greater Periwinkle. (*Vinca major*)
5. Variegated Periwinkle. (*Vinca major var.*)
6. Jewelweed. (*Impatiens fulva*)
7. Soapwort. (*Saponaria officinalis*)
8. Woodruff. (*Asperula odorata*)
9. Small Yellow Balsam. (*Impatiens parviflora*)
10. Dane's Elder. (*Sambucus ebulus*)

PLATE 30 VARIOUS PLANTS
1. Bugloss. (*Lycopsis arvensis*)
2. Viper's Bugloss. (*Echium vulgare*)
3. *Arnica montana*.
4. *Plumbago capensis*.
5. Scullcap. (*Scutellaria lateriflora*)
6. Yellow Gentian. (*Gentiana lutea*)
7. Juniper. (*Juniperus communis*) A. male. B. female.
8. Butterfly-Weed. (*Asclepias tuberosa*)
9. Jacob's Ladder. (*Polemonium caeruleum*)

PLATE 31 VARIOUS PLANTS
1. Insect Powder Plant. (*Tanacetum cinerarifolium*)
2. *Nicandra physaloides.*
3. Turkish Tobacco. (*Nicotiana rustica*)
4. Calamint. (*Calamintha officinalis*)
5. Caper-Spurge. (*Euphorbia lathyris*)
6. Sweet Flag. (*Acorus calamus*)
7. *Lobelia syphilitica.*
8. Musk. (*Mimulus moschatus*)
9. Woad. (*Isatis tinctoria*)

PLATE 32 VARIOUS PLANTS
1. Indian Basil. (*Ocimum gratissimum*)
2. *Solanum sisymbrifolium.*
3. *Salpichroa rhomboides.*
4. *Molucella laevis.*
5. Dwarf Pomegranate. (*Punica granatum nanum*)
6. American Spikenard. (*Aralia racemosa*)
7. True Saffron. (*Crocus sativus*)
8. *Sideritis hyssopifolius.*
9. *Artemisia rupestris.*

makes the aroma thoroughly enjoyable. The flowers are like those of a Rosemary on a large scale, dashingly curved and soft-lavender-blue in colour. This shrub flourishes in the south-west, either to train up a south-facing wall or ramble at the foot, and will grow outside in similar situations nearer London if really favoured. *Teucrium* makes a good pot-plant for the cool greenhouse or conservatory, obliging with its cool flowers from April to June under glass. Propagation is by cuttings in spring or autumn, and pruning after flowering consists in shortening back some shoots that have flowered to encourage new growth where required.

THISTLES (Plate 10) [*Compositae*]
    Silybum marianum (Our Lady's Milk Thistle)
    Cricus benedictus, Carduus benedictus (Holy or Blessed Thistle)
These two Thistles are sometimes confused, as Our Lady's Milk Thistle is also on occasion called Holy Thistle.

The true Holy Thistle has papery involucral bracts, armed with painful spines, and yellow composite flowers tinged with purple. It is an annual, some 2 ft. high, grown from seed sown outside in April, the whole herb being collected in July, just when flowering begins, and dried. The infusion of the dried herb at the usual rate, 1 oz. to 1 pint of boiling water, in wineglassful doses, is esteemed to relieve fevers.

Silybum marianum (*Carduus marianus*) has white spotted foliage and purple thistle-flowers. This thistle is a hardy annual, growing 4 ft. high, and propagated by seed. Gerard considered the plant excellent against melancholy diseases, and it has had many other uses.

THORNAPPLE   *Datura stramonium* (Plate 11) [*Solanaceae*]
This plant, occasionally found naturalized in waste places, has a curiously foreign appearance, with stiff side-stems radiating out, rather carelessly toothed leaves, and twisted white convolvulus-like flowers, followed by the thorned capsules, the size of a small apple, which split to reveal large black chiselled seeds.

Thornapple is an annual, when self-sown germinating late, in May or June, as the soil gets warmer, and reaching the flowering stage in August and September. Thornapple grows some 2–3½ ft. high. Various exotic decorative Daturas are grown as shrubs and small trees some 6–7 ft. or more in height, and may be seen amongst other places in the Scilly Isles. Their pendulous trumpet-flowers are distinctive. *D.suaveolens* is one normally grown under glass.

Many myths surround Thornapple, and it was formerly thought to be fatal to sleep under its shade. The plants give off a rather foetid aroma and one could easily imagine this to have narcotic properties on the air, particularly if the scent from the flowers is inhaled for too long.

This plant has had, owing to its narcotic properties, diverse uses, through the centuries, especially in the East, where it is believed that the priests of Apollo at Delphi valued the plant, and used the leaves to give inspiration for their prophecies. In India, the Thugs and other nefarious people used various Daturas to stupefy their victims.

The seeds are the most potent part of the plant and are official in some pharmacopoeias, but the dried leaves are chiefly used. The leaves are smoked alone, or mixed with belladonna, sage and other herbs. Or the leaves are blended into a special igniting mixture from which the beneficial smoke is inhaled to relieve asthma.

If there should be a demand for the leaves, Thornapple can be sown in the open in spring, and the plants cut with a hook when mature, about August, and the leaves dried.

THYMES *Thymus sp*. (Plates 5, 6, 27) [*Labiatae*]

The Thymes form a closely-linked genus with strong family resemblances between the different species. They are low or even (*Thymus serpyllum*) prostrate shrublets with evergreen or evergrey foliage. Common Thyme (*T.vulgaris*) and Lemon Thyme (*T.citriodorus*) provide two of the most-used and popular culinary flavours after Mint, Parsley, Sage and perhaps Chives.

The Greek name for Thyme is said to be derived from a word meaning 'to fumigate', from its uses as incense and as a sweet-smelling herb. It has also been considered to have invigorating properties, promoting courage, and vitality, and has been taken as the symbol of these qualities. Thymes are beloved by bees, and honey from nectar in which Thyme predominates has a characteristically aromatic flavour. There is Kipling's lovely description in his poem *Sussex* of Wild Thyme smelling 'like dawn in Paradise'.

A sprig of Common Thyme is a usual ingredient in the *bouquet-garni* for flavouring. Lemon Thyme can be substituted for a change. Common Thyme, dried and rubbed, is potent in flavour, and while it is excellent added in very small amounts to meat dishes, care should be taken that it does not mask the true taste of the meat, but enhance it in the background. Dried Thyme is a frequent ingredient in potted meat pastes and similar preparations.

Lemon Thyme has a refreshing, fruity flavour, less pungent than Common Thyme, and is a welcome and safe ingredient in all stuffings to go with veal and poultry, and forcemeat used with baked fish. A fresh sprig, with a sprig of Fennel, is excellent with white fish boiled in milk with butter. Finely chopped fresh Lemon Thyme is also good on salads and in herb butter.

Common Thyme is distilled on the Continent to give the Oil of Thyme which contains, amongst other phenols, Thymol, a mild but effective antiseptic, used in gargles, for nasal catarrh and wound disinfection.

Propagation of Garden Thymes

This is usually done by cuttings during spring and summer, put in pans under glass; or by division and planting-out small rooted offsets, particularly for the creeping kinds, in spring or autumn, depending on the conditions, favourable or otherwise, of the garden.

General Cultivation of Garden Thymes

Thymes like sunny sheltered sites and abhor whistling and piercing winds, especially in March and April, after cold weather. Unfortunately, a moist summer and autumn may on a cold damp soil cause lush growth, more liable to frost damage. Therefore a well-drained soil to which compost has been added but which is not too rich is best. On very rich soils, the Golden Thymes particularly tend to lose their variegation and look green.

The prostrate and creeping Thymes lend charm to the rock-garden bank, for cascading over dry walls, and making informal carpets to edge paths, and the shrubby Thymes flower in the rock-garden at a welcome time, after the first blaze of colour is over.

Thyme paths and lawns are an interesting feature. For a path that has continual treading it is good to sink paving-stones (such as Noelite) about half an inch below the surface, to take the main pressure, and plant Thymes between and at the sides.

Thyme lawns (as at Sissinghurst) have distinction, and require little in the way of mowing. It is a counsel of perfection to hold that, without weeding, Thyme will win completely, but any rosette weeds can be removed and fine grasses will help to knit the surface. Preparation should be thorough, with digging, and the incorporation of compost, and a good dressing of lime; also on heavy soils, grit and sand. Rooted pieces put in from 6 in. to 1 ft. apart (depending on how patience and economics resolve the question) in spring or early autumn while the soil is still warm should (at 6 in.) meet by July or so.

Any or, rather pleasantly, a blend of *T.serpyllum* varieties listed can be used for such a lawn, and to make a complete scented lawn, areas can be devoted to Chamomile and Pennyroyal. Irregular drifts of half a dozen or more each of contrasting kinds, crimson, pink, white and mauve, can be planted.

T. vulgaris (Plate 6), Common or Black Thyme, is a native of Mediterranean countries. There is an English broad-leafed green form (9–12 in. high) and French Thyme (12–18 in. high), which when grown from seed produces progeny with foliage ranging from narrow and grey to deep green and moderately broad; the flowers showing a similar range from very pale mauve-pink to quite a rich colour, with deeper bracts, with small two-lipped flowers in the characteristic rounded heads. French Thyme usually flowers from mid-May to June, the English broad-leaf later, in July.

Seed of the French type is minute. It may be sown $\frac{1}{10}$ in. deep and 8 in. apart in watered drills in a sandy seedbed in April–May or in seedboxes, just lightly covering the seed with soil. The seedboxes or pans are put into a frame or greenhouse, where it is easier to control conditions for germination. Seedlings are pricked out and may be planted out in suitable weather, 1 ft. apart and 2 ft. between the rows, for cropping in June and July. Distance, however, depends on the length of time the plantation is to be kept, and facilities available for mechanical cultivation. Beds may be left two to three years, after which production is apt to fall off.

For an economic crop when market conditions are suitable, a reasonably rich but well-drained soil, light in texture but plenty of organic matter, is necessary. Thymes need full sun to develop a good flavour.

Broad-leaf English Thyme and Lemon Thyme are propagated not by seed but by division of plants in autumn or spring, or by cuttings taken in sandy prepared beds outside or in pans under glass during summer and autumn. Cuttings may be 2–5 in. long, depending on available material, and an application of rooting powder is helpful. When well rooted, the cuttings may be planted out as outlined for French Common Thyme.

Harvesting takes place before flowering and therefore proceeds in succession from May till late August. Later crops may be difficult to cut if a dry summer has brought little new growth after the first cut. An application of a nitrogenous fertilizer such as nitrate of soda in showery weather after the first cut, at 2 oz. per sq. yd., can be useful, but must be kept well away from the spreading foliage of the plants or damage will occur.

T. citriodorus (Plate 5), the Lemon Thyme, has rich green foliage and grows some 9–14 in. high. There are at least two forms, one with broad dark-green foliage, excellent for carpet work in knot-gardening; the other form with slightly smaller leaves, of mid-green colour. Both have the delightful lemon scent and flavour. Confusion often arises when people expect Lemon Thyme to be yellow or golden in foliage. There is a Golden Lemon Thyme as described in due course, but the true commercial Lemon Thyme has the green foliage.

Thymes are the easiest of the culinary crops to dry, being spriggy and containing comparatively little moisture. The crop should be spread out as thinly as drying capacity allows. In five days or so the stems will snap, showing that it is ready for sifting. This, done in hand-sieves, can be more laborious than with many herbs, as the stems are brittle and, once they are broken, small, it is hard to separate them from the leaves. Care should be taken to rub lightly to keep them as intact as possible. As Thyme grows close to the ground there may be grit, washed up on to the foliage in wet weather. At some stage this should be shaken out by placing the rubbed Thyme in a suspended hessian tray, and moving it over the tray surface till the grit is worked through the mesh of the hessian; or by shaking in a hair-sieve.

T.albus compactus has very narrow, linear leaves, close, spriggy growth, forming a shrublet some 6 in. high, with a strong aroma, white flowers and hardiness to most winter conditions. It is therefore desirable for the Thyme collection.

T.caespitius.—This Thyme has compact cushion-growth, some 2 in. high, with awl-shaped leaves closely set in the manner of pine-needles on a terminal twig, and with a scent reminiscent of pines with a dash of orange. The flowers are pale purple. Propagation is by rooted offsets or cuttings.

T.citriodorus aureus.—Golden Lemon Thyme. This Thyme forms an erect small bush some 6–8 in. high, with green leaves dappled pleasingly with gold, most apparent in winter and early spring, when the terminal buds are usually orange-bronze when closely inspected. Since such detailed appreciation palls in a stabbing north-east breeze, it is recommended to have at least one plant under glass. The scent is delightful, and of course the plant can be enjoyed during spring and summer in the herb border or rock-garden, and will give mauve-pink flowers in late June and July. This kind is rather liable to revert to a green form. Sometimes differentiated as *T.aureus citriodorus*, there is another lemon-scented form of compacter growth and resembling ordinary Golden Thyme (*T.vulg.* Aureus), except that it has the fruit scent. The golden colour is suffused through the foliage, and growth is some 3–6 in., flowers being purplish, in July.

T.citriodorus, Silver Queen. Great confusion occurs between this plant and *T.vulgaris* Silver Posie, and the only way for the connoisseur to be sure of getting the real lemon-scented kind is by personal choice. The degree of variegation in Silver Queen varies considerably from a very fine cream-marbled kind to a dull silver, and reversion tendencies are noticeable. But Silver Queen is a most desirable kind, charming in winter when the terminal leaf-buds turn rose-pink. As with *T.cit.* Aureus, it is wise to grow a plant under glass, though it will grow reasonably outside in a favourable spot.

T.doerfleri is a prostrate Thyme with woolly grey foliage, some long and narrow, and flowers early, having pink-purple flowers.

T.erectus (*T.carnosus*) has distinctive growth, like a slow-growing miniature Irish yew, valuable for sink garden design, and the rock-garden. The scent is camphoraceous and strong. Foliage is narrow, and green-grey, and the terminal heads of flowers are white, and open in summer. Propagation is by cuttings.

T.ericaefolius grows 6 in. high and has heath-like, golden-green leaves and pale flowers. It is not very robust in our less restrained winters.

T.fragrantissimus is one of the gems. It is sometimes considered to be a differently fragrant form of *T.vulgaris*, and in plunge-beds hybrid seedlings or forms arise. In some cases these have a stronger constitution than the type, and provided the characteristic scent (sometimes evanescent and less perceptible under weather or seasonal conditions) is present, seedlings are valuable. The scent is a delicious blend of balsam and oranges. The foliage is small, spoon-shaped, narrow towards the tip, and there are both upright and laxer forms of growth. A sprig may be used to give variety in a stew or ragout and the foliage dried is good in pot-pourri. *T.fragrantissimus* gives constant pleasure in an accessible spot in the herb garden or rock-garden, where the leaves can be rubbed and the scent enjoyed; or as a pot-plant under glass, flowering from spring onwards; or, outside, in June and July.

T.herba-barona is another intriguing Thyme. The name indicates that the leaves were at one time rubbed on the baron of beef, to impart the distinctive caraway flavour. The scent is a strange and evocative blend of caraway, polish, and Christmas of three decades ago, perhaps in the combination of varnished toys, ginger and Christmas fir-trees.

The growth is semi-prostrate, with sprays fanning out and arching 1 in. from the ground, and rooting energetically at the tips. The leaves are small and shining green and the flowers, in June and July, fairly deep rose-purple. Apart from culinary ventures with the roast joint, *T.herba-barona* is pleasing for the rock-garden, the front of a herb bed to form a carpet, crannies in paving and as a pot-plant for the cool greenhouse. It is a reasonably hardy Thyme, coming from Corsica.

T.hyemalis is a worthy Thyme from Spain, for as its name suggests it has to do with winter, and is one of the hardiest and greenest during the taxing and grim months for vegetation and mankind. The leaves have a scent rather like Common Thyme, warm and suggestive of aromatic oil, and could be used in cooking in the same way. Growth is somewhat straggling, some 6 in. high, and flowers rather sparsely produced.

T.mastachinus.—The type is upright, with greyish foliage, with a slightly camphoraceous scent. The interesting kind is R. Armstrong's form, with a more trailing habit, and the grey, slightly hairy foliage has a refreshing scent of lavender. Again, hybrids and intermediate forms occur, but this is an unusual plant for the rock-garden and front of the herb border, or crevices in paving. The mauve-pink flowers come in June. *T.mastachinus* is enjoyable in the cool greenhouse.

T.membranaceus is a distinguished Thyme for the whitish, tissue-paper-like bracts and long tubular white flowers that surmount the shrublet rather unexpectedly in July and August. The leaves are very small, grey-green and with a pungent Common Thyme aroma, and the plant grows some 9 in. high. It does, however, react unhappily to our English winters and is best helped to surmount the dim days by growing as a pot-plant indoors from October till May, and plunging outside for the summer; or keeping in a frame.

T.nitidus.—For many years the plant widely described and sold under this name has been one with narrow grey-green foliage, forming a shrublet up to 1 ft. high, closely resembling the grey form of French Thyme, and flowering generously in May and June.

W. Ingwersen of Gravetye distributes the type considered to be the true one with wider green foliage, a laxer form of growth and mauve flowers.

Both these Thymes are useful for the rock-garden or herb border.

T.odoratissimus has rather longish leaves in green-grey for a Thyme, with prostrate stems, not compact as in *T.serpyllum*, but tending to arch. The rather large very pale mauve flowers open early, in May. The scent varies with the forms and intermediates, but the pleasantest is of a fruity blend, with the characteristic Thyme aroma underneath. *T.adamovitschii* is rather similar.

T.serpyllum, our native Wild Thyme, brings the distinctive atmosphere of Ruskin's 'Thymy slopes of Down overlooked by the blue line of lifted sea'. The fragrant carpet intermingles naturally with fine-bladed grasses, with the blue and pink of Milkwort, the yellow stars of *Helianthemum* and the delicate Eyebright.

There are numerous varieties of *T.serpyllum* in cultivation, and the nomenclature can be botanically confusing.

The scents in the coloured varieties vary considerably in strength.

T.serp.albus and Snowdrift have very small, close, bright-green foliage, and white flower-heads in June and July. Growth is reasonably fast.

T.Annie Hall has moderately bright green smooth foliage and pale flesh-pink flowers.

T.serp.citriodorus has small close mid-green foliage, a good lemon scent and mauve-pink flowers.

T.serp. Coccineus is one of the best for the rich crimson, purple-spotted flowers over very small, rather bronze-green foliage, blooming in June and July. There is not much scent.

T.serp. Coccineus Major has larger, rounded leaves with a pleasing lemon scent and crimson flowers. This is a very hardy form.

T.comosus hirsutus lives up to its names, for it is hairy with rather large leaves for a creeping form, and a strong habit of growth.

T.serp.lanuginosus is well-known for making sheets or cushions of woolly grey foliage, gemmed with pale mauve flowers in July.

T. Lemon Curd is a valuable kind with moderate-sized leaves with a really fine fruit scent and mauve flowers.

T.serp. Minus is, next to *Mentha requienii*, the smallest and closest-growing of the aromatic plants in this book, with small mauve flowers in July.

T.s. Nosegay has very small narrow leaves, with a really delightful fragrance as the name suggests. The flowers are mauve-pink.

T.s. Pink Chintz has grey-green somewhat hairy foliage and pale pink flowers.

T.s.roseus has pink flowers.

T.s. Russettings has greyish foliage and rose pink flowers with a rather russet overall effect.

T.vulgaris Golden. This is a good-tempered hardy and decorative variety, with yellow-gold foliage, most conspicuous in winter, forming large clumps, 6 in. or so high, and rose-purple flowers in July. The scent is warm and slightly balsamic. This Golden Thyme is excellent for edgings and carpet work.

T.vulgaris Silver Posie. This kind is often confused with Silver Queen. Silver Posie, however, has the ordinary warm Thyme scent, with silver variegated leaves. It tends to be hardier than *T.cit.* Silver Queen, and grows some 8–10 in. high, with delicate mauve flowers in June and July. It is most useful for edgings to beds, in the rock-garden, and for contrast in the herb garden.

T.zygis from Spain and Portugal has a distinctive fan-like growth, some 6 in. high, small rather gold-green leaves and pale flowers late in the season.

TOBACCO   *Nicotiana tabacum*   [*Solanaceae*]
   T. TURKISH   *N.rustica* (Plate 31)

Ordinary Tobacco is well known, having large ovate, lanceolate green leaves, slightly viscid and narcotic in aroma, and growing some 3–6 ft. high. *N.rustica*, possibly the first kind to be used for smoking in Europe, has small yellow flowers, interesting as they closely resemble *Atropa*, a close relative in the *Solanaceae* family. Tobaccos are half-hardy annuals grown from seed.

When tobacco was introduced into England by Sir Walter Raleigh in 1586, considerable controversy raged over its use, and it was condemned by various Popes. Three hundred years later it was to become official in the British Pharmacopoeia. Today it is officially regarded as a health hazard.

Gerard (*c.*1597) improves the occasion delightfully with his salty humour and sense of values. 'The priest and Inchanters of the hot countries do take the fume thereof until they be drunke, that after they have lien for dead three or foure houres, they may tell the people what wonders, visions or illusions they have seen, and so give them a prophetical direction or foretelling (if we may trust the Divell) of the successe of their businesse.'

He says that tobacco 'is taken of some physically in a pipe once a day at most and that in the morning fasting, against paines in the head, stomack and griefe in the brest and lungs; against catarrs and rheums and such as have gotten cold and hoarsenesse'. He recommends Tobacco foliage to make a balm to cure deep wounds and against toothache.

Nicotine extract is used in horticulture as an insecticide.

ULEX EUROPAEUS   Gorse   Sc. S.   [*Leguminosae*]

The Gorse or Furze is not always considered as a flowering shrub, but the delicate almond scent is reminiscent of cliffs, commons and downland. The main flowering season is March to June, but there are often golden tokens in other months, particularly during the winter. The double-flowered form is sometimes used as a hedging plant. Propagation may be by cuttings.

VALERIAN   *Valeriana officinalis* (Plate 22)   [*Valerianaceae*]

The delightful so-called Valerian, with rounded heads of small carmine, pink or white flowers, often adorned with tortoiseshell butterflies, which beautifies the cliffs of seaside resorts, festoons chalk railway cuttings, and leans over countless walls in the West Country, is not the true medicinal Valerian, but *Centranthus ruber* (Plate 22).

The true Valerian is a less gay plant with ash-like foliage and flat heads of pale flesh-pink flowers with a sweetish smell. The rhizomes are much divided, and have an aroma earning the plant the name of 'Phu'. Nard, an Eastern perfume, came from a species of Valerian, with a sweeter scent.

The medicinal Valerian is a hardy perennial, found wild in swampy places, and grows 3–4 ft. high.

In times of emergency Valerian is a useful crop. To get rhizomes of economic size, a moist but not waterlogged soil, with plenty of compost or well-decayed manure added, is good. The rhizomes are planted riding a slight ridge made in a furrow with the roots hanging on each side, the pieces being 8 in. apart and the rows 18 in. to 2 ft. The roots can be dug one or two years after planting, depending on the growth made, which can be judged by leaf-size.

Valerian rhizomes are dug in late autumn, and washed either under a jet of a strong hose or, first, immersed in wire-netting baskets in a tank until they can be rinsed clean with the hose.

Valerian needs a reasonable temperature for effective drying, special slow ovens with a steady heat of 90–100°F. being suitable.

The scent of the dried rhizomes is terrific. From them an excellent nervine is produced, used to quiet nervous unrest, induce sleep and help those suffering from overstrain.

VERBENA, LEMON *Lippia citriodora* (= *Aloysia cit.*) (Plate 5) [*Verbenaceae*]
This aromatic shrub is one of the pleasantest and most popular of all scented plants. It is, however, often confused with Lemon Balm, but has a richer scent and, of course, is very different when examined. The leaves are long, pointed and crinkled, and the small mauve flowers are in scattered spikes. The height can reach 6–8 ft.

Lemon Verbena can be grown against a south wall in a sheltered sunny garden in the Home Counties, but flourishes in the south-west. The soil needs to be light, warm and well drained. Winter protection such as bracken or sacking over the shoots and over the ground around the roots is helpful, provided it is not overdone so that the whole affair becomes sodden and decay sets in during cold, damp weather.

If outdoor cultivations is unsuccessful, Lemon Verbena can be grown in tubs which can be stood outside for the summer and moved under glass for the winter; or in large pots which can be plunged in a garden bed for the summer and brought in at the end of September.

Propagation is by new young shoots taken as cuttings, some 3–5 in. long, during summer. Pruning is best done in spring. The Lemon Verbena is deciduous, to many people's dismay, and looks excessively dead till March or April, when minute knobs of green buds arise and grow into fresh shoots. Shortening of shoots back to new growth and the removal of weak wood and crossing branches may be carried out in early spring.

Lemon Verbena leaves may be harvested in July to September, or whenever they are mature, and they dry well to retain their inimitable scent and flavour. If warmed up till crisp, they can easily be rubbed down to a fine powder and used for culinary purposes, to give a lemon flavour wherever required, in veal and poultry forcemeat, to stuff fish and in fish cakes, with parsley.

Lemon Verbena is also valuable in pot-pourri and, instead of lavender, for a change, in sachets. The scent is brought out by crushing the leaves in the sachets occasionally.

VERONICA CUPRESSOIDES (now HEBE CUPRESSOIDES) (Plate 22)
[*Scrophulariaceae*]

This shrub has cypress-like foliage and a similar habit, growing some 4–5 ft. high and enjoying a sheltered sunny spot. The minute speedwell-shaped flowers are palest mauve, in July. The whole shrub, which is increased by cuttings, has an aromatic, warm scent. It is attractive as a specimen shrub.

V.salicifolia has long leaves and spikes of pale mauve sweetly fragrant flowers, borne in summer, also in autumn and occasionally in winter also. It is a most hardy shrub, propagated by cuttings.

VERVAIN *Verbena officinalis* (Plate 10) [*Verbenaceae*]

This perennial is found on downland and by waysides, but although in former days it has been considered of great symbolic and mystic importance, few would take an interest in the plant seen growing naturally. Vervain grows some 18 in. high, and the very small pale mauve flowers open in turn up a slender spike, over lobed leaves. There is no particular aroma to the plant. Propagation is by seed sown in spring outside, or self-sown seedlings usually materialize.

Vervain was much esteemed to keep evil powers at bay. The English name is an adaptation of *herba veneris*, the herb dedicated to Venus. The herb was closely connected with altar worship and ceremonies in Roman times, and worn as a chaplet by heralds announcing war or peace.

Medicinally, probably in consequence of its symbolic usages, Vervain was considered efficacious to cure numerous ills, such as eye troubles, gout and jaundice. Vervain has, however, almost entirely fallen into disuse in modern times; though it is stated to be helpful in dispelling fevers; and the infusion good for inflamed eyes.

VIBURNUM (Plate 18)   Sc. S.   [*Caprifoliaceae*]

While some members of this genus are grown mainly for their appearance, it also comprises some of the finest scented shrubs. *V.burkwoodii* and *V.carlesii* have pink buds and white flowers with a hint of pink, in clusters with a far-flung spicy perfume in April and May. *V.carlecephalum* has large trusses of scented flowers in

May, and is a vigorous grower. *V.farreri* (*V.fragrans*) delights the autumn with perfumed pale pink flower-clusters as the leaves fall, and enjoys a sheltered corner. *V.bodnantense* also has fragrant pale pink flowers in winter, and is a robust grower. Propagation may be by cuttings or layering, and the bushes can be thinned out if necessary after flowering.

VIPER'S BUGLOSS *Echium vulgare* (Plate 30) [*Boraginaceae*]

An attractive plant, with the family characteristic of pink buds that open into blue flowers, it is found on downs and sandy waste places. According to the Doctrine of Signatures, as the stems are mottled like a snake's skin, this herb was considered a good remedy for snake-bite. An infusion has been used to alleviate headaches and fevers.

BUGLOSS *Lycopsis arvensis* (Plate 30)

Is found as a weed of cultivation, and is a more prostrate plant than the Viper's Bugloss, with much smaller flowers.

WALL GERMANDER *Teucrium chamaedrys* (Plate 7) [*Labiatae*]

This herb is a low-growing shrub some 12 in. high, spreading by creeping rootstocks. The smallish leaves are ovate and slightly toothed, of tough texture and deep green. The flowers are two-lipped, reddish-purple and open in July and August. In the herb garden, they associate well with blue herbs such as Hyssop. Wall Germander is occasionally found naturalized near old ruins. This plant has been used from early days medicinally and was famous as a cure for gout; also for coughs and asthmatic troubles.

Wood Sage (Plate 22) is sometimes called Sage-leaved Germander, and is a close relative—*Teucrium scorodonia*. It is one of those wild British plants frequenting every lane, as accepted as grass, cows and sunshine, and when the name is mentioned, being greeted invariably with 'So *that's* it!' It has sage-like foliage and spikes of green two-lipped flowers. It has been used as a hops substitute; and in country medicines to help in colds and fevers, also in chronic rheumatism, usually taken as an infusion of 1 oz. to 1 pint of boiling water taken in wineglassful doses.

T.marum, a small shrub with pungently aromatic, silvery leaves, is sometimes called Cat-Thyme, and said to be attractive to cats, but my gingers are unmoved by it.

WINTERGREEN *Gaultheria procumbens* (Plate 16) Ar. S. [*Ericaceae*]

This low shrub is a native of the United States and Canada. It grows some 6–12 in. high, with oval, shining green leaves, tinged with bronze when young, and small white bell-shaped flowers, followed by red berries. The leaves have the characteristic wintergreen scent, due to the presence of Methyl Salicylate, and the distilled oil is used for external rheumatic complaints (or the synthetic product is on occasion preferred). The leaves have been used as a tea substitute. The oil is used to flavour toothpastes and powders.

English Wintergreen is *Pyrola rotundifolia*, a plant of very different appearance, sometimes formerly used to heal wounds. The various species of *Pyrola* have white flowers, sometimes solitary, sometimes in spikes, and almost radical leaves.

WINTER HELIOTROPE *Petasites fragrans* (Plate 23) [*Compositae*]

This plant, a relative of Coltsfoot and Butterbur, has the travelling characteristics of the former, as the underground growths spread. The deliciously scented quiet lilac flowers appear in winter and spring. This plant could be naturalized on a bank or woodland, where encroachments do not matter, and the flowers can be enjoyed in peace.

WISTERIA Sc. S. [*Leguminosae*]

Wisteria sinensis has hanging racemes of lavender-mauve pea-flowers, with a delicious musky fragrance. In addition to the spring blossoms, more flower-trusses often delight the late summer months. The old name is Grape-flower Vine. An ideal position for this climbing shrub, which has twining branches, is against a south wall, or on a pergola, but it can also be grown as a standard tree. In this position, however, there is more liability to frost damage of the young flower-buds. Pot-grown plants should be obtained. Propagation may be by layering, and a deep sandy loam is a suitable soil. Summer-pruning is advisable, to pinch back side-shoots, to help in the formation of flowering spurs, also winter shortening-back of young shoots.

WITCH HAZEL *Hamamelis virginiana* [*Hamamelidaceae*]

The Witch Hazels are delightful plants for the winter garden, with their curious spidery yellow flowers with dark centres, on leafless branches. *H. virginiana* is a native of North America and flowers in autumn.

Both leaves and bark have the same active principles and the qualities are astringent, sedative and tonic. Witch Hazel lotion is used for scalds, burns, skin inflammation and to improve its general condition. Suitably prepared, Witch Hazel decoction is also used in ophthalmic trouble, and is soothing. *H. japonica* (Plate 16) is decorative and scented.

WOAD *Isatis tinctoria* (Plate 31) [*Cruciferae*]

The name Woad conjures up (with a certain hint of private pride at remembering so much history learnt aeons of years ago, and of having such a vivid imagination), a composite picture of a British warrior-queen, barbaric chariots, blue-painted and wild hordes and a confused *mêlée*. Is it not so?

The plant disappoints many at first acquaintance, as (except in hints of blue-black when the leaves are dying) there is no blue about it. The Woad is a biennial, with longish, spoon-shaped leaves of glaucous green-grey, and flower-stems some 4 ft. high in May, with clouds of small yellow four-petalled flowers followed by decorative sprays of 'key-fruits', green, then turning blue-black when ripe, and excellent for flower arrangements.

Woad is grown from seed sown outside in May–June or under glass in April. It is pleasing to give colour in the herb garden in spring.

Woad used formerly to be much cultivated in this country, particularly in East Anglia, but indigo has largely superseded it. It is found naturalized in various parts of this country. Apart from its use to dye wool, Woad was valued medicinally, amongst other uses, the ointment being used to heal ulcers.

A fermentation process is applied to the slightly dried and ground leaves before the dye is used, and the colour is obtained by mixing with lime-water.

WOODRUFF *Asperula odorata* (Plate 29) [*Rubiaceae*]

A fragile woodland plant with whorls of smooth green leaves (in common with the Bedstraws, Madders, Cleavers and other members of the family), and sprays of small four-petalled white flowers. On strong soils, Woodruff has been recommended as a cover-plant in shrubberies, where there is plenty of leaf-mould to encourage its growth. It may be increased by division. The thin underground shoots are not easy to replant.

The whole herb dried has a scent of new-mown hay, due to Coumarin, and bunches may be put amongst linen to impart the pleasing scent. Fresh bunches of the herb were hung up in houses in the Middle Ages, to refresh the air. It was also used as a vulnerary.

YARROW (Milfoil) *Achillea millefolium* [*Compositae*]

This well-known wild plant of waysides and lawns has fine-cut foliage and grows some 18 in. high, with flat heads of white flowers, sometimes tinged with pink. The rootstocks are creeping. Yarrow was valued for staunching wounds, and Yarrow Tea, made from the dried herb, is now used on occasion for easing severe colds.

Bibliography

A Modern Herbal. Mrs M. Grieve (Jonathan Cape).
Leaves from Gerard's Herbal. Marcus Woodward (Gerald Howe).
The Old English Herbals. Eleanour Sinclair Rohde (Longmans, Green).
Herbs and Herb Gardening. Eleanour Sinclair Rohde (Medici Society).
Practical Herb Growing. D. G. Hewer, B.Sc. (George Bell).
Herbs: How to Grow, Treat and Use Them. Ethelind Fearon (Herbert Jenkins).
Come into the Garden, Cook. Constance Spry (J. M. Dent).
Herbal Simples. W. T. Fernie, M.D. (Simpkin, Marshall, Hamilton & Kent).
Wild and Garden Herbs. Sanecki (Collingridge).
The Herbarist—Annual publication of the Herb Society of America, Boston, Mass.
Gardening with Herbs for Flavor and Fragrance. Helen Morgenthau Fox (Macmillan, New York).
The Living Garden. Sir Edward Salisbury (Chapter on plant scents). (George Bell).
British Herbs. Florence Ranson (Penguin).
Constance Spry Cookery Book (J. M. Dent).
A Fresh Herb Platter. Dorothy Childs Hogner (Doubleday, New York).
Profitable Herbs. Philippa Back (Darton, Longman and Todd).
A Book of Aromatics. Roy Genders (Darton, Longman and Todd).
A Book of Herbs. Dawn Macleod (Duckworth).
Pleasure of Herbs. Audrey Wynne Hatfield (Museum Press).
Herb Gardening. Claire Loewenfeld (Faber).

INDEX

[Where there are several alternative English names for a plant, an index entry is provided for each name. The English alternative names will be found grouped together in the entry under the Latin name.]

Acanthus 28, *A.spinosus* pl. 9
Achillea decolorans ('Mace') pl. 2; 150f., *A. millefolium* (Yarrow, Milfoil) 206
Aconite (*Aconitum napellus*) pl. 12; 95
Aconitum napellus (Aconite, Monkshood, Wolf's Bane) pl. 12; 95
Acorus calamus (Sweet Flag, Sweet Rush) pl. 31; 28, 190
Adam and Eve (*Pulmonaria officinalis*) 150
Adonis autumnalis (False Hellebore, Pheasant's Eye) 133, *A.vernalis* 133
Agastache anethiodora (Anise-Hyssop) 99, *A.cana* 148, *A.mexicana* (Lion's Tail) pl. 20; 148, *A.foeniculum* pl. 20; 99
Agave 27
Agrimony (*Agrimonia eupatoria*) 95
Agrimonia eupatoria (Agrimony, Church Steeples) 95
Alchemilla alpina 140, *A.arvensis* (Parsley-Piert) pl. 8; 140, *A.vulgaris* (Lady's Mantle) pl. 8; 140
Alecost (*Chrysanthemum balsamita* = *Tanacetum balsamita*) pl. 3; 33, 54, 81, 96, Alecost, as ointment 39
Alexander's Black Lovage (*Smyrnium olusatrum*) 59, 96
Alkanets (*Anchusa sp., Pentaglottis sp.*) pl. 6; 18, 96
Alleluia (*Oxalis acetosella*) 33
'All good' (*Chenopodium bonus-henricus*) 130
Allium cepa var. (Tree Onion) pl. 5; 167, *A.fistulosum* (Welsh Onion) pl. 5; 167, *A.moly* 167, *A.sativum* (Garlic) pl. 5; 128, *A.schoenoprasum* (Chives) pl. 6; 116
Allspice (*Calycanthus sp.*) pl. 16; 97
'Almond March-Bane' 37
Aloes (*Aloe vera*) 27
Althaea rosea (Hollyhock) 152
Althaea officinalis (Marsh Mallow) pl. 9; 151f.
America 70f.
American Hellebore (*Veratrum viride*) pl. 14; 97
American Land Cress 165

American Liver Wort (*Hepatica triloba var. Americana*) pl. 14; 97, 170
American Mandrake (*Podophyllum peltatum*) pl. 13; 97f., 153
American Sarsaparilla (*Aralia sp.*) 189
American Spikenard (*Aralia racemosa*) pl. 32; 189
Anethum graveolens (Dill) pl. 3; 123
Anchusa 18, *A.officinalis* (Common Alkanet) 96, *A.italica* 96, *A.sempervirens* (Evergreen Alkanet) pl. 6; 44, 96
Anemone hepatica (American Liverwort) pl. 14; 97, 170, *A.pulsatilla* (Pasque-Flower) pl. 11; 170
Angelica pl. 2; 18, 24, 35, 49, 55, 60, 62, 98, *A.archangelica* pl. 2; 98
Anglicus, Bartholomaeus, author of 'De Proprietatibus Rerum' 32, 33
Anise (*Pimpinella anisum*) pl. 3; 99, 109f.
Anise-Hyssop (*Agastache anethiodora*) 99
Anthemis nobilis (Chamomile) pl. 8; 113, *A.tinctoria* 113
Anthriscus cerefolium (Cerfeuil, Chervil) pl. 3; 115
Apium graveolens (Smallage, Wild Celery) 150
Apple Mint (*Mentha rotundifolia variegata*) pl. 26; 157, 161
Apple Ringie (*Artemisia abrotanum*) 101
Aralia racemosa (American Spikenard) pl. 32; 189
Aristotle 29
Armoracea rusticana (Horseradish) 135
Arnica 99, *A.montana* pl. 30; 99
Aromatic plants 51f.
Aromatic shrubs pl. 15 and 16; 50, 93
Artemisias 99f., *A.abrotanum* (Apple Ringie, Garde-Robe, Lad's Love, Old Man, Southernwood) pl. 19; 101, *A.absinthium* (Old Woman, Wormwood) pl. 19; 100, *A.borealis* (Old Lady) pl. 19; 99, *A.chamaemelifolia* (Lady's Maid) pl. 19; 100, *A.dracunculoides* (Russian Tarragon) pl. 6;

191, *A.dracunculus* (true French Tarragon) pl. 6; 191, *A*. Lambrook Silver 101, *A.lanata pedemontana* pl. 19; 51, 100, *A.pontica* (Old Warrior, Roman Wormwood) 100, *A.rupestris* pl. 32; 51, 100, *A.sericea* 100, *A.stellerana* 100, *A.vulgaris* (Mugwort) 100
Asarum canadense (Indian Ginger) pl. 13; 137
Asclepias 101f., pl. 30; *A.tuberosa* (Butterfly Weed) pl. 30
Asperula odorata (Woodruff) pl. 29; 206
Atriplex hortensis (Orach) pl. 4; 168
Atropa 200, *A.belladonna* (Belladonna, Deadly Nightshade) pl.11; 105, *Madragora officinarum* pl. 12; 152f.
Australia 71f.
Australian Blue Gum (*Eucalyptus globulus*) 126
Austrian Copper Briar 190
Autumn Crocus (*Colchicum autumnale*) pl. 12; 102
Azaleas 53, 90
Azara microphylla 89, 102

Bacon's *Of Gardens* 34
'Bac-peat' for town gardens 54
Ballota nigra (Black Horehound) 134
Balm of Gilead (*Cedronella triphylla*) pl. 22; 28, 103
Balm, Lemon (*Melissa officinalis*) pl. 5; 102, Golden (*M. off.var.*) pl. 4; 103
Balsams (*Impatiens sp.*) pl. 29; 62, 103, 138, B. of Gilead (*Commiphora opobalsamum*) 28, 103, B.Poplar (*Populus balsamifera*) pl. 10; 103
Balsamita major ('Camphor-Plant') pl. 23; 110
Banckes's *Herbal*, sixteenth century 33
Basils (*Ocimum sp.*) pl. 4 and 32; 56, 61, 63, 77, 78, 79, 103, Dark Opal basil 104, purple basil 104
Basil-Thyme (*Calamintha acinos*) 110
Bay, sweet (*Laurus nobilis*) pl. 3; 104
Bay leaves 75, 76
Bearcabbage (*Veratrum viride*) pl. 14; 97
Bears Foot (*Helleborus foetidus*) 132
Bee Balm, see Bergamot (*Monarda sp.*)
Belladonna (*Atropa belladonna*) pl. 11; 105 belladonna in Knole Park 20

Bells of Ireland (*Moluccella laevis*) 163
Berberis japonica 89
Bergamots (*Monarda sp.*) pl. 1; 17, 52, 54, 55, 60, 65, 91, 106, B. orange 107
Betony, Wood (*Stachys betonica*) pl. 10; 107
Bible and herbs 19, 27f.
Bistort (*Polygonum bistorta*) pl. 4; 24, 107
Bittersweet pl. 11; see *Solanum dulcamara*
Black Cohosh (*Cimicifuga racemosa*) pl. 13; 107f.
Black Horehound (*Ballota nigra*) 134
Black Lovage (*Smyrnium olusatrum*) 96
Blackwell, Eliz., engravings (1737) 37f., Alex. B., *Herbal* 38
Black Thyme (*Thymus vulgaris*) pl. 6; 196
Blessed Thistle (*Carbenia benedicta*) 193
Blind children and scented plants 19
Bloodroot (*Sanguinaria canadensis*) pl. 13; 108
Blue Comfrey (*Symphytum caucasicum*) pl. 6; 119
Bluebeard, annual (*Salvia horminum*) pl. 6 and 25; 118
Bluebells 90
Borage (*Borago officinalis*) pl. 6; 18, 33, 55, 108, 'for courage' 31f.
Borago officinalis (Borage) pl. 6; 108, *B.laxiflora* pl. 29; 108
Bouncing Bet. (*Saponaria officinalis*) pl. 29; 188
Bowles mint (*Mentha rotundifolia*) pl. 26; 64, 79, 157f.
Bowman's Root (*Porteranthus trifoliatus*) pl. 14; 137
Box hedges 44
Braille, plant names labelled in 19
Brittonastrum mexicanum (Lion's Tail) pl. 20; 91, 148, *B.canum* 148
Broadleaf English Thyme (*Thymus vulgaris*) 196
Broadleaf sage (*Salvia officinalis*) 182
Broadleaf sorrel (*Rumex acetosa*) 24, 188
Brompton stocks (*Matthiola sp.*) 90
Broom (*Cytisus sp.*) 122
Bryonia dioica, pl. 12; 108, 153
Bryony, black (*Tamus communis*) pl. 7; 109, B.white (*Bryonia dioica*) pl. 12; 108
Buddleia davidii (Butterfly Bush) 91, 109
Bugle (*Ajuga reptans*) 34

INDEX

Bugloss (*Lycopsis arvensis*) pl. 30; 204
Burnet Rose 34
Burnet Salad (*Poterium sanguisorba*) pl. 2; 34, 54, 109, B.saxifrage (*Pimpinella saxifraga*) 109
Burning bush (*Dictamnus fraxinella*) pl. 19; 124
Bush basil (*Ocimum minimum*) pl. 4; 103
Butterfly bush (*Buddleia davidii*) 91; 109

Cakes, herbs for use with 81
Calamint (*Calamintha sp.*) pl. 20 and 31; 51, 110
Calamintha grandiflora (Calamint) pl. 20; 110, *C.officinalis* pl. 31; 110
Calamus, acorus or *C.aromaticus* (Sweet flag) pl. 31; 28, 190
Calendula officinalis (Marigold) 153
California 71
Californian Laurel (*Umbellularia californica*) pl. 22; 110
Calycanthus floridus (Allspice) 97, *C.occidentalis* (Allspice) pl. 16; 51, 97, *C.praecox* (Winter Sweet) 51, 89, 97
Campanula rapunculoides (Rampion) 176, *C.rapunculus* (Rampion) pl. 4; 176
Camphor-Plant (*Balsamita vulgaris* or *Chrysanthemum balsamita*) pl. 23; 24, 96, 110
Canella alba (Cinnamon) 28
Caper plant (*Capparis spinosa*) 136, C.spurge (*Euphorbia lathyrus*) pl. 31; 110, 189
Cannabis sativa (Indian Hemp) 133
Capparis spinosa (Caper Plant) 111, 136
Carbenia benedicta=Carduus benedictus (Holy or Blessed Thistle) pl. 10; 193
Carduus marianus=Silybum marianum (Our Lady's Milk Thistle) pl. 10; 193
Carnations 34, 35, 43, 90
Caraway (*Carum carvi*) pl. 2; 18, 24, 54, 81, 111, C.seeds 77, C.thyme (*Thymus herba-barona*) 54
Carum carvi (Caraway) pl. 2; 18, 24, 44, 77, 81, 111, *C.petroselinum* (Parsley) pl. 3; 168f.
Caryopteris clandonensis (Moustache Plant) pl. 15; 91, 111, *C.mastacanthus* 111
Catmints (*Nepeta sp.*) pl. 10 and 21; 112
Ceanothus (Mountain Sweet) 91, 112, *C.americanus* (Red-Root, New Jersey Tea) pl. 13; 176

Cedronella triphylla (Balm of Gilead) pl. 22; 28, 103
Celandine, Greater (*Chelidonium majus*) pl. 7; 20, 113
Centranthus ruber (Red-spurred Valerian) pl. 22; 201
Cerfeuil, see also Chervil (*Anthriscus cerefolium*) pl. 3; 18, 115
Chamomile (*Anthemis nobilis*, see also *Matricaria chamomilla*) pl. 8; 50, 51, 52, 54, 65, 81, 113f., 162, C.non-flowering Treneague 113, C. and thyme lawns for herb seats 51, lawns 19
Chartreuse flavoured with herbs 33
Chelidonium majus (Greater Celandine) pl. 7; 36, 113
Chequer-board lily (*Fritillaria meleagris*) pl. 11; 128, 'chequered daffodil' 128
Chenopodium bonus-henricus (Good King Henry, All-Good, Mercury) pl. 3; 130
Chervil, see also Cerfeuil (*Anthriscus cerefolium*) pl. 3; 18, 55, 56, 75, 77, 78, 81, 115
Chicory (*Cichorium intybus*) pl. 4; 80, 115
Chimonanthus praecox (Winter Sweet) pl. 18; 89, 97, 116
Chives (*Allium schoenoprasum*) pl. 6; 23, 50, 56, 75, 76, 79, 80, 116, 194
Choisya (Mexican Orange blossom) 53, *C. ternata* pl. 18; 90, 116f.
Chorley Scented Garden 19
Christchurch 72
Christmas Rose (*Helleborus niger*) 132
Chrysanthemum parthenium (Feverfew) pl. 8; 127
Church steeples (*Agrimonia eupatoria*) 95
Cichorium intybus (Chicory, Succory) pl. 4; 115
Cimichifuga racemosa (Black Cohosh, Black Snakeroot) pl. 13; 107
Cinnamon (*Canella alba*) 28
Cinnamonum camphora (True Camphor) 110
Circaea lutetiana (Enchanter's Nightshade) 166
Cistus (Sun-Rose) pl. 15; 90, 117, *C.cyprius* 117, *C.ladanifer* 51, 90, 117, *C.laurifolius* 117, *C.purpureus* 51, 90, 117
Citrus mint (*Mentha citrata*) 161, 162

Clary (*Salvia sclarea, S.horminum,* etc.) 34, C., perennial pl. 24; 118
Clary Sages (*Salvia sclarea, S.horminum*) pl. 24 and 25; 52, 54, 91, 118, 181
Clematis montana 44, *C.flammula* 119
Clerodendron trichotomum pl. 17; 91, 119
Cloth of Silver (tulips) 35
Cloves 43, 81
Clove gilliflowers 35, 43
Cochlearia armoracea (Horseradish) 135
Colchicum autumnale (Autumn Crocus, Meadow Saffron) pl. 12; 102
Colocynth 28
Colorado 70
Coltsfoot (*Tussilago farfara*) 107
Comfrey (*Symphytum sp.*) pl. 6; 119, C., Russian (*S.peregrinum*) 119
Commiphora myrrha (Myrrh) 27, *C.opobalsamum* (Balm or Balsam of Gilead) 28, 103
Common Elder (*Sambucus nigra*) 124
Common Thyme (*Thymus vulgaris*) 194
Conium maculatum (Hemlock) pl. 12; 133
Connecticut 70
Coriander (*Coriandrum sativum*) pl. 4; 28, 120
Coriandrum sativum (Coriander) pl. 4; 28, 120
Corn Salad (*Valerianella olitoria*) 120
Cornmint (*Mentha arvensis*) 157, 159
Corylopsis pauciflora 89, *C.spicata* pl. 18; 120
Costmary (*Chrysanthemum balsamita* or *Tanecetum balsamita*) pl. 3; 20, 96, mentioned by Spenser 33
Cotton Lavenders, dwarf (*Santolina sp.*) pl. 21; 49, 50, 90, 120, 191
Cow parsley, 24
Cowslip (*Primula veris*) 121, C. wine 33
Crataegus (*C.monogyna* = Hawthorn, May) 90, 121
Crithmum maritimum (Samphire) pl. 3; 185
Crocus, autumn (*Colchicum autumnale*) pl. 12; 102
Crocus sativus (True Saffron Crocus) pl. 32; 102
Cucurbitae family 108
Culinary herbs, imports 40, in war time 18
Culinary mints (*Mentha sp.*) 158
Culpeper 36, 84
Cultivation, harvesting and drying of herbs 59

Cumin (*Cuminum cyminum*) pl. 2; 121
Cuminum cyminum (Cumin) pl. 2; 121
Currant, Golden (*Ribes aureum*) pl. 16; 177
Curryplant (*Helichrysum angustifolium*) pl. 20; 24, 49, 50, 60, 89, 131
Cynoglossum officinale (Hound's Tongue) pl. 8; 135
Cypress hedges 44
Cytisus praecox (Broom) 89, 122, *C.battandieri* 122

Daisies as asthma relief 20
Dandelion (*Taraxacum officinale*) 26, 122
Danes' Elder (*Sambucus ebulus*) pl. 29; 124
Danewort (*Sambucus ebulus*) pl. 29; 124
Daphne 123, *D.burkwoodii* pl. 18; 123, *D.japonica* 89, *D.laureola* (Spurge-Laurel), Green Daphne pl. 12; 89, 123, *D.mezereum* (Mezereon) pl. 16; 89, 123, *D.odora* pl. 18; 123, *D.pontica* pl. 18; 123
Datura 20, *D.stramonium* (Thornapple) pl. 11; 193, *D.suaveolens* 193
Deadly nightshade (*Atropa belladonna*) pl. 11; 35, 105, as relief in gout 21, in Knole Park 20
'Denbigh's Almond March-Bane' 37
De Proprietatibus Rerum (thirteenth cent.) 32
Dianthus (Pinks) 90, D.rainbow 43
Dictamnus fraxinella (Burning Bush, False Dittany) pl. 19; 124
Digby, Sir Kenelm, author 'Still Room Book' 37
Digitalis purpurea (Foxglove) pl. 11; 128
Dill (*Anethum graveolens*) pl. 3; 56, 123
Dittany-of-Crete (*Origanum dictamnus*) pl. 19; 124
Doctrine of Signatures 36, 113
Doedens' *Pemptades* 35
Douglas fir (*Pseudo tsuga douglasi*) 44
Dropwort, or Dropwort Meadowsweet (*Spiraea filipendula*) pl. 8; 155, dropwort, Hemlock Water (*Oenanthe Crocata*) 133
Dry walls 51
Drying of herbs 66
Duke of Argyll's Tea Tree (*Lycium halimifolium*) pl. 29; 192
Dunster Church herb border 49
Dutch Lavender 144, 146

INDEX

Dwarf Munstead Lavender (*Lavandula off. var.*) pl. 1; 143

Easter puddings 107
Eau de Cologne Mint (*Mentha citrata*) pl. 26; 54, 65, 81, 157, 161
Echinops ritro (Globe Thistle) 129
Echium vulgare (Viper's Bugloss) pl. 30; 204
Edging herbs 50
Educational value of herbs 19f.
Eggs, herbs for use with 79
Eglantine (*Rosa eglanteria*, or *R. rubiginosa*) pl. 15; 34, 189
Elder, Common (*Sambucus nigra*) 124
Elder and honey tablets 39
Elderberry wine 33
Elecampane (*Inula helenium*) pl. 7; 17, 49, 60, 62, 125
Elsholtzia stauntonii pl. 16; 91, 125
Enchanter's nightshade (*Circaea lutetiana*) 166
Endive 80
English mandrake (*Bryonia dioica*) 108, 153
English marjoram (*Origanum vulgare*) 153
English scullcap (*Scutellaria galericulata*) 187
English wild thyme (*Thymus serpyllum*) 199, English broad-leaf thyme (*Thymus vulgaris*) 196
Erica mediterranea (Heath) pl. 17; 126
Eryngium amethystinum 126, *E. maritimum* (Sea-Holly) pl. 7; 126
Eryngo (Sea-Holly) pl. 7; 126
Estragon, or Tarragon (*Artemisia dracunculus*) 18, 191
Etna Broom (*Genista aetnensis*) 129
Eucalyptol 59
Eucalyptus pl. 16; 126, *E. globulus* (Australian Blue Gum) 126, *E. gunnii* 126, *E. smithii* 126
Eupatorium cannabinum (Hemp Agrimony) 95
Euphorbia (Spurges) 189, *E. amygdaloides* (Wood S.) pl. 12; 189, *E. lathyris* pl. 31; 110, *E. polychroma* 189
Euphrasia officinalis (Eyebright) pl. 7; 107, 127
Evening Primrose (*Oenothera biennis*) 126
Eyebright (*Euphrasia officinalis*) pl. 7; 107, 127

False Dittany (*Dictamnus fraxinella*) pl. 19; 124

Fennell, Green (*Foeniculum officinale* (pl. 2; 52, 55, 77, 78, 80, 127; Bronze F. pl. 2; 127, Florence F. (*F. dulce*) 127, F., mention by Chaucer 33
Feverfew (*Chrysanthemum parthenium*) pl. 8; 127
Filipendula vulgaris see *Spiraea f.*
Fish, use of herbs with 78
Flax (*Linum usitatissimum*) pl. 10; 148
Flora Medica (1838) 38
Florence fennel (*Foeniculum officianale*) 127
Foeniculum officinale (Green Fennel) pl. 2; 127, *F. dulce* (Florence F.) 127
Folgate blue lavender 49, 143
Fool's Coat (tulips) 35
Foster, Mrs. G. M. 70
Foxglove (*Digitalis purpurea*) pl. 11; 128
Frankincense (*Boswellia thurifera*) 27
Freesias 90
French Common Thyme (*Thymus vulgaris*) 64, 196
French lavenders, dwarf (*Santolina*) pl. 21; 49, 50, 90, 120, 191
French marjoram (*Origanum onites*) 153, 154
French parsley (*Petroselinum crispum var.*) 169
French sorrel (*Rumex acetosa* or *R. scutatus*) pl. 2 and 4; 188f.
Fritillaria (Fritillary) pl. 11; 128, *F. imperialis* (Crown Imperial) 128, *F. meleagris* (Fritillary, Snake's Head Lily) pl. 11; 128

Galega officinalis (Goat's Rue) pl. 8; 130
Galen on medicinal plants 30
'Galenick and Chymick' 37
Gall 20
Garde-Robe (*Artemisia abrotanum*) 101
Garlic (*Allium sativum*) pl. 5; 77, 78, 79, 128
Gaultheria procumbens (Wintergreen) pl. 16; 204f.
Genista aetnensis (Mount Etna Broom) 90, 129
Gentiana lutea (Yellow Gentian) pl. 30; 129
Geranium dissectum 129, *G. macrorrhizum* pl. 22; 129, G., oak-leaf (scented *Pelargonium*) 171, 172, *G. robertianum* 129, G., scented pl. 22; 129
Gerard's *Herbal* 31, 35, 37, 84, G., garden in Fetter Lane, London (sixteenth cent.) 34, Gerard 132

Germander, Sage-leaved (*Teucrium scorodonia*) pl. 22; 204, Wall (*T. chamaedrys*) pl. 7, 204
Giant Grappenhall lavender 145
Gilead, Balm or Balsam of (*Commiphora opobalsamum*) 28
Ginger mint (*Mentha gentilis*) pl. 26; 162
Ginseng (*Panax quinquefolius*) 129
Globe Thistle (*Echinops ritro*) 129
Glycyrrhiza glabra (Liquorice) pl. 10; 148f.
Goat's Rue (*Galega officinalis*) pl. 8; 130
Golden balm (*Melissa off. var.*) pl. 4; 103
Golden currant (*Ribes odoratum*) pl. 16; 177
Golden lemon thyme (*Thymus citriodorus aureus*) 197
Golden marjoram (*Origanum aureum*, etc.) pl. 20; 154
Golden purslane (*Portulaca sativa*) 175
Golden sage (*Salvia officinalis* variety) pl. 22; 182, 183
Golden samphire (*Inula crithmoides*) 185
Golden Seal (*Hydrastis canadensis*) 130
Good King Henry (*Chenopodium bonus-henricus*) pl. 3; 130
Greater celandine (*Chelidonium majus*) pl. 7; 20, 21, as cure for warts 21
Green American Hellebore (*Veratrum viride*) pl. 14; 97
Green Daphne (*Daphne laureola*) pl. 12; 89, 123
Green fennel (*Foeniculum officinale*) 127
Green hellebore (*Helleborus viridis*) 132
Green purslane (*Portulaca oleracea*) pl. 3; 175
Greek valerian (*Polemonium caeruleum*) pl. 30; 137
Grey hedge lavender (*Lavandula sp.*) 145
Grieve, Mrs. M. of Chalfont St. Giles (*Modern Herbal*) 38, ref. in poem, 84
Grindelia pl. 7; 131

Hamamelis mollis (Witch Hazel) 89, 131, *H.virginiana* 205, *H.japonica* pl. 16; 131
Hampton Court Knot Garden 51
Harvesting, correct time for 64
Hawthorn (*Crataegus monogyna*) 90, 121
Heartsease (*Viola tricolor*) pl. 9; 131
Heath, Heather (*Erica* and *Calluna sp.*) pl. 17; 126

Helichrysum angustifolium (Curry Plant) pl. 20; 131
Heliotrope (*Heliotropium sp.*) 44, 91
Hellebore (*Helleborus sp.*; see also *Veratrum*) pl. 12; 132, H., False (*Adonis autumnalis*) 133, *H.foetidus* (Bear's Foot) 132, *H.niger* (Christmas Rose) 132, *H.orientalis* 132, *H.viridis* (Green Hellebore) 132, H., white (*Veratrum album*) 132
Hepatica triloba (American Liverwort) 170, *H.triloba* var. *americana* pl. 14; 97
Hemlock (*Conium maculatum*) pl. 12; 133
Hemp (*Eupatorium cannabinum*) 95, H., Indian (*Cannabis sativa*) 133
Henbane (*Hyoscyamus niger*) pl. 11; 20, 134
Hewer, Miss D. G., founder of Seal Herb Farm 38, ref. in poem 85
Herb(s): in the Bible 19, biscuits recipe 78, butters 80, as cosmetics 39, definition of 24, educational value of 19, Farm at Seal 38, 39, garden 43–56, garden designs 52, garden plans 45–48, in history 19, and Lord Mayor 40, pancakes 79, Peter 121, Robert 129, savouries 80, seats at Sissinghurst 51, as substitutes for tea etc. 38, in war time 40
Herbarist, The 70
Herbarium Apuleii Platonica (fifteenth cent.) 31
Herbe de St. Fiacre (*Verbascum thapsus*) 164
Herbe Trinitatis 131
Herb Grower, The 70
History of Herbs 27
Hidcote Giant Lavender (*Lavandula sp.*) 146 H., purple 49, 144
High Tapers (*Verbascum thapsus*) 164
Hippocrates and the virtues of plants 29
Hollyhocks, related to mallows 152
Honeysuckle (*Lonicera sp.*), 34, 43, 44, 51, 53 90
'Hop Plant' (*Origanum dictamnus*) 124
Horehound, Black (*Ballota nigra*) 134 H., white (*Marrubium vulgare*) pl. 10; 134
Horsemint (*Mentha sylvestris*) pl. 26; 158
Horseradish (*Cochlearia armoracea* or *Armoracea rusticana*) 135
Hound's Tongue (*Cynoglossum officinale*) pl. 8; 135
House Leek (*Sempervivum tectorum*) 135
Hove 19, scented garden 19, 53

Hundreds and thousands (*Pulmonaria officinalis*) 150
Humea elegans (Incense Plant) pl. 23; 44, 136f.
Hyacinths 44, 54, 90
Hydrastis canadensis (Golden Seal) 130
Hyssop (*Hyssopus officinalis*) pl. 5; 20, 33, 50, 51, 136, at Beaulieu Abbey 21, Rock H. (*H.aristatus*) 136
Hyssopus officinalis (Hyssop) pl. 5; 20, 33, 50, 51, 136, *H.aristatus* (Rock Hyssop) 136
Hypericum pseudohenryi pl. 16; 18, 91, 136
Hyoscyamus 20, *H.niger* (Henbane) pl. 11; 134

Impatiens sp., (Balsam, Jewelweed) pl. 29; 138, *I.capensis* 138, *I.fulva* pl. 29; 138, *I.glandulifera* 138, *I.parviflora* pl. 29; 138, *I.noli-me-tangere* 138, *I.roylei* 138
Incense in 3000 B.C. 27
Incense Plant (*Humea elegans*) pl. 23; 136f.
Indian Cress (*Tropaeolum majus*) 165
Indian Ginger (*Asarum canadense*) pl. 13; 137
Indian Physic (*Gillenia trifoliata*) pl. 14; 137
Indian Basil (*Ocimum gratissimum*) pl. 32; 104
Insect Powder Plant (*Pyrethrum cinerariifolium*) pl. 31; 137
Insects and other fauna wanted for West End firm 40
Inula helenium (Elecampane) pl. 7; 125
Iris florentina (Orris) pl. 21; 168, *I.germanica* 168, *I.pallida* 168, *I.reticulata* 89
Isatis tinctoria (Woad) pl. 31; 206
Ivy-leafed toadflax at St. Nicholas Church, Sevenoaks (*Linaria cymbalaria*) 21

Jacob's Ladder (*Polemonium caeruleum*) pl. 30; 137
Japanese honeysuckle (*Lonicera japonica*) 51
Japanese mint (*Mentha arvensis var. piperascens*) pl. 26; 171
Jasminum (Jasmine) 44, 90
Jasmine 44, 90, J., white (*Jasminum officinale*) 44, 138
Jerusalem Cowslip (*Pulmonaria officinalis*) 150
Jerusalem Sage (*Phlomis fruticosa*) pl. 21; 138
Jewelweed (*Impatiens sp.*) pl. 29; 29, 103, 138
John Innes potting compost 55
Joseph and Mary (*Pulmonaria officinalis*) 150

Joseph's Coat (*Pulmonaria officinalis*) 150
Juniper (*Juniperus communis*) pl. 30; 139
Juniperus communis (Juniper) pl. 30; 139

Kalmia latifolia (Mountain Laurel) pl. 14; 164
Kerria japonica (Jew's Mallow) 90, 139
'Key Flower' (*Primula veris*) 121
'Knit-bone' (*Symphytum officinale*) 120
Knives for cutting herbs 65
Knole House 20, 21
Knot-gardens 19, beds 50, in Elizabethan and Stuart days 34
Knotted marjoram (*Origanum marjorana* or *Marjorana hortensis*) pl. 6; 153, 154

Labiatae 21
Labrador Tea (*Ledum groenlandicum*) pl. 13 139
Lactuca virosa (Opium Lettuce) pl. 12; 147
Lad's Love (*Artemisia abrotanum*) 101
Lady's maid (*Artemisia chamaemelifolia*) pl. 19; 100
Lady's mantle (*Alchemilla vulgaris*) pl. 8; 140
Lamb's Lettuce (*Valerianella olitoria*) 120
Lavatera arborea (Tree Mallow) 152
Laurus nobilis (Sweet Bay) pl. 3; 104
Lavender (*Lavandula sp.*) pl. 1 and 20; 33, 49, 55, 60, 64, 65, 90, Baby Blue, 143, as dwarf hedge 49, dwarf white (*L.nana alba*) 143, Folgate Blue 143, hedges 49, 50, 51, 52, Hidcote Purple 144, Hidcote Giant 146, Munstead dwarf 143, Old English 145, pink (*L.nana rosea*) 143, semi-dwarf 144, spike (*L.spica*) 140, Summerland Supreme 144, tall 145, Twickle 144, white (*L.alba*) 145
Lavenders, Cotton (*Santolina sp.*) pl. 21; 120
Lavandula sp. pl. 1 and 20; *L. alba* (White Lavender) 145, *L.atropurpurea nana* 144, *L.dentata* 146, *L.multifida* 147, *L.nana alba* (Dwarf White L.) 143, *L.nana rosea* (Pink L.) 143, *L.angustifolia*) pl. 1; 140, *L.pendunculata* 146, *L.pinnata* 147, *L.spica* (Spike L.) 140, *L.stoechas* 140, 146, *L.viridis* 147
Leech Book of Bald 30, 31, 82
Le Grant Herbier 33
Leicester, City of, herb garden 52
Lemon balm (*Melissa officinalis*) pl. 5; 18, 33, 54, 55, 60, 64, 81, 102, 202

Lemon curd 50
Lemon pelargonium (*Pelargonium citriodorum*) 54
Lemon thyme (*Thymus citriodorus*) 18, 49, 54, 55, 59, 64, 75, 76, 78, 79, 80, 127, 194, 195, 196
Lemon verbena (*Lippia citriodora*) pl. 5; 18, 43, 56, 59, 81, 202
Leonorus cardiaca (Lion's Tail, Motherwort) pl. 8; 163
Lettuce, opium (*Lactuca virosa*) pl. 12; 147
Levisticum officinale (Lovage) pl. 3; 149
Leyel, Mrs., ref. in poem 84
Ligusticum scoticum (Scotch Lovage) 150
Lilac (*Syringa sp.*) 43, 53, 90
Lilies 91
Lily of the valley (*Convallaria majalis*) 43, 90 L., Snake's Head (*Fritillaria meleagris*) 128
Lime Flowers (*Tilia europea*, etc.) 148
Linaria cymbalaria (Ivy-leafed Toadflax) at St. Nicholas Church, Sevenoaks 21
Lindley, Dr. John, *Flora Medica* 38
Linseed (*Linum usitatissimum*) pl. 10; 148
Linum usitatissimum (Flax, Linseed) pl. 10; 148
Lion's Tail (*Brittonastrum mexicanum* or *Agastache mexicana*) pl. 20; 148, = Motherwort (*Leonurus cardiaca*) pl. 8; 163
Lion's tooth (*Taraxacum officinale*) 122
Lippia citriodora (Lemon Verbena) pl. 5; 202
Liquorice (*Glycyrrhiza glabra*) pl. 10; 148
Liverwort, American (*Hepatica triloba var. americana*) pl. 14; 97
Lobelia 149, *L.cardinalis* pl. 14; 149, *L.dortmanna* 149, *L.dresdeniana* 149, *L.inflata* 149, *L.syphilitica* pl. 31; 149, *L.uren* 149
Long term planting 53
Lonicera fragrantissima pl. 17; 89, 149, *L.japonica* 51, *L.periclymenum* (Honeysuckle) 51, 90, 149
Lovage (*Levisticum officinale*) pl. 3; 20, 33, 49, 60, 79, 81, 149f., Scotch (*Ligusticum scoticum*) 150
Love-in-idleness (*Viola tricolor*) pl. 9; 131
Low hedges 50
Lungwort (*Pulmonaria officinalis*) pl. 6; 18, 36, 44, 150
Lycium barbarum (Duke of Argyll's Tea Tree) pl. 29; 192, *L.halimifolium* pl. 29; 192
Lycopsis arvensis (Bugloss) pl. 30; 204

'Mace' (*Achillea decolorans*) pl. 2; 54, 150, alecost as 'Mace' 96
Magnolias pl. 17; 90, 151, *M.grandiflora* 151, *M.soulangeana* 151, *M.stellata* 151, *M.watsonii* 151, *M.wilsoni* 151
Mahonia (*Berberis*) *bealii* pl. 17; 151
Mallows (*Malva sp.*) pl. 9; 151, M., Common or Blue (*M.sylvestris*) 151, M., Musk (*M.moschata*) 151
Malva sp. pl. 9; 151, *M.moschata* (Musk Mallow) 151, *M.sylvestris* (Common or Blue Mallow) 151
Mandragora officinarum see *Atropa mandragora* (Mandrake)
Mandrake (*Atropa mandragora* or *Mandragora officinarum*) pl. 12; 21, 27, 31, 152, see also *Podophyllum* and *Bryonia*
Manna from heaven, resembling coriander seed 28
Marigold (*Calendula officinalis*) 153
Marjorams (*Origanum sp.*) pl. 6 and 20; 18, 23, 24, 33, 43, 50, 52, 54, 56, 59, 60, 63, 64, 65, 68, 75, 76, 79, 80, 81, 89, 153
Marrubium vulgare (White Horehound) pl. 10; 134
Marshmallow (*Althaea officinalis*) pl. 9; 65, 140, 151
Matricaria chamomilla (German Chamomile) pl. 21; 113
May (*Crataegus monogyna*) 90, 121
Mayweeds (*Matricaria sp.*, etc.) 113
Meadow saffron (*Colchicum autumnale*) pl. 12; 102
Meadowsweet (*Spiraea ulmaria*) pl. 8; 32, 43, 155
Meat, herbs to use with 77
Medicinal herbs in wartime 18
Medicinal mints (*Mentha sp.*) 160
Melilot (*Melilotus officinalis*) pl. 5; 156
Melilotus alba 156, *M.officinalis* (Melilot) pl. 5; 156
Melissa officinalis (Lemon Balm) pl. 5; 102, (Golden B.) pl. 4;, 103
Mentha sp. pl. 26, *M.aquatica* (Water Mint) 157, *M.arvensis* (Corn M.) 157, 161, 162, *M.citrata* (Citrus, Eau-de-Cologne, Pineapple M.) 161, *M.cordifolia* 157, 158, *M.gattefossei* 50, 163, *M.gentilis* (Ginger

Mint) 162, *M.longifolia weineriana* 157, 162, *M.piperita* (Peppermint) 160f., *M. piperita crispula* 161, *M.pulegium* (Pennyroyal) 162, *M.requieni* (Spanish Mint) 50, 163, *M.rotundifolia* (Bowles Mint) 158, *M.suavolens variegata* (Apple Mint) 157, 161, *M.rubra raripila* 158, *M.spicata* see *M.Viridis*, *M.spicata crispata* (Crisped Spearmint) 159 (see also *M.viridis*), *M.flongifolia* (Horsemint) 158, *M.viridis* or *M.spicata* (Green Lamb Mint, Peamint, Spearmint) 158

Menthol 59
'Mercury' (*Chenopodium bonus-henricus*) 130
Mexican Orange (*Choisya ternata*) pl. 18; 90, 116
Mezereon (*Daphne mezereum*) pl. 16; 89, 123
Micromeria pl. 20; 156, *M.corsica* pl. 20; 156, *M.piperella* 156
Milfoil (*Achillea millefolium*) 206
Milton and herbs 34
'Mind your own business' (*Helxine* or *Saxifraga sarmentosa*) 157, 163
Mint pl. 26; 24, 33, 52, 56, 60, 62, 64, 68, 69, 75, 81, 89, Apple (*Mentha rotundifolia variegata*) 157, 161, Bowles (*M.rotundifolia* Bowles) 158, Citrus (*M.citrata*) 161, Corn (*M.arvensis*) 157, 161, 162, Crisped Spearmint (*M.spicata crispata*, also *M. viridis*) 159, Eau-de-Cologne (*M.citrata*) 161, Ginger (*M.gentilis*) 162, Green Lamb (*M.viridis* or *spicata*) 158, Horsemint *M.longifolia*) 158, Pea (*M.viridis* or *spicata*) 158, Pennyroyal (*M.pulegium*) 162, Peppermint (*M.piperata*) 150f., Pineapple (*M.citrata*) 161, Spanish 163, Spearmint (*M.viridis* or *spicata*) 158, Water (*M.aquatica*) 157, demand for dried 62, for egg flavouring 79, jelly recipe 160, seats 51, at Sissinghurst 163
Mixed herbs recipe 77
Mock orange (*Philadelphus sp.*) p. 17; 43, 90, 174
Moluccella pl. 32; 163, *M.laevis* (Bells of Ireland, Shell-Flower) 163
Monarda didyma (Bergamot, Bee Balm, Oswego Tea) pl. 1; 106, *M.fistulosa* 106, *M.menthifolia* 107

Monkshood (*Aconitum napellus*) pl. 12; 95
'Mother of Thousands' (*Helxine* or *Saxifraga sarmentosa*) 163
Motherwort (*Leonorus cardiaca*) pl. 8; 163
Mountain Laurel (*Kalmial atifolia*) pl. 14; 164
Moustache plant (*Caryopteris sp.*) 111
Mt. Etna broom (*Genista aetnensis*) 90, 129
Mugwort (*Artemisia vulgaris*) 100
Mullein (*Verbascum thapsus*) pl. 10; 140, 164
Munstead Lavender 50, 143
Musk (*Mimulus moschatus*) pl. 31; 62
Musk hybrid roses 43, 51, 54, 90
Musk Mallow (*Malva moschata*) 151
Myrtle, Bog (*Myrica gale*) pl. 22; 165
Myrrh (*Commiphora myrrha*) 27
Myrica gale (Bog Myrtle) pl. 22; 165
Myristica fruit 150
Myrrhis odorata (Sweet Cicely) pl. 21; 190
Myrtle (*Myrtus communis*) pl. 15; 91, 164
Myrtle shrubs 55
Myrtus communis (Myrtle) pl. 15; 91, 164

Narcissus 44, 54, 90
Nard 140
Narrow leafed sage (*Salvia officinalis*) pl. 25; 182
Nasturtium (*Tropaeolum majus;* also Latin name for Watercress) 165
Neal, Sir Paul, way of making cider 37
Nepeta cataria (Catmint) pl. 10; 24, 112, *N.mussini* 112, *N.grandiflora* 112, *N.* six hills giant pl. 21; 112
Nettles (*Urtica sp.*) 165f.
New Jersey 70
New Jersey Tea (*Ceanothus americanus*) pl. 13; 176
Nicandra pl. 31; 166, *N.physaloides* (Shoo Plant) pl. 31; 22, 166
Nicotiana (Tobacco Plant) 44, 53, 91, *N.rustica* (Turkish Tobacco) pl. 31; 200, *N.tabacum* 200
Nightshade, black (*Solanum nigrum*) pl. 11; 166, enchanter's (*Circaea lutetiana*) 166, woody (*Solanum dulcamara*) 105, see also Belladonna
Nutmeg geranium (*Pelargonium fragrans*) pl. 28; 173

INDEX

Nymphaea coerulea (Blue Water Lily) 28, *N.odorata* (Water Lily) 90

Oak leaf geranium (*Pelargonium capitatum*) pl. 28; 171, 172
Ocimum basilicum (Sweet Basil) pl. 4; 103f., *O.gratissimum* (Indian Basil) pl. 32; 104f., *O.minimum* (Bush Basil) pl. 4; 103f.
Oenanthe crocata (Hemlock Water Dropwort) 133
Oenothera 91, *O.biennis* (Evening Primrose) 126
Old English lavender 145f.
Old lady (*Artemisia borealis*) pl. 19; 52, 99, 101
Old man (*Artemisia abrotanum*) 101
Old warrior (*Artemisia pontica*) 100
Omelette herbs 80
Onions 167, tree (*Allium cepa var.*) 55
Opium poppy (*Papaver somniferum*) pl. 11; 175
Orach (*Atriplex hortensis*) pl. 4; 168
Oregano (*Origanum marjorana*) pl. 6; 18, 56, 75, 76, 78, 79, 81, 153
Origanum pl. 6 and 20; 136, 153, *O.aureum* (Golden Marjoram) 154, *O.dictamnus* (Dittany-of-Crete) pl. 19; 124, 154, *O.marjorana* (Knotted M.) 154, *O.microphyllum* 154, *O.onites* (French M.) 154f., *O.vulgare* (English M.) 154f., see also Origano (*O.marjorana*)
Orris root (*Iris florentina*) pl. 21; 168, 81
Osmanthus delavayi pl. 18; 90, 168
Osmarea burkwoodii pl. 18; 168
Oswego tea (*Monarda didyma*) pl. 1; 106
Our Lady's flannel (*Verbascum thapsus*) 164
Our Lady's milk thistle (*Carduus marianus* or *Silybum marianum*) pl. 10; 193
Oxalis acetosella (Wood Sorrel) 189
Oxford botanic gardens 21, 108

'Paigles' (*Primula veris*) 121
Panax quinquefolius (Ginseng) 129
Pansies 51
'*Paradisi in Sole*' (Parkinson) 35
Parietaria officinalis (Pellitory-of-the-Wall) 173f.
Papaver somniferum (Opium Poppy) pl. 11; 175, *P.rhoeas* (Red Field Poppy) 175
Parkinson's '*Paradisi in Sole*' 35

Parkinson's '*Theatrum Botanicum*' (1640) 35
Parsley (*Petroselinum* or *P.crispum*) pl. 3; 50, 55, 60, 63, 67, 75, 76, 78, 79, 80, 168f., for egg flavouring 79
Parsley-Piert (*Alchemilla arvensis*) pl. 8; 140
Pasque flower (*Anemone pulsatilla*) pl. 11; 170
Pastry cases, herbs for use in 79
Paths, plants for 50
Patience 35
Paving plants 50
Pea mint (*Mentha viridis*) 158
Pelargoniums pl. 28; 32, 43, 44, 54, 90, 170f., *P.acetosum* pl. 20; 173, P. Attar of Roses 173, *P.capitatum* (Oak-Leaf geranium) 172, *P.citriodorum* 173, *P.crispum* 172, *P.crispum variegatum* 172f., *P.filicifolium* 173, *P.fragrans* (Nutmeg Geranium) 173, *P.graveolens* 172, P. Lady Plymouth 172, P. 'Mabel Grey' pl. 19; P. Madame Nonon pl. 19; 173, P. Oakleaf 56, 172, *P.odoratissimum* 173, *P.quercifolium* 172, *P.radula* 172, P. Rose Unique 173, P. Scarlet Pet 172, *P.tomentosum* 173
Pellitory-of-the-wall (*Parietaria officinalis*) 20, 21, 173, as cough mixture 21
Pennyroyal (*Mentha pulegium*) pl. 26; 20, 50, 53, 162
Pentaglottis sempervirens see Alkanets
Penzance briars pl. 15; 90, 190
Peppermint (*Mentha piperita*) pl. 26; 24, 54, 65, 160f.
Perfumes in worship of tabernacle 27
Periwinkles (*Vinca major, V.minor*) pl. 29; 21, 31, 174, protection from evil spirits 21
Perowskia abrotanifolia pl. 15; 174, *P.atriplicifolia* (Russian Sage) pl. 15; 18, 91, 174
Petasites fragrans (Winter Heliotrope) pl. 23; 89, 205
Petroselinum crispum see Parsley
Peucedanum graveolens (Dill) 123
Pheasant's eye (*Adonis autumnalis*) 133
Pheasant's eye narcissus (*poeticus*) 90
Philadelphus (Mock Orange, 'Syringa') 43, 53, *P.*Belle Etoile pl. 17; 175, *P.microphyllus* pl. 17; 174, *P.purpureo-maculata* 90
Phlomis 60, *P.fruticosa* (Jerusalem Sage) pl. 21; 138
Phytolacca octandra (Pigeon-Berry, Red-ink

Plant, Virginian Poke) pl. 9; 175, *P.decandra* pl. 9; 175
Phyteuma spicatum (Rampion) 176, *P.orbiculare* (Rampion) 176
Pigeon-berry (*Phytolacca decandra*) 175
Pimpernels 109, P., rose 34
Pimpinella anisum (Anise) pl. 3; 99, *P.saxifraga* (Burnet Saxifrage) 109f.
Pineapple mint (*Mentha citrata*) 161, 162
Pineapple sage (*Salvia rutilans*) pl. 24; 44, 56, 81, 91, 181, 184f.
Pinks(*Dianthus*) 44, 51, 54, P., chintz, thyme 50
Pink hyssop (*Hyssopus officinalis var.*) 136, P. lavender (*Lavandula*) 49
Plants for paths 50
Plumbago capensis (Leadwort) pl. 30; 32, 52
Podophyllum peltatum (American Mandrake) pl. 13; 97f., 153
Poems, 'Chelsea' 41, 'For use and delight' 2, 'My herb garden' 11, 'Passover herbs' 26, 'Sir Thomas More' 57, 'Tradition' 83
Pokeweed (*Phytolacca decandra*) pl. 9; 175
Polemonium caeruleum (Greek Valerian, Jacob's Ladder) pl. 30; 137f.
Polyanthus narcissus 89
Polygonum bistorta (Bistort) pl. 4; 107
Pomanders 29, in Elizabethan days 39, in modern times 39
Pomegranate (*Punica granatum*) pl. 32; 28
Poppies (*Papaver sp.*) pl. 11; 175
Populus balsamifera (Balsam Poplar) pl. 10; 103, *P.candicans* 103
Porteranthus trifoliatus (Bowman's Root, Indian Physic) pl. 14; 137
Portugal laurel (*Prunus lusitanica*) 104
Portulaca oleracea (Green Purslane) pl. 3; 175, *P.sativa* (Golden Purslane) 175
Potato, introduction of 35
Poterium sanguisorba (Salad Burnet) pl. 2; 109
Pot-pourri 39, 81, flowers for 81
Preparation after drying 69
Priest's crown (*Taraxacum officinale*) 122f.
Primroses 90
Primula auricula (Auricula) 90, *P.veris* (Cowslip, 'Paigles') 121
Privet aroma 43
Prostrate Rosemary (*Rosmarinus prostrate var.*) 178

Prunella vulgaris (Self-Heal, Prunella) pl. 10; 187
Prunus laurocerasus (Laurel) 104, *P.lusitanica* (Portugal Laurel) 104
Psalms, mention of herbs in 27
Pseudotsuga douglasi (Douglas Fir) 44
Pulmonaria officinalis (Adam and Eve, Joseph and Mary, Joseph's Coat, Hundreds and Thousands, Lungwort, Soldiers and Sailors, William and Mary) pl. 6; 150
Pulsatilla vulgaris (Pasque Flower) 170
Punica granatum nanum (Dwarf Pomegranate) pl. 32; 28
Purple bergamot (*Monarda fistulosa*) pl. 1; 106
Purslane (*Portulaca sp.*) pl. 3; 33, 175
Pyrethrum cinerarifolium (Insect-Powder Plant) pl. 31; 137
Pyrola rotundifolia (English Wintergreen) 205

Queen's barley cream 37
Queensland 72
Quest of herbs, the 17

Rampion (*Campanula rapunculus*, etc.) pl. 4; 176
Ramsons (*Allium ursinum*) 167
Red Bergamot (*Monarda didyma*) pl. 1; 106
Red field poppy (*Papaver rhoeas*) 175
Red ink plant (*Phytolacca decandra*) 175
Red-root (*Ceanothus americanus*) pl. 13; 176
Red sage (*Salvia officinalis var.*) pl. 24; 181, 183, variegated 182, 183
Rhododendron pl. 17; 177, *R.augustinii* 177, *R.fragrans* 177
Ribes odoratum (Golden Currant) pl. 16; 90, 177
Rock roses (*Helianthemum*) 117, hyssop (*Hyssopus aristatus*) 136
Rohde, Miss, ref. in poem 84, *Old English Herbals* 32
Rosa eglanteria (Sweetbriar) pl. 15; 189, *R.rubinginosa* (Sweetbriar) pl. 15; 189, R. of Sharon (*Hypericum sp.*) 136
Rosa primula pl. 15; 190, varieties 179
Roman wormwood (*Artemisia pontica*) 100
Rosemary (*Rosmarinus sp.*) pl. 6; 23, 24, 35, 43, 50, 51, 55, 60, 77, 79, 89, 177, Miss Jessup 50, 178, Seven Seas 178, Tuscan Blue 178, white 178

Roses 90, 91, rose petals 81
Rosmarinus corsicus 178, *R.officinalis* pl. 6; 177f.
Rubus odoratus pl. 15; 89, 91, 179
Rue (*Ruta graveolens*) pl. 7; 50, 52, 54, 65, 179f., carried at Assizes 39, variegated pl. 20; 180
Rumex acetosa (French Sorrel) pl. 2; 188, *R.scutatus* (French Shield-Leaf Sorrel) pl. 4; 189
Russian comfrey (*Symphytum peregrinum*) 119
Russian sage (*Perowskia atriplicifolia*) pl. 15; 174
Ruta graveolens (Rue) pls. 7 and 20; 179f.

Sackville West, Victoria, ref. in poem 85
Saffron crocus (*Crocus sativus*) pl. 32; 102
Sages (*Salvia sp.*) pl. 22; 23, 24 and 25; 18, 24, 38, 39, 40, 56, 60, 62, 64, 65, 75, 76, 79, Russian (*Perowskia sp.*) pl. 15; 174
Sage-leaved germander (*Teucrium scorodonia*) pl. 22; 204
St. John's wort (*Hypericum sp.*) 136
St. Leonard's Braille and Scented Garden 19, 53
Salad burnet (*Poterium sanquisorba*) pl. 2; 59, 80, 109
Salads 80
Salmon's herbal (1710) 37
Salpichroa rhomboides pl. 32; 166
Salter, Mrs., garden at Hassocks 108
Satureia hortensis (Summer Savory) pl. 5; 186, *S.montana* (Winter Savory) pl. 6 186
Salvia sp. pls. 22, 23, 24 and 25; 180–185, *S.ambigens* 180, 183, *S.argentea* 185, *S. bethelli* 21, 184, *S.chamaedrioides* 183, *S. coccinea* 185, *S.farinacea* 185, *S.glutinosa* 181, 183, *S.grahamii* 91, 181, 184, *S.greggei* 184, *S.haematodes* 184, *S.horminum* (Annual Clary Sage) pls. 6 and 25; 118, *S. involucrata bethelli* 184, *S.juriscii* 185, *S.lavandulifolia* 182, *S.officinalis* (Sage) 181, 183, *S.grahamii* 91, 181, 184, *S.greggei* 184, *S.haematodes* 184, *S.horminum* (Annual 181, 184, *S.sclarea* (Clary Sage) pl. 24; 118, *S.splendens* 180, *S.superba* or *S.virgata nemorosa* 185, *S.turkestanica* 118, *S.uliginosa* 185, *S.verbenacea* 119, 181, *S.verticillata* 185, *S.nemorosa* or *S.superba* 185
Sambucus nigra (Common Elder) 124
Samphire (*Crithmum maritimum*) pl. 3; 185
Sanguinaria canadensis (Bloodroot, Indian Paint) pl. 13; 108
Sanguisorba officinalis (Greater Burnet) 109
Santolina (Cotton Lavender) pl. 21; 34, 41, 50, 52, 60, 89, 90, 120, 191, *S.chamaecyparissus* pl. 21; 120, *S.* Cotton lavender or French lavender 50, *S.incana* 120, *S.* Lemon Queen 121, *S.neapolitanica* pl. 21; 121, *S.viridis* 121
Saponaria officinalis (Bouncing Bet, Soapwort, Wild Sweet William) pl. 29; 188
Sarcococca humilis pl. 18; 44, 89, 186
Sassafras, used in Spain, etc., for medicinal purposes 35
Savory (*Satureia sp.*) Summer, pl. 5, Winter pl. 6 ; 33, 34, 50, 52, 54, 55, 56, 60, 63, 64, 75, 76, 186, 186, at Beaulieu Abbey 21
Savouries, herb 80
Saxifraga sarmentosa or *Helxine* (Mind-your-own-Business) 157, 163
Scabious (*Scabiosa sp.*) 91
Scent of plants 43f.
Scented and aromatic plants 89, 93
Scented gardens for the blind 19, 53
Scented geranium pl. 22; 129
Scotch lovage (*Ligusticum scoticum*) 150
Scullcap, English (*Scutellaria galericulata*) 187, S., Virginian (*S.lateriflora*) pl. 30; 187
Scutellaria alpina 187, *S.galericulata* (English Scullcap) 187, *S.lateriflora* (Virginian S.) pl. 30; 187, *S.minor* 187
Sea Holly (*Eryngium maritimum*) pl. 7; 126
Sea Purslane (*Atriplex portulacoides*) 176
Sea wormwood (*Artemisia maritima*) 100
Seal Herb Farm, history of 38, ref. in poem 85f.
Seal lavender (*Lavandula sp.*) pl. 1; 49, 145
Self Heal (*Prunella vulgaris*) pl. 10; 187
Sempervivum tectorum (Houseleek, Welcome-home-husband-however-drunk-you-be) 135
Shakespeare and plants 20, on herbs 33
Shepherd's purse 34
Shell flower (*Moluccella laevis*) pl. 32; 163

INDEX

Shittah tree 28
Shoo plant (*Nicandra physaloides*) pl. 31; 22, 166
Short term planting 53
Shrubs, aromatic 187
Sideritis hyssopifolius pl. 32
Silver Posie thyme (*Thymus vulgaris var.*) pl. 27; 197, 200, S. Queen thyme (*Thymus citriodorus var.*) pl. 27; 197, 200
Silybum marianum (Our Lady's Milk Thistle) pl. 10; 193
Sissinghurst herb seats 51
Sium sisarum (Skirret) pl. 2; 188
Skimmia japonica pl. 16; 89, 187, *S.foremanii* 187
Skirret (*Sium sisarum*) pl. 2; 188
Skunk cabbage (*Symplocarpus foetidus* or *Spathyema foetida*) pl. 14; 188
'Sleepy nightshade' (*Atropa belladonna*) 35
Smallage (*Apium graveolens*) 150
Smyrnium olusatrum (Alexanders, Black Lovage) 96
Snake's head lily (*Fritillaria meleagris*) pl. 11; 128
Snowdrift thyme (*Thymus serpyllum var.*) 199
Soapwort (*Saponaria officinalis*) pl. 29; 188
Solanaceae 20
Solanum nigrum (Black Nightshade) pl. 11; 166, *S.sisymbrifolium* pl. 32; 166, *S.dulcamara* (Woody Nightshade, Bittersweet) pl. 11; 105
Soldiers and sailors (*Pulmonaria officinalis*) 150
'Sorcerer's violet' (*Vinca major, V.minor*) 174
Sorrel (*Rumex sp.*) pl. 2 and 4; 78, 81, 188
Soups, herbs for use in 77
South Africa 72
Southernwood (*Artemisia abrotanum*) pl. 19; 50, 55, 81, 101
Spanish mint (*Mentha requienii*) 163
Spathyema foetida or *Symplocarpus foetidus* (Skunk-Cabbage) pl. 14; 188
Spearmint (*Mentha viridis*) pl. 26; 64, 158
Spice tree (*Umbellularia californica*) pl. 22; 110
Spiders sold to West End firm 40
Spikenard 29, 140
Spikenard, American (*Aralia racemosa*) pl. 32; 189

Spike lavender (*Lavendula spica*) 140
Spiraea filipendula or *Filipendula vulgaris* (Dropwort Meadowsweet) pl. 8; 155, *S.japonica* 112, *S.ulmaria* (Meadowsweet, Queen of the Meadows) 155
Spurge-Laurel (*Daphne laureola*) pl. 12; 89, 123
Spurges (*Euphorbia sp.*) pl. 12; 189
Stachys betonica (Wood Betony) pl. 10; 107
Stacte 27
Staphylea colchica 90, 189
'Sticadore' 141
Still-room books 36, 37
Stock (*Matthiola sp.*) 43, 53, nightscented 90, ten-week 91
Storax (*Styrax officinalis*) 27
Succory (*Cichorium intybus*) pl. 4; 115
Sun roses (*Cistus sp.*) pl. 15; 117
Sweet Basil (*Ocimum basilicum*) pl. 4; 103
Sweet bay (*Laurus nobilis*) pl. 3; 55, 104
Sweet briar (*Rosa eglanteria* or *R.rubiginosa*) pl. 15; 34, 89, 189
Sweet Cicely (*Myrrhis odorata*) pl. 21; 190
Sweet Flag (*Acorus calamus*) pl. 31; 28, 190
Sweet green basil (*Ocimum basilicum*) pl. 4; 104
Sweet marjoram (*Origanum marjorana*) pl. 6; 153
Sweet peas 43, 53, 91
Sweet roses 54
Sweet Rush (*Acorus calamus*) pl. 31; 28, 190
Sweet scabious (*Scabiosa sp.*) 91
Sweet Sultan 91
Symphytum caucasicum (Blue Comfrey) pl. 6; 119, *S.officinale* (Common Comfrey) 119, *S.uplandicum* (Russian Comfrey) 119
Symplocarpus foetidus (Skunk-Cabbage) pl. 14; 188
'Syringa' (*Philadelphus sp.*) pl. 17; 174

Tamus communis (Black Bryony) pl. 7; 109
Tanecetum balsamita now *Chrysanthemum balsamita* (Alecost, Costmary, 'Mace') pl. 3; 96, *T.vulgare* (Tansy) pl. 9; 52, 54, 191
Tansy (*Tanecetum vulgare* or *Chrysanthemum vulgare*) pl. 9; 52, 54, 191
Taraxacum officinale (Dandelion) 122

Tarragon, French (*Artemisia dracunculus*) pl. 6; 18, 24, 35, 54, 55, 56, 60, 62, 63, 65, 76, 77, 78, 79, 81, 99, 191, Russian (*A.dracunculoides*) pl. 6; 191
'Tea Plant' (*Lycium halimifolium*) pl. 29; 192
Ten-week stocks (*Matthiola*) 91
Teucrium chamaedrys (Wall Germander) pl. 7; 204, *T.fruticans* pl. 15; 192, *T.marum* (Cat-Thyme) 204, *T.scorodonia* (Wood Sage, Sage-leaved Germander) pl. 22; 204
Theophrastus of Athens 29
Thistles (*Silybum sp.*, *Carbenia sp.*, *Carduus sp.*) pl. 10; 193
Thornapple (*Datura stramonium*) pl. 11; 39, 134, 193
Thuja 44
Thyme lawns, 19, 195, at Sissinghurst 51
Thymes (*Thymus sp.*) pl. 5, 6 and 27; 23, 38, 49, 50, 51, 52, 53, 54, 55, 59, 60, 64, 65, 68, 69, 75, 76, 77, 78, 79, 80, 194–200
Thymus sp. pl. 5, 6 and 27; 194–200, *T.albus compactus* 197, *T.* Annie Hall 199, *T.carnosus* 198, *T.citriodorus* (Lemon Thyme) 194, 196, *T.cit. aureus* 197, *T.cit.* Silver Queen 197, *T.comosus hirsutus* 200, *T. doerfleri* 198, *T.erectus* 198, *T.ericifolius* 198, *T.fragrantissimus* 198, *T.herba-barona* (Caraway Thyme) 198, *T.hyemalis* 198, *T.* Lemon curd 200, *T.mastachinus* 198, *T.nitidus* 199, *T.odoratissimus* 199, *T.serpyllum* 194, 195, 196, *T.serp. albus* 199, *T.serp. citriodorus* 199, *T.serp. coccineus* 200, *T.serp. coccineus major* 18, 50, 200, *T.serp. lanuginosus* 200, *T.serp. minus* 200, *T.serp.* Nosegay 200, *T.serp.* Pink Chintz 200, *T.serp. roseus* 200, *T.serp.* Russettings 200, *T.vulgaris* 194, *T.vul.* Golden 200, *T.vul.* Silver Posie 200, *T.zygis* 200
Tilia europaea (Lime) 148
Tobacco pl. 31; 200, introduction of 35
Town garden 54
Tradition—a poem 83
Tree mallow (*Lavatera arborea*) 152
Tree onions (*Allium cepa var.*) pl. 5; 167
Treveris, P., author of *Grete Herbal* (fifteenth cent.) 33
Tropaeolum majus (Nasturtium) 165
Troughs 55

True French tarragon (*Artemisia dracunculus*) pl. 6; 191
Tubs 55
Turner's *Herbal* 34
Turner on cornflowers 34
Tutti-Frutti (*Teucrium fruticans*) pl. 15; 192
Twickle Purple Lavender 144

Ulex europaeus (Gorse) 89, 201
Umbelliferae, economic value of 20
Umbellularia californica (Californian Laurel, 'Spice-Tree') pl. 22; 110
Urtica dioica (Perennial Nettle) 165, *U.urens* (Annual Nettle) 165
Uses of herbs 75–82

Valerian (*Valeriana officinalis*) pl. 22; 201 V., Greek (*Polemonium caeruleum*) pl. 30; 137
Valeriana officinalis (Valerian) pl. 22; 201
Valerianella locusta (Corn Salad, Lamb's Lettuce) 120
Variegated rue (*Ruta graveolens var.*) pl. 20
Vatican clary 118
Veratrum album (White Hellebore) 132
Veratrum viride (American Hellebore, Bear-cabbage) pl. 14; 97
Verbascum thapsus (High Tapers, Herbe de St. Fiacre, Mullein, Our Lady's Flannel) pl. 10; 164
Verbena, lemon (*Lippia citriodora*) pl. 5; 202, *V.officinalis* (Vervain, Wild Verbena) pl. 10; 30, 202
Vermuth, Roman Wormwood used in preparation of 100
Veronica cupressoides pl. 22; 203, *V.salicifolia* 90, 203
Verticillium wilt, plant disease 183
Vervain (*Verbena officinalis*) pl. 10; 30, 203
Viburnum bodnantense 204, *V.burkwoodii* 203, *V.carlecephalum* 203, *V.carlesii* pl. 18; 203, *V.farneri* pl. 18; 204
Victoria 71
Vinca major and *minor* (Periwinkle, Sorcerer's Violet) pl. 29; 174
Viola 44, *V.tricolor* (Call-Me-to-You) Three-Faces-under-a-Hood, Love-in-Idleness, Herbe Trinitatis, Wild Pansy) pl. 9; 131

INDEX

Violets (*Viola odorata*, etc.) 37, 43
Viper's bugloss (*Echium vulgare*) pl. 30; 204
Virginian creeper 21, V. poke (*Phytolacca decandra*) 175, V. scullcap (*Scutellaria lateriflora*) pl. 30; 187

Wallflower 35, 43, 54, 84, 90
Wall germander (*Teucrium chamaedrys*) pl. 7; 204
Warburton Gem lavender 144, 146
Watercress (*Nasturtium officinale*) 165
Watermint (*Mentha aquatica*) 32, 34, 52, 157
Water-lilies (*Nymphaea odorata*) 90
Welsh onion (*Allium fistulosum*) pl. 5; 167
Westminster Abbey, use of herbs 40f.
White Hellebore (*Veratrum album*) 132
White horehound (*Marrubium vulgare*) pl. 10; 134
White jasmine (*Jasminum officinale*) 44, 51, 90
White lavender 145
'White Metheglin of My Lady Hungerford' 37
Wild Celery (*Apium graveolens*) 150
Wild garlic (*Allium vineale*) 167
Wild Sweet William (*Saponaria officinalis*) pl. 29; 188
Wild thyme (*Thymus serpyllum*) 33, 52
William and Mary (*Pulmonaria officinalis*) 150
Window boxes 55

Winter aconite (*Eranthis hyemalis*) 95
Wintergreen (*Gaultheria procumbens*) pl. 16; 24, 44, 204
Winter heliotrope (*Petasites fragrans*) pl. 23; 89, 205
Winter savory (*Satureia montana*) pl. 6; 80, 186
Wintersweet (*Chimonanthus fragrans* or *Calycanthus praecox*) pl. 18; 51, 89, 97, 116
Wisteria (Grape-Flower Vine) 44, 51, 90, 205
Witch Hazel (*Hamamelis sp.*) pl. 16; 89, 205
Woad (*Isatis tinctoria*) pl. 31; 206
Wolfbane (*Aconitum napellus*) pl. 12; 95
Wood garlic (*Allium ursinum*) 167
Wood sorrel (*Oxalis acetosella*) 189
Woodbine (*Lonicera sp.*) 34
Woodburn, Miss E. 70
Woodruff (*Asperula odorata*) pl. 29; 206
Woodsage (*Teucrium scorodonia*) pl. 22; 204
Woody nightshade (*Solanum dulcamara*) pl. 11; 105, 166
Wormwood (*Artemisia absinthium*) pl. 19; 20, 49, 52, 59, 65, 100, 191, W. and gall 27
'Wort' meaning herb 31
Wyrtzerds 31

Yam family 109
Yarrow (*Achillea millefolium*) 206
Yellow gentian (*Gentiana lutea*) pl. 30; 129